Southern Shepherds, Savage Wolves

Southern Shepherds, Savage Wolves

Presbyterian Domestic Missionaries and Race in South Carolina, 1802–1874

Otis Westbrook Pickett Sr.

THE UNIVERSITY OF
SOUTH CAROLINA PRESS

Published by the University of South Carolina Press
Columbia, South Carolina 29208

uscpress.com

Printed in the United States of America

Library of Congress Cataloging-in-Publication Data
can be found at http://catalog.loc.gov/.

ISBN: 978-1-64336-614-2 (hardcover)
ISBN: 978-1-64336-637-1 (paperback)
ISBN: 978-1-64336-638-8 (ebook)
DOI: https://doi.org/10.61162/9781643366388

The publication of this book, as well as its inclusion in the Open Carolina collection, received generous funding support from The Division of Research and the Clemson Libraries at Clemson University.

The Open Carolina collection is made possible by the generous funding of the University of South Carolina Libraries.

For Jules

CONTENTS

Introduction

Southern Religion and Domestic Missions to Enslaved Persons

The driving questions behind this book have been with me ever since I formally began the study of the history of southern religion. One of my chief questions was, "Why is 11 o'clock on Sunday morning the most segregated hour in American life?" As I became a Presbyterian and was training for full-time ministry in seminary, I began asking, "Were there any southern Presbyterians who were anti-enslavement or who desired an integrated church?" I possessed a desire to work one day in a multiethnic church, and this was a part of my inward call to ministry. In a way I was attempting to discern whether Presbyterians in the US South possessed any history of integrated worship. My search led me to Southern Presbyterian domestic missionaries and shepherds of marginalized flocks in nineteenth-century South Carolina. I was so interested in this question that I left training for full-time ministry and pursued training to become a full-time professional historian.

I found out that Southern Presbyterians played an outsized role in creating segregated churches in the US South, laying the theological groundwork and the ecclesiastical practices in the antebellum era that would come to dominate the postbellum landscape up to the modern Civil Rights movement and beyond. I found that Southern Presbyterians became one of the first denominations to vote for racial separation as an official practice in a church court and thereby providing the theological and moral justification for segregation in other spaces both public and civic. I found that there were some anti-enslavement Presbyterians, and there were some Presbyterians who desired integrated churches, but those individuals lost ground to an entrenched economic system driven by enslavement, a divisive political climate, an entrenched view of the inferiority of non-White persons and, ultimately to a Lost Cause, a cause that continued into the twentieth century and has had reverberations into the twenty-first century. In Joshua 4, the Lord commanded Joshua to "take twelve men from the people, from each tribe a man, and command them saying 'Take twelve stones from here out of the midst of the Jordan.' After this was done the Lord said, 'When your children ask in time to come [What do these stones mean to you?] then you shall tell them that the waters of the Jordan were cut off before the ark of the covenant of the Lord. So these stones shall be to the people of Israel a memorial forever."[1] It is my hope that this book is a memorial stone or a stone of remembrance of the work that happened in South Carolina and that it might stand as a memorial to the ways in which some Presbyterian missionaries and pastors attempted to push back against these systems, but ultimately succumbed to the system's entrenched grasp on the southern landscape.

As historians of southern religion have examined nineteenth-century pastors, I think it is important not to overlook the connections that the Bible repeatedly makes to pastors as shepherds. Jesus of Nazareth once said, "Rejoice with me, for I have found my sheep that was lost,"[2] and there are numerous other passages that make this connection. As someone who has trained for this calling and later served as an ordained ruling elder or "shepherd" alongside a team of pastors and other ruling elders on a church court that Presbyterians call a "session" for an intentionally planted multiethnic church, I have given a great deal of thought to this verbiage and what it means regarding race. The calling of Christian ministers or "shepherds" regarding pastoral oversight is to care for the flock of God and to protect the flock at all costs. According to the Presbyterian Church in America in the Book of Church Order "the office (of Ruling Elder) is one of dignity and usefulness" and it is the "duty to be spiritually fruitful, dignified, and prudent, an example to the flock, and to govern well in the house of the Kingdom of Christ."[3]

In South Carolina in the nineteenth century there were Presbyterian missionaries who shepherded recent European settlers or immigrants, Native Americans, and enslaved African Americans. These "southern shepherds" or missionaries served as shepherds or undershepherds of integrated flocks while also recognizing that some in their churches had privileges based on their race that others did not. These southern shepherds often served in a mission church, which meant that the oversight of the church belonged to a governing body known as the Presbytery until the church particularized or created a local governing body known as a session.

The Presbyterian Church in South Carolina was evangelical, cared deeply about missions, and saw that domestic missions along with foreign missions were an integral part of a practicing Christians' duty. Domestic missions would have included a pastor or missionary being sent to evangelize, set up a church, and minister to what were considered "foreigners" to the faith within the landscape or close to major settlements that were a part of the then fledgling United States. These "domestic missions" spaces included people on the frontier who lived in territory the United States did not formally recognize, Indigenous communities, enslaved people, as well as large populations of immigrants who might or might not have known about the teachings of Christianity.

Southern Shepherds, Savage Wolves displays how the ecclesiastical body of the Presbyterian Church in the United States in South Carolina attempted to "shepherd" marginalized flocks in the nineteenth century, which mostly occurred in what was considered the South Carolina backcountry, western frontier, and coastal lowlands. This book tells the story of missionaries who attempted to minister to and shepherd racially, ethnically and culturally diverse flocks. But ultimately they violated their own principles of ecclesiology, church membership structures, and even their views on education to accommodate the savage wolves of race-based chattel enslavement, a pursuit of mammon over love of neighbor, and later racial segregation. These mission churches, while providing some opportunities for limited emancipationist experiences, ultimately laid the groundwork for separate but unequal church memberships and would later play a role in "organic separation" or racial segregation in 1874. These shepherds allowed the "savage wolves" of enslavers, their worldview, and their overwhelming desire for mammon at the expense of human life to enter the flock and lead the church to make accommodations for the institution of enslavement and segregation. The antebellum mission churches developed a racialized membership hierarchy that would reverberate into a postbellum separation along racial lines. In short, racial hierarchies in southern Presbyterian domestic mission churches helped pave the way for ecclesiastical racial separatism in 1874, which helped create "the most segregated hour in American life" on Sunday mornings. By the time *Plessy v. Ferguson* and de jure segregation come along in 1896, southern Presbyterians had been practicing and laying the moral justification for racial segregation for almost half a century.

In 1955, C. Vann Woodward, the great historian of the US South, wrote *The Strange Career of Jim Crow*, which laid out in almost blueprint fashion the laws, systems, and structures of racial segregation. Dr. Martin Luther King Jr. called it "the historical bible of the Civil Rights movement" because it was cited so often to counter arguments for segregation and because it provided a road map for civil rights activists to begin to attack systems that created racial segregation. Woodward argued that racial segregation in the US South dated to the late nineteenth century and that African Americans and Whites had not been divided before the 1890s. My hope is that this book can offer similar insights for scholars of southern religion and southern Presbyterianism about the Presbyterian systems, church courts, ecclesiastical practices, and laws and that created Christian segregation in 1874, a full twenty-two years before *Plessy v. Ferguson*. I want us to remember that speaking humans historically have always been together in community and are meant to be together. Humans manufacture systems that create racial separation. The future, as the Apostle John reminds us in Revelation is "a great multitude that no one could number, from every nation, from all tribes and peoples and languages standing before the throne and before the Lamb."[4] In the US South, and in South Carolina in the 1870s, it was church leaders in church courts who made decisions to vote for separation along racial lines. The American Christian church has suffered from the ramifications of this decision ever since

Southern shepherds, PCUS pastors, churches, ecclesiastical bodies, and regional church leaders made accommodations on an antebellum racialized ecclesiology and postbellum racial segregation culminating in an 1874 decision to pursue "organic separation" along racial lines for the entire denomination. Many churches and denominations in the US South advocated for enslavement from a biblical position, and several made theological arguments supporting the institution of enslavement as it existed in the United States. However Presbyterians in South Carolina took this work a step further: They created a church structure and racialized ecclesiology to make accommodations for the institution of enslavement in day-to-day life, practices, church government, and church activities. These accommodations have had reverberations into Reconstruction, the era of segregation, and the Jim Crow south. The accommodations make southern or at least South Carolina Presbyterians, early adopters in the southern landscape on accepting segregation as a practical, "biblical," and therefore an acceptable practice. Any understanding of trying to discern Dr. King's quote, "We must face the sad fact that at eleven o'clock on Sunday morning when we stand to sing 'In Christ there is no East or West,' we stand in the most segregated hour of America" must start with an understanding of Southern Presbyterian domestic missions and their ecclesiology on race during Reconstruction. The antebellum Presbyterian mission churches had intentionally integrated worship, that worship contained many elements of racial segregation, that worship continued into Reconstruction, and it was formally severed by a church court in 1874. Finally in the years following Reconstruction the Lost Cause put to death and buried what was only severed.

This leadership in South Carolina on segregation has left a legacy that continues into the twentieth and twenty-first centuries. The PCA or Presbyterian Church in America developed largely as a southeastern denomination that was a "continuing church" out of the PCUS or Presbyterian Church United States.[5] Often modern disagreements in the denomination dating back to the early nineteen seventies have roots in how antebellum southern missionaries viewed enslaved African Americans and how those views continued into the Reconstruction era and beyond. The PCA was born alongside a long tradition in the PCUS, which consistently viewed African American members as inferior. When a new denomination formed (the Presbyterian Church in America) in December 1973 in Birmingham, Alabama, as a "continuing church" out of the PCUS, the context consisted of several significant civil rights activities of the late 1960s and the desegregation of several schools in the US South. The new denomination also led to the development of small, private, segregationist academies often clothed in religious language. Further many moderate and conservative White pastors were concerned that the PCUSA had moved toward a theologically, biblically, and culturally "liberal" position. These positions also included the PCUSA's views on race. The ordained African Americans in the PCUSA who were pro-civil rights were often labeled as Marxists or Communists, and the more moderate or conservative pastors delegitimized them as theologically inaccurate. The critique of the White moderate, which King detailed in his *Letter from a Birmingham Jail*, saw these individuals approaching the civil rights movement from a cultural and political position, but certainly not a biblical one. From the modern civil rights movement to today there is continuity over how African Americans, or generally people of color, are treated within southern Presbyterianism.

A part of the historian's work is to evaluate continuity and change over time. There has largely been a consistent refrain among southern Presbyterians when it comes to issues of race from the antebellum context, up to Reconstruction, Jim Crow, and into the twentieth century. Indeed many of the themes explored in this book, such as how the church created an inferior form of church membership for enslaved African Americans and how this continued into the church's views during the Jim Crow era are examples of this continuity. To continue to see the church's resistance to be an active agent during the civil rights movement, its resistance to reconciliation movements in the 1980s and

'90s as "theologically liberal," and its ongoing battle with discussions of race even today continue to resonate.

Today (2020–24), the language of anyone discussing race in the church is that they are "woke" (meant as a pejorative) and that they eschew biblical arguments for sociological and historical ones. There have been a few moments like 2002, 2015, and 2016–18, when the PCA passed a resolution on repenting of its connection to enslavement and racism, a personal resolution confessing the denomination's failures during the civil rights movement, and the creation of the Ad-Interim Committee on Racial and Ethnic Reconciliation to research and give a report to the 2018 General Assembly on its findings. However there has been more continuity rather than change over time.[6] Indeed the experiences of these missionaries and the actions of southern Presbyterians in the nineteenth century is largely consistent with southern Presbyterian engagement on issues of race into the late nineteenth, twentieth and with few exceptions twenty-first centuries. There has been some needed and long-awaited change. For instance the PCA began as an integrated body at its beginning in 1974. However the denomination has a supermajority White membership; it continues to be resistant to discussions of race since 2020; and it treats those who wish to discuss these topics as potential threats to theological orthodoxy, unity, peace, and the current status quo.[7] In contrast to how individuals discussing race today are viewed as "woke, progressive, theological liberals," those discussing race in the nineteenth century were considered "conservative, orthodox, and biblically informed." Ironically, it was the latter who were truly the theological liberals in that they were reading their racist views onto biblical texts and applying them in an unbiblical manner in the church courts.

In southern Presbyterianism in the nineteenth century, many shepherds ended up letting, as the Apostle Paul warned in Acts 20, "wolves" in among the flock who "will come in among you not sparing the flock; and from among your own selves will arise men speaking twisted things, to draw away the disciples after them."[8] Indeed the Apostle Paul was concerned here with the ways in which pastors might shift the true application of the gospel of Jesus Christ to fit within their specific culture, political ideology, or economic system, thereby marring the gospel of Jesus with a human system with which the gospel must be syncretized. Paul also had in mind those coming into the flock to preach a false gospel. In America the southern Presbyterian Church has excused the abuse of enslaved African Americans to protect the economic system of slavery, the gaining of wealth at the expense of fellow human beings and therefore subjecting fellow Christians to dehumanization and suffering for the pursuit of mammon.

This syncretism, a worshipping of mammon and protecting economic systems over one's neighbor, protecting a racial hierarchy within the church, and pursuing a political agenda over biblical fidelity was merged with gospel preaching and has largely been consistent with southern Presbyterian rhetoric and action toward people of color since the early nineteenth century. This approach also contained a false gospel. The gospel of Jesus Christ is completely wrapped up in a love of God; love of neighbor as thyself; and to serve, not to be served. Jesus spoke these words in his first public presentation, "'The Spirit of the Lord is upon me, because he has anointed me to proclaim good news to the poor. He has sent me to proclaim liberty to the captives and recovering of sight to the blind, to set at liberty those who are oppressed, to proclaim the year of the Lord's favor.' And he rolled up the scroll and gave it back to the attendant and sat down. And the eyes of all in the synagogue were fixed on him"[9] A church that preached enslaved people and all their descendants to stay in perpetual bondage because of their race and to buttress systems of racial oppression by making room for them in church in second-class membership because of their race was preaching a false gospel in direct contradiction to Jesus's own proclamation. It should also be noted that this syncretism had a civil religious component as the pursuit of mammon over love of neighbor are deeply connected with South Carolina's and later the Confederate States of America's political goals of protecting enslavement and later perpetuating a Lost Cause narrative into the late nineteenth century. The three were intertwined and southern Presbyterianism will become a place that accepted and upheld the economic, political, and civil religious goals of the Lost Cause.

Ecclesiologically speaking the southern Presbyterian church was a place in which enslaved and free had a distinct and unique status before God, before the elders of the church, and as members based on their race. To be sure White members were preferred, given the highest positions, and "ruled" over members of African American heritage. Non-White individuals were seen as non-Christians or "heathens," were suitable only for labor, and for the lowest forms of un-ordained ecclesiastical service. Enslaved African American Christians could never be ordained deacons, elders, or pastors with authority and oversight over White members. Finally it would have been unthinkable for White missionaries to challenge southern enslavement as it was practiced in South Carolina. If a pastor taught that enslavement, as it existed in the US South, was unbiblical, and therefore the money gotten from enslavement was to be considered sinful, ill-gotten or connected with human stealing, then the pastor would have been fired, removed, and disciplined. If pastors persisted, then they would have been threatened with violence and likely killed. The powers of wealth, racism, and politics could not be overcome even with the strongest biblical or theological arguments.

Some in the PCA believe that if a church is being faithful to the scriptures, preaching truth, and engaging in the courts of the church judiciously, then all sin can be rooted out by the power and work of the Holy Spirit and dealt with. While this is theoretically possible, what southern Presbyterianism has shown is that without outside actors, activists, or national events, such as the massacre of nine victims at Mother Emmanuel AME (ironically directly across the street from the mission churches featured in the later chapters of this text), the death of Michael Brown, or the murder of George Floyd, the church is largely satisfied with the status quo and will perpetuate preaching that does not address a fixation on love of wealth over neighbor, a commitment to racism over unity and/or an obsession with politics and making sure those politics fit within a "biblical truth" for their particular tribe. It is interesting to note that two of the three actions taken by the PCA (mentioned earlier) were directly after two of the aforementioned events (Mother Emmanuel and Michael Brown).

After Reconstruction, southern Presbyterians would lead the national landscape on legal segregation by voting for racial segregation or what was referred to as "organic separation" in 1874, developing a theology of "racial purity," fears around "racial amalgamation" (a word created to understand "race mixing" and the dangers of what some would call "mongrelization" of the White race by intermarriage with African Americans), and antagonism toward the civil rights movement. In the last fifty years, Southern Presbyterians have been resistant to cultural changes in racial reconciliation. When they address racial injustice they have referred to those within the church who participate in these activities as "Marxists, social justice warriors" and "woke Christians," who really are not concerned about the gospel, but are simply activists, radicals, progressives, theological liberals, or the ultimate irony, "wolves in sheep's clothing." These are all pejorative terms used within the PCA in the twenty-first century to describe individuals who care about these issues and display empathy toward their neighbors of color.

Indeed it was not until 2015, when Drs. Ligon Duncan and Sean Lucas, supported by Jim Baird,[10] openly stated that the PCA's founders had no interest in civil rights and failed their African American brothers and sisters in this regard. What followed was a posture of repentance and the work of the Ad-Interim Committee on Racial and Ethnic Reconciliation, whose report was accepted in omnibus at the 2018 General Assembly of the PCA.[11] With few exceptions the experiences of Southern Presbyterians over the last two centuries have been consistent regarding injustice toward the marginalized, especially African Americans and Native Americans, in the southern United States.

While the call of the spirit no doubt caused these missionaries to labor among and minister to enslaved people, their understanding of race; their views on the inferiority of African Americans and Native Americans; and the fears of change, racial equality, and loss of political, social and economic dominance inherent within the overwhelmingly White membership overcame any biblical or theological understanding of how Christians should relate to fellow church members of another race. For Southern Presbyterians the pursuit of mammon, protecting a racial hierarchy, and politics predetermined what the status of non-White members in the church would be. These three (greed, race, and politics) make up a sort of "holy trinity of American idolatry" and informed an enslaved person's membership status in the church. Rather than being an antebellum anomaly, this has been a largely consistent pattern in Southern Presbyterianism from its early inception up to the civil rights movement, with the exception of a few South Carolina Presbyterians like James McBride Dabbs who were active in the Presbyterian Church (USA).

Indeed a racially cohesive theology driven by the understanding that Africans were inferior; protecting one's wealth, status, and social mobility by putting down people of color; and following a specific political narrative on race has been continuous for almost three centuries. This theology of racial cohesion moves from a paternalistic structure during the antebellum period to an attempt at racial equity from 1869–74, only to withdraw from biracial equitable leadership and to buttress a staunch racial hierarchy in the face of post-1874 political change moving toward the creation of a segregated church along racial lines. The "organic separation" vote in 1874 should be seen as an example of Southern Presbyterian churches leading the way or modeling to the region that racial segregation was biblical, acceptable, and the proper way in which the races ought to interact. To be sure, twenty-two years ahead of *Plessy v. Ferguson*, Southern Presbyterians provided the moral authority the courts and broader public needed to make segregation an acceptable public practice in the US South.

However a tension existed during the early part of the nineteenth century regarding the ambiguous status of enslaved African Americans and Native Americans who attended and became members of nineteenth-century Presbyterian mission churches in the US South. These African Americans and Native

Americans were simultaneously experiencing limited freedoms as members in a Christian[12] community and some measured ecclesiastical equalities, while also experiencing the effects of dehumanizing enslavement. Scholars of southern religion have attempted to understand how and why a church could at one point acknowledge one's humanity, soul, and membership in a religious institution while also buttressing a "peculiar institution" that treated enslaved African Americans not as humans, but as property. In seemingly direct contrast to Galatians 3:28, in nineteenth-century South Carolina, a Christian African American enslaved person was two things at once: both enslaved and free. He or she was both chattel (nonhuman) property and a human who possessed a soul and was "free from sin in Christ." Such distinctions should not exist in the Christian church or the Christian worldview. Yet in mission churches in South Carolina they did exist and were held in an unbiblical and heterodox tension for more than two centuries.

Enslaved communities in the contexts of an urban space like Charleston, South Carolina, and a frontier space like northeast Mississippi (considered part of South Carolina territory in the very early part of the nineteenth century) were, in some ways, distinct from enslavement in other spaces across the southern landscape. Enslaved African Americans in urban spaces typically had more freedom of movement; more skilled, artisanal tasks; and the ability to interact with a broader swath of people coming in and out of a port city. This environment provided unique opportunities compared to an isolated, rural plantation. Further as an enslaved member of a mission church, the enslaved individual experienced some measure of ecclesiastical support. The individual was not free but might have experienced measured ecclesiastical equalities, which were not apparent in many other spaces across the US South. Similar experiences were also common on the South Carolina frontier. There was a complexity to these spaces in which enslavement and a race-based social hierarchy mixed and existed alongside a variety of uncommon and unexpected opportunities.

Galatians 3:28 is a passage the Apostle Paul used to speak to first-century Greek Christians in Galatia. Later a young missionary from Charleston, South Carolina, named John Lafayette Girardeau used it to speak to nineteenth-century White Southern Presbyterians, defending the tenor and thrust of the biblical position on this issue. In Christ and in the church, no human being should have a substandard status based on his or her race, position in society, or gender. According to the Apostle Paul and to Girardeau interpreting Paul, in Christ they are all one or equals. However the relationship between enslaved African Americans and White Presbyterians in the US South before the Civil War did not, in function or in practice, reflect this interpretation. Indeed most churches, theologians, missionaries, and pastors working in the US South used the Bible to defend slavery and did so adamantly. What is apparent throughout American history, from the Puritans in the colonial era to the segregationists in the 1960s is that the exegesis of this text or interpreting it to mean that all races were equal in Christ was not practiced.

In a slight departure from this reality missionaries like Girardeau used an interpretation of Galatians 3:28 to defend the rights of newly freed African American men to join the Presbyterian Church in the United States (PCUS) in full membership with equal membership rights in 1866 and with rights to be elected to positions of full church office in 1869. Likewise the South Carolina missionary T. C. Stuart used these sentiments to grant membership, education, and leadership positions in the church to both Native Americans and enslaved African Americans. However Girardeau and Stuart were not willing to make this argument publicly in 1859 or any time before the Civil War. For instance Girardeau's mission church in Charleston, called Zion, and Stuart's mission church in northwest South Carolina (now Mississippi), called Monroe, were composed of Whites, free African Americans, enslaved African Americans, Native Americans, and was a unique space where spiritual freedom, enslavement, and measured ecclesiastical equalities mingled awkwardly together. However neither Girardeau nor Stuart were ever advocates of abolition or freedom of enslaved African Americans in the antebellum context.

Southern Shepherds, Savage Wolves is an attempt to understand these missionaries and the Native American as well as African American mission church members in South Carolina. This book's purpose is to enhance our understanding of the complexity of religion's role and the institution of slavery in South Carolina and in nineteenth-century religious spaces of multiethnic interaction. Further this work will endeavor to understand Presbyterian mission churches as multiracial spaces with interracial activities between Native Americans, particularly individuals of the Chickasaw nation; enslaved African Americans; Whites; and peoples of mixed ancestry. This book not only focuses on the expanded role of Presbyterian mission churches as spaces that formalized pro-enslavement theology into practice, but also delves into larger discussions of religion, race, gender, and the nature of pro-slavery ecclesiology in the context of nineteenth-century South Carolina. Moreover it also considers the connections of complex relationships forged in an antebellum context and how those relationships bridged the Civil War, continued into

Reconstruction and beyond into a well-formulated and robustly articulated Lost Cause ideology.

Indeed, while the Civil War left a tremendous impact on our nation's history, it did not serve to completely sever relationships forged in the antebellum context. For instance many of the relationships that began at Zion Presbyterian Church from 1850 to 1864 continued in a variety of different ways from 1865 to 1874. Likewise removal of the Chickasaw from Mississippi to Arkansas and Oklahoma left a massive imprint on mid-South Native American culture and history. However it did not destroy relationships formed between missionaries and members in the preremoval era. Figuring most prominently in this work however is the question of race and the role the church played in perpetuating, while also at times questioning, entrenched racial attitudes and perspectives. Finally, human relationships are complex and messy, and this book attempts to understand the complexities of the multiracial relationships forged in the context of nineteenth-century mission churches in South Carolina.

Multiracial mission communities shed light on nineteenth-century perspectives on race, how church membership affected racial identity, and how race changed the status of that membership. Few works have tried to consider the multiracial makeup of both frontier and urban missionary structures as spaces that provided opportunities for interracial ecclesiastical activities based on church membership as well as on the spaces themselves. Further while the historiography is full of scholarship examining pro-enslavement theology, few books examine the way this theology took root in a practiced ecclesiology or theology applied to the nature, structures, and function of the church membership, its polity, and government. This work will display how mission churches were spaces in which a theology of race was applied to church ecclesiological structures to accommodate and make room in the church for pro-enslavement views and therefore separate church activities and membership based on one's race. Finally it will show that race was not linear in South Carolina Presbyterianism. The fluidity of racial categories, combined with the pragmatic nature of missionary survival on the southwestern South Carolina frontier, as well as in urban spaces, often made missionary churches spaces that both entrenched and occasionally challenged racial hierarchies.

Further few historians have attempted to make connections between antebellum and postbellum periods using mission schools, churches, and ecclesiastical spaces as links providing relationships in the antebellum context, which carried over into the postwar period and into Reconstruction. Similar connections can be made between preremoval and postremoval periods regarding the missionary's relationship to the Chickasaw. For instance Presbyterian churches for free African Americans in Charleston, set up in 1865, provided glimpses into the agency and autonomy of African American communities apart from White communities but still had a similar membership base, ecclesiastical structure, and even some of the same leaders as antebellum churches under the "enslavement mission" model in the 1850s.[13] Therefore the connection in the prewar and postwar periods must be examined more closely.

Finally, today, many individuals think conversations on race in the church are new and that church leaders didn't care about issues like race in the past, but that forwarding the gospel was the only concern. Nothing could be further from the truth. One might even say that nineteenth-century Southern Presbyterians were absolutely obsessed with the question of race and did their best theological gymnastics to defend it and apply it to the life of the church in a thoroughly unbiblical and heterodox manner by imputing their regions' entrenched economic, political, and racial views onto church structures. Therefore when modern Presbyterians discuss race in the church, it is coming from a long history and tradition of this conversation dating back to the late eighteenth century. In fact nothing is probably more Southern Presbyterian, historically speaking, than talking about race and the church through biblical and theological lenses.

Indeed nowhere is this more apparent than in what John Lafayette Girardeau called "ecclesiastical equality" and what Robert Lewis Dabney called our "ecclesiastical equality of negroes." Girardeau used this term in 1866 to describe what he believed was equal status between African Americans and Whites regarding church membership and ecclesiastical rights. Indeed Girardeau used biblical precepts to point the Presbyterian Church in the United States toward addressing issues of inequality with regard to church membership for individuals of non-White heritage. Thus ecclesiology and theological principles rooted firmly in antebellum interracial relationships pushed Girardeau's position on race to one of ecclesiastical equality during Reconstruction. Dabney worked to destroy Girardeau's position at every point. The two men spent years on this subject in their writing and discourse. This is probably just as much if not more than anyone in the modern Presbyterianism has spent on the topic in the last sixty years.

The historiography included in this book is robust[14] as many of the historical conversations and threads throughout the book cover a variety of subjects ranging from a host of issues tied up with southern history, which make their way into southern religious history.[15] The experiences of religion among southerners[16] is especially central to the work as African Americans, Native Americans, and individuals of European descent as well as individuals with a variety of ethnic ancestral threads. These groups are centrally placed as practitioners of southern religion. The historiography of religion in the South,[17] missions, pro-enslavement ideology,[18] and particularly missions to enslaved African Americans play a central role in the analysis of this context.[19] Further, African American religious experiences in the Atlantic world shed light on nineteenth-century Presbyterian mission churches and provide context for mission churches as biracial communities.[20] The eras and topics covered include and speak to historiographies related to the colonial South,[21] the nineteenth-century institution of enslavement and race,[22] southern religion,[23] African American history, Native American history, southern Presbyterian churches,[24] and the US South broadly. To deal with all the nuances of these various historiographical debates would be its own book. However one prominent theme throughout the book is examined through the lens of John Boles's notion of a "limited emancipationist impulse.[25] The book explores the ways in which Southern Presbyterians used mission churches as a means of control, but also as spaces in which the enslaved were active agents. As Janet Cornelius argued, African Americans were active participants in these churches and quickly seized opportunities.[26] Cornelius also makes the argument that the foundation for post–Civil War congregations have their roots in antebellum mission churches in the South.[27] Further, the connection of antebellum mission churches to the Lost Cause was strong as Girardeau and other southern shepherds engaged as Confederate chaplains and later as ministers and practitioners of Lost Cause rhetoric.[28] Last, broader historiographical debates dealing with religion,[29] race,[30] and church membership as it applied to Whites, African Americans, and Native Americans in church mission spaces across US history is instructive of our understanding of the US South.

Indeed, the lives of individuals like Thomas Donnelly, T. C. Stuart, Charles Colcock Jones, John Adger, and John Girardeau, have shown that missions to European immigrants, African Americans and Native Americans upheld a racialized vision for the role of people of color within the church. However at times these mission churches also served as avenues for sympathetic Whites to attempt to mitigate the harsh treatment of enslaved African Americans or Native Americans. Indeed there are many inconsistencies, nuances, and complexities inherent within the study of enslavement missions. As Donald Mathews has stated,

> Identified with the efforts of antebellum southerners to vindicate their social system, the mission as a historical institution and idea has suffered from the sentimentality of conservatives and the righteous indignation of radicals. Awareness of class interest, religious self-delusion, and racial fears, however, should not prevent historians from considering the ironies and almost hopeless contradictions that bemired southern evangelicals. If the mission was a movement to impose social control, it nevertheless sprang from some of the best inclinations of White southerners. And if the best was inadequate to deal with social problems, perhaps the monumental quality of the inadequacy is worth remembering.[31]

While no doubt bemired, the example of Presbyterian missionaries in urban and frontier spaces in South Carolina presents similar issues toward Native Americans and the institution of enslavement among southern evangelicals to which Mathews refers. Indeed internal and sometimes external contradictions "bemired southern evangelicals" and the lives and work of Thomas Donnelly, T. C. Stuart, Charles C. Jones, John B. Adger, and John Lafayette Girardeau bear witness to that struggle.[32]

Chapter 1 examines the work of Thomas Donnelly at Rocky Creek Presbyterian Church in the South Carolina Backcountry and missions to the peoples of the northeastern section of South Carolina who were largely recent immigrants to South Carolina as well as enslaved African Americans. It traces the movement of a Presbyterian church pastor from Pennsylvania down to South Carolina in 1802 and how the writing of Alexander McCleod influenced the experiences of enslaved African Americans in South Carolina.

Chapter 2 investigates the life of Thomas C. Stuart and the missions to the Chickasaw in western South Carolina. Stuart became one of the earliest missionaries in western South Carolina, which would later become a part of the Mississippi territory. In 1820, the Synod of South Carolina sent Stuart to establish the Monroe Mission, and he served as a missionary to the Chickasaw of northeastern Mississippi for decades. The chapter examines Stuart's relationships with church members: African Americans, Whites, Native Americans, and those of "mixed heritage." Later, Chickasaw College grew out of a need for educational institutions outside of Monroe. The chapter traces the ways in which Stuart's preaching, the ministry of enslaved African Americans, and the work of Chickasaw members complicate our understanding of southern mission churches on frontier spaces.[33]

Chapter 3 analyzes the genesis of missions to enslaved African Americans in the southeast by understanding the work of missionary to the enslaved Charles Colcock Jones. The chapter begins with an examination of the father of enslavement missions and his work in Liberty County, Georgia and makes connections between Jones and the later work of John B. Adger out of Second Presbyterian Church in Charleston, South Carolina. The chapter examines the philosophies of Jones and how his work undergirded the efforts in the South Carolina Lowcountry.

Chapter 4 then moves into an in-depth analysis of the early mission work of John Lafayette Girardeau. The chapter then follows the mission from its home on Anson Street to the larger mission structure on Calhoun Street. Examining this antebellum structure of mission churches, interracial ecclesiastical activity, and the system of complex human relationships at the Zion Mission is central to understanding the overall thrust of enslaved missions in South Carolina as it was the largest mission to enslaved African Americans that South Carolina ever produced. The chapter traces the history of the Zion mission church up to 1860 and the beginning of the Civil War as Girardeau would go on to serve in the Confederate Army as a chaplain for the Twenty-Third South Carolina Volunteers.

Chapter 5 explores Girardeau, Zion Church, and the postwar interracial church, which existed from 1866 up to 1874 in Charleston, South Carolina. This chapter addresses Girardeau's philosophy of "ecclesiastical equality," and postwar philosophies, for ecclesiastical equality and his work in trying to keep the Presbyterian Church United States together as an integrated body into the late 1870s. Finally the chapter examines how an antebellum multiethnic mission church lead by paternalistic White southern Presbyterians left a space for an autonomous racial, political, and even economic identity among Zion's African American membership into the mid-twentieth century and beyond.

The book concludes with an examination of Girardeau's rhetoric and the South Carolina Presbyterian Church's contribution to Lost Cause ideology toward the end of Reconstruction. The connection between Girardeau's Lost Cause sentiments and his postbellum work on ecclesiastical equality ultimately serves to reinforce Southern Presbyterian missionaries' antebellum views on race and incorporates language that is both unbiblical and heterodox. Indeed it is possible that many southern shepherds, including the ones who might have had the best possible intentions, were continuing to let wolves in, disguised as sheep, that would have ramifications on racial segregation for the next century and beyond.

Chapter 1

"A Black Swan in the Flock"

Race and Enslavement in Rocky Creek, South Carolina, 1801–2

Ernest Trice Thompson, an early twentieth century Presbyterian Church historian once mentioned that missions in the Southern Presbyterian Church "recognized its responsibility to certain needy classes located within its bounds—Indians, Negroes, Foreigners, isolated Mountain folk, and others." Thompson was discussing the Presbyterian impulse toward "domestic missions" or peoples that urban, property-owning Presbyterians thought were on the margins and needed to hear the gospel. Presbyterian ministers throughout the nineteenth century labored as domestic missionaries to Backcountry immigrant populations, enslaved African American populations, Native Americans, and those considered "needy." While evangelicalism certainly drove this sense of "responsibility" there were other characteristics that typified Presbyterian mission work. Presbyterians were noted for their belief in education, and so literacy was a prime focus of missions work—as well as theological training, ecclesiastical organization, and development of ecclesiastical leadership.[1] However as the missionaries brought their version of the gospel, they also brought with them expectations on culture, racial hierarchy, and the importance of profit through enslaved labor.

The Reverend Thomas Donnelly, pastor of the "Carolina Covenanters" in Rocky Creek, South Carolina, once wrote that there may be such a thing as a Christian holder of enslaved persons, "but a slaveholder among Christians is like a black swan in the flock."[2] This is a unique perspective among South Carolinians in the early nineteenth century. The "peculiar institution" in South Carolina goes back to 1691 when Sir John Yeamans, a Barbados planter, first governor of Carolina, and one of the founders of Charleston, brought enslaved African people from Barbados to clear his plantation on the Ashley River.[3] Enslavement as an institution is interwoven in the state's history and culture but also deeply embedded within the religious consciousness of its people.

However one South Carolina Presbyterian, Thomas Donnelly, seeing the dehumanizing effect that enslavement had on enslaved African Americans, began a process among a group of Presbyterians in Rocky Creek, South Carolina, to consider the ecclesiastical rights of enslaved members of their church and the issue of enslaved person ownership itself. In a rare move among South Carolinians in the early nineteenth century, Donnelly and his congregants strove to consider their own duties within their small ecclesiastical context to enslaved African Americans within their flock.

It is important to note that while later chapters focus on Presbyterian missions to Native Americans and African Americans, this chapter displays the intent of a Reformed Presbyterian Church to spread missions to southerners and individuals in the US South who had recently emigrated from Europe. So while domestic missions might include missionary efforts to people considered "heathens" such as the African Americans or Native Americans, there were also domestic missions attempts to recent immigrant communities without a church of their own.

The Carolina Covenanters, or members of the Reformed Presbyterian Church in South Carolina, looked upon the institution of enslavement as "an evil of enormous magnitude."[4] In 1802 a Reformed Presbyterian Church (RPC) pastor and theologian living in Albany, New York, Reverend Alexander McLeod, authored a pamphlet entitled *Negro Slavery Unjustifiable*. This document was not only groundbreaking for its time, but it also employed biblically based arguments that would go on to benefit the abolitionist cause some thirty years later. In South Carolina, Donnelly, acting under the Coldenham Presbytery's vote for acceptance of McLeod's views on enslavement, would oversee the process of making sure his church implemented the decisions of the presbytery. Indeed some thirty years before the height of the abolitionist movement and sixty years before emancipation, a handful of families in Rocky Creek, Chester District, South Carolina, decided to free enslaved African Americans in response to the work of McLeod and Donnelly. This event, while a small representation of South Carolina Presbyterianism, is significant for the history of Reformed Presbyterians and their impact on anti-enslavement in American society. It helped to frame an ideological stance against American enslavement as unbiblical and out of accord with historic Christian practice and Christian theology in a stronghold of American slavery: South Carolina.

Many northern abolitionists would later cede biblical arguments to southern theologians because there were verses in the Bible defending enslavement and southern theologians were experts in the exegesis, and sometimes exegetical gymnastics, it took to apply these verses to a modern context. As Eugene Genovese has mentioned, "intellectual historians and northern thinkers such as the Emersons and the Adamses" thought "that southerners had no minds, only temperaments," but "on one subject after another the intellectuals of the Old South matched and in some cases overmatched the best the North had to offer."[5] This would most certainly include the southern theological arguments for the biblical justification of enslavement from the pens of men like James Henley Thornwell, Benjamin Morgan Palmer, and Robert Lewis Dabney.

As a result, numerous abolitionists withdrew from making biblical arguments to defend abolition in favor of arguments proposing social reform influenced by Thomas Paine's *The Age of Reason*. David B. Davis, in his book *The Problem of Slavery in the Age of Revolution 1770–1823*, seems to imply that the abolitionists did not think so highly of the biblical arguments for anti-enslavement. Davis mentioned "Garrison's disciple, Henry Clarke Wright, summed up the radical abolitionist view in the title of an essay, 'The Bible, if opposed to Self-Evident Truth, is Self-Evident Falsehood.'" For another abolitionist, Charles Sterns, this meant that the Old Testament was a tissue of lies, "no more the work of God than the Koran, or the Book of Mormon."[6] William Llyod Garrison asserted that the Bible "must be judged by 'its reasonableness and utility, by the probabilities of the case, by historical confirmation, by human experience and observation, by the facts of science, by the intuition of the spirit. Truth is older than any Parchment."[7]

In contrast the examples of Mcleod and Donnelly provide a historical precedent of a biblically rooted and well-developed biblical exegesis and theology of anti-enslavement. This work would influence a denomination that had experienced some measure of success with freeing enslaved people in South Carolina. The example of Rocky Creek can provide us with fresh insight as to how a biblically orthodox denomination successfully challenged the entrenched system of enslavement in the South, where so many other denominations failed. To be sure understanding Mcleod's groundbreaking *Negro Slavery Unjustifiable* is central to gauging what happened in Rocky Creek, South Carolina, in 1801–2. Further exploration into this unique historical episode and document displays the Presbyterian Church's function as it related to anti-enslavement and domestic missions in South Carolina.

In "1763 the Peace of Paris marked the end of the Great War for Empire (the French and Indian War in America and the Seven Years War in Europe)."[8] This was a time of radical change in America as the new colony was seeking to legitimize itself as a recognized entity. Thomas Paine's rationalistic writings ushered in a time of conflicting ideologies in American thought between an English Enlightenment and Calvinistic theology. In the latter half of the eighteenth century the United States was just coming off a devastating revolution and war. Revolution had also broken out in France, and the political landscape of the world was changing dramatically. After the American Revolution John Locke, "whose doctrine of natural rights was the keystone of revolutionary ideology," and who had a hand in the early documents forming Charles Town as a colony while serving as a secretary to one of the founding Lord's Proprietors Ashley Cooper, and had simultaneously "justified slavery as a continuation of a state of war in which a captive was enslaved rather than killed."[9]

A few states, such as Vermont in 1777, had gone so far as to outlaw slavery.[10] In 1779, John Laurens of South Carolina proposed the arming of three thousand enslaved African Americans promising them freedom if they fought for the cause of the Americans. The Continental Congress approved his proposal, but the South Carolina legislature rejected it.[11] James Madsion, who after the war recaptured his enslaved African Americans who had tried to run away under British protection, stated: "I will not punish a slave merely for coveting that liberty for which we have paid the price of so much blood, and have proclaimed so often to be the right, and worthy pursuit, of every human being."[12] The Northwest Ordinance of 1787 provided a means by which new states could be created and therefore western lands added to the Union. Article VI held that there should be no slavery received in those new states and there were "no southern members of the Congress of Confederation" who "voiced the slightest disapproval of Article VI, which a committee of five, including a South Carolinian and two Virginians" approved.[13]

In 1787, South Carolina enacted a temporary ban on the enslaved persons trade and later in 1788 Connecticut, New York, Massachusetts, and Pennsylvania forbade their citizens from participating in the slave trade.[14] In 1793, Eli Whitney's cotton gin paved the way for the "cultivation of short-staple cotton through much of the South."[15] This invention helped make enslavement an embedded institution in the southern landscape because of the profitability that the cotton gin provided. Southern Christians began to see a more entrenched view of slavery at this time within the confines of the church because most, if not all, of the landed elites serving in the churches as elders were enslavers or had business interests that benefited directly from the institution of enslavement. As enslavement became more and more entrenched in the southern landscape, Presbyterian churches in the South began justifying American slavery as biblically supported even though there were important distinctions between enslavement in the near east (BCE), in the Greco-Roman world, and in the Atlantic world and US South. The most important distinctions were that in the seventeenth century sub-Saharan African people were targeted for enslavement because of their race, a trade market developed on the coast of West Africa with European vessels as market drivers, and this market required that human stealing take place to provide the "commodities" for this market.

The abolitionist movement had its early beginnings in 1794 in Philadelphia where the first meeting of the Convention of Delegates from the Abolition Societies met.[16] In 1800, John Rutledge Jr. of South Carolina opposed an anti-enslavement petition in Congress referring to "this new-fangled French philosophy of liberty and equality."[17] As the nineteenth century began, Gabriel Prosser's plot to take over Richmond, Virginia, via armed enslaved persons, was discovered. William Henry Harrison called a convention and appealed to Congress to suspend the Northwest Ordinance and allow enslaved persons to be in the Indiana Territory. In 1803, after the purchase of the Louisiana Territory from France, South Carolina opened its ports to the African enslavement trade once again after an act of Congress, passed in 1800, made it illegal for Americans to engage in the enslavement trade between two or more nations.[18] There was also a heightened sense of fear throughout the South of enslaved person insurrections. It is in this context that Alexander McLeod made his way into the United States from the highlands of Scotland and penned the discourse entitled *Negro Slavery Unjustifiable*.

Alexander McLeod was one of twelve McLeod children on the Island of Mull in the Scottish Highlands. There on a small farm on the southwest coast of the island of Ardchrisinish, McLeod grew up. The farm included the southern boundary of the district known as Borlas, which the Duke of Argyle rented to the family. Here Alexander was born on June 12, 1774.[19] His father was a pastor who died when Alexander was young. His mother oversaw his formal education with the help of many tutors. Mcleod's biographer, Samuel Brown Wylie, wrote, "he was remarkably a child of prayer, and had been devoted to the ministry of the gospel from his birth; and of this object, amidst all the vicissitudes of his early life, he never once lost sight."[20]

A letter from Alexander's brother, a colonel in the army, corroborates this description of McLeod. Colonel McLeod wrote, "From early infancy, my brother was fond of study; and while I was engaged in boisterous and sometimes dangerous sports, he would be picking up scraps and leaves of books. He had a most retentive memory, and as far as I can recollect, he was eager to become a minister of the gospel."[21] In 1792, McLeod left from Liverpool to America. He settled in Albany close to the Mohawk River. He soon became connected with other Scottish Highlanders who had emigrated to America. Wylie mentioned that "his manners were agreeable; his mind noble, generous, and ardent. He was affable, condescending, and national. He loved the country of his birth; he loved and cherished his countrymen wherever he met them."[22]

McLeod was a Presbyterian, but he came to this conclusion only from extensive investigation, reasoning, and reflection. After much consideration in the late eighteenth century, he and several of the Scottish immigrants from the Mohawk and Schenectady vicinity adopted the articles and testimony of the RPC. This denomination was ardently biblically orthodox in its focus and held to the Westminster Confession of Faith and the *Larger* and *Shorter Catechism* as the creed of their church. Most notably the denomination was famous for its musical worship employing only the Bible; therefore it only sang the psalms and without the aid of instruments. The other noteworthy distinction of the PRC was the "Old Scottish Covenanter" view that Jesus was Lord and King over all the earth and therefore any state or nation's constitution must include this as a basic tenet.[23] Members of the RPC did not run for public office, nor did many of the members vote in elections for a representative that did not hold to these tenets.

Alexander McLeod then came under the tutelage of the Reverend James McKinney, a member of the RPC who had come from Ireland. Alexander attended Union College in Schenectady and graduated with distinguished honors in 1798.[24] McLeod then studied theology under Reverend McKinney and read the Bible as well as Francis Turretin's theology and commentaries. At his ordination McLeod was called upon "to deliver, viva voce, his answers to the Presbytery's inquiries. Mr. McCleod's . . . grasp of his subject; his arrangement; his manner of delivery; his self-possession, and the tout ensemble, could leave no doubt on the mind of any intelligent auditor, that he possessed talents of the first order."[25] At this time the RPC denomination was small and mostly located in the Northeast in Vermont, Pennsylvania, and lower New York, but there was also a small covenanter community in South Carolina under the direction of a Mr. King, "who had some time before, as a member of Committee of Scotch Presbytery, arrived in South Carolina."[26]

While McLeod was studying theology under McKinney; King had also received a student of divinity in South Carolina, Thomas Donnelly. In 1800, Donnelly became the main pastor for the covenanters in South Carolina, and McLeod labored in the southern part of New York. Later that year "in the fall of 1800, a call was made on Mr. McLeod to the pastoral charge of the united congregations of the City of New York and Coldenham, in Orange County, in the same State. Mr. McLeod demurred, on the plea that there were slaveholders among the subscribers to the call."[27] The issue of enslavement was now before the presbytery, which included a church in the enslavement state of South Carolina.

Wylie noted that "at Mr. Mcleod's suggestion, the subject was acted upon and this inhuman and demoralizing practice was purged from our connection."[28] Presbytery minutes from February 11, 1801, mentioned that "a petition came in requesting a reconsideration of the business respecting slaveholders, so far as this species of traffic might be supposed to affect Christian communion."[29] The minutes showed "it was agreed upon prior to the further consideration of this subject that all slave-holders in the communion of this church should be warned to attend the next meeting of the committee."[30] On February 18, the presbytery met, and the minutes recorded "it was unanimously agreed that enslaving these, our African brethren, is an evil of enormous magnitude, and that none who continue in such a gross departure, from humanity and the dictates of our benevolent religion, can have any just title to communion in this church."[31]

Wylie described the presbytery's position: "It only required to be mentioned. There was no dissenting voice in condemning the nefarious traffic in human flesh. From that period forward, none either practicing or abetting slavery in any shape, has been found on the records of our ecclesiastical connection."[32] What would this mean for the RPC in South Carolina, most of whose membership were practicing holders of enslaved persons? First, it is important to understand McLeod's position, which became the accepted RPC view on enslavement. Indeed examining *Negro Slavery Unjustifiable*, it is important to understand that this was McLeod's first publication. Yet as Wylie noted "It is true, the style and phraseology, have a few vestiges of the author's juvenescence; but many characteristics of powerful discrimination and cogent deduction exist."[33]

Dwight Lowell Dumond discussed McCleod's discourse in *Antislavery: The Crusade for Freedom in America*. Dumond mentioned McLeod as one who fought for anti-enslavement in the early nineteenth century: "He went on to become one of the leading preachers in the country, a powerful champion of individual freedom." Further "he denounced slavery as immoral, contrary to the rights of man, and destructive of intellectual powers and finer sensibilities. The most important part of his argument, however, was his emphasis upon the way in which the inferiority of the Negroes to the whites had been so grossly exaggerated."[34] Dumond emphasized the importance of the discourse by pointing out that it was "published in eleven separate editions, the last in 1863." Dumond also noted that the discourse was important because "it went beyond slavery itself to the more fundamental and lasting doctrine of racial inferiority."[35]

After Alexander McLeod received a call to pastor a church in Orange County, New York, "he perceived among the subscribers the names of some whom he knew to be holders of slaves. He doubted the consistency of enslaving the Negroes with the Christian system, and was unwilling to enter into a full ecclesiastic communion with those who continued the practice."[36] C. Vann Woodward argued that "the party that led the Northern crusade against slavery has not come off well at the hands of the new revisionists who have been emphasizing the pervasiveness of anti-Negro sentiment in Northern society."[37] Indeed McLeod was reacting just as much against the New York view of the enslaved African Americans as much he was the southern and South Carolina view.

Negro Slavery Unjustifiable is a discourse that McLeod intended for the elders, the members of the church, as well as the greater denomination about his sentiments regarding enslavement. As his prime text, McLeod chose Exodus 21:16: "He that stealeth a man, and selleth him, or if he be found in his hand, shall surely be put to death." McLeod went on to argue against American enslavement from several passages in the Bible, which made his discourse novel and ahead of his time. McLeod made many arguments against enslavement in the discourse, but there are five which should be given particular attention.

The first argument McLeod presented was that to hold any man in perpetual enslavement was sinful. McLeod here presented the natural rights of humans whom God made in the image of him and as a bearer of the *imago dei*. Therefore "one's life and his faculties are the gift of God. Considering man a free agent, by the constitution of nature he has a right to the exercise of freedom, in conformity to the precepts of that law by which the author of nature has ordered him to regulate his actions."[38] McLeod here addressed the deeper issue of the total removal of freedom that the American peculiar institution inherently lacked. For McLeod this went against God's nature, which gave humans freedom and made them active agents. To be sure, enslavement was "an attempt to reduce a moral agent to a mere machine, whose motions are to be regulated by external force; and, consequently a denial of his right to the person enslaved."[39] It is important to note that this was another distinction from ancient slavery in the Near East or in the Greco-Roman period. Both societies held enslaved persons for a time, but neither held people in bondage for their entire lives with no hope of manumission or that of their children or children's children. In American enslavement, one's race meant that enslavement was forever and generational down to one's children's children with no hope of freedom.

A second argument from McLeod's discourse was that American enslavement had a definite and clearly defined racial element. McLeod noted that "right stands opposite and contrary to right" and that if "I have a right to enslave and sell you, you have an equal right to enslave and sell me. The British have a right to enslave the French, and the French the British—the Americans the Africans, and the Africans the Americans." [40] Very few if any pro-enslavement advocates would have been willing to admit that Americans, British, or French citizens could be forced into enslavement by Africans. Indeed the notion that an Anglo of European descent could be taken in bondage into enslavement by an African was both unthinkable and preposterous in the context of the nineteenth century. This meant that pro-enslavement Europeans and Americans believed that there was an inherent subservience within the African race, that somehow Africans were a debased form of humanity who should be treated as animals or livestock. As McLeod insightfully noted, "Such absurdity will meet with few advocates to plead its cause in theory."[41] Thus, McLeod was arguing that the entire system of enslavement in the Atlantic world, beginning in the early seventeenth century, was racially driven and therefore constructed based on the perceived racial inferiority of the sub-Saharan African. It is important to note here that to believe in this system and practice it, one had to believe in White or European superiority and African or African American inferiority. This system therefore makes it a racially driven or White supremacist system.[42]

A third argument, made by many later abolitionists, was that the practice of enslaving men and women stood equally opposed to the general tenor of scripture as well as against four precepts of the Decalogue. As the abolitionist and Virginian Presbyterian George Bourne stated in 1845, "Slavery, however supported by use of 'isolated passages,' is against the spirit of the Scriptures."[43] Here McLeod made use of various texts such as Acts 17:26; Jesus's statements of the golden rule; James 2:10; as well as the fifth, sixth, eighth and tenth commandments to show the general crux of scripture as against enslavement. McCleod found it clear from the overall theme of Jesus' teachings as well as of God's character throughout the Bible that holding men in perpetual bondage without the hope of freedom based solely on race was inimical to the biblical and Judeo-Christian ethic as well as to the overall thrust of scripture: freedom in Christ.

The last argument from McLeod was "the pernicious consequences of the system of slavery"[44] on humans and a society in which enslavement was prevalent. This was a rather large category in McLeod's argument but is also the most cogent and inventive. The first point under this larger framework was that "this practice has a tendency to destroy the finer feelings and render the heart of man more obdurate."[45] McLeod compared the owner of enslaved persons to the butcher or the executioner who becomes desensitized to death and blood. He described their demeanors in detail: how their attitudes remained immovable even when faced with physical torture and cries of those killed, lashed, and beaten. Mcleod again referred to the racial aspect of enslavement in the midst of this argument mentioning that, "the slave-holder views all the Ethiopian race as born to serve. His heart is steeled against them."[46] This argument contained much depth and foresight in that it not only mentioned the hardened heart toward physical violence, but it also provided an understanding of a racist worldview undergirding the ethos of American enslavement and how this racist worldview ran counter to biblical teaching. Thus McLeod seemed to possess a very full understanding of enslavement in the nineteenth century. To be sure men like McLeod and others knew that race was a major factor, and this was evidenced in his argument.[47]

For McLeod, one race could not hold another in perpetual enslavement for centuries without developing some demented, backward, and hateful views of another race. The owner's heart was not only hardened to the physical torture that he or she was implementing but also became hardened to the possibility that the African American could be just as free, imaginative, intelligent, and industrious as himself or herself. This would also have implications for the role of the African American church member. There would be questions by many White southerners as to the ability of African Americans to serves as pastors, teachers, and elders. Thus sown into the fiber of the American enslaver's understanding of the enslaved African American were the seeds of a racist ideology that have blossomed into poisoned fruit even into today's cultural, political, social, economic, and religious landscape.

McLeod concluded that enslavement "debases a part of the human race and tends to destroy their intellectual and active powers."[48] Wherever Christianity has gone, in the post-Reformation period, it has encouraged education and literacy among the people exposed to it. For McLeod enslavement in America was inconsistent with church history and the church's interest in promoting biblical literacy and understanding. McLeod wrote, "The slave, from his infancy, is obliged implicitly to obey the will of another. There is no circumstance, which can stimulate him to exercise his own intellectual powers. The energies of his mind are left to slumber. Every attempt is made to smother them."[49] Not only is this treatment inconsistent with the history of the Christian church, but it is also inconsistent with the orthodox Christian teaching of God's design in Genesis of humans as thinking, acting, and creative individuals made in God's image. For McLeod the dehumanizing effects of American enslavement were a direct contradiction to the creation ordinances of God. According to Genesis God created humans to have dominion over creation and to exercise their talents, gifts, and creative powers over the earth as a reflection of and image bearer of God. American enslavement, as McLeod pointed out, robbed humans of this privilege intended for them by God and stood in stark contradiction to the most basic principles of the biblical creation ordinances. For McLeod then the Christian church could not tolerate American enslavement as it existed in early nineteenth-century America.

McLeod then went on to anticipate expected objections and answers. One of the points was an answer to the distinction between humans and enslaved humans. McLeod asserted that "the inferiority of the blacks to the whites has been greatly exaggerated."[50] Americans at this time thought that a less technologically advanced civilization possessed an inherent incapability in the human intellect of that given civilization. McLeod disposed of this argument by citing the works of Phillis Wheatly, the eighteenth-century American poet, which evidenced for McLeod that "the negroes are not destitute of poetic genius."[51] McLeod also rightly noted that it did not matter what the intellectual capabilities of a certain civilization were; humans inherently possess "moral sentiments, and a free agent. He has a right, from the constitution given him by the Author of Nature, to dispose of himself, and be his own master in all respects, except in violating the will of heaven."[52]

McLeod also made use of a very modern argument for his time. He referenced recent studies of New Guinea's inhabitants. These studies displayed that all humans around the world were different in appearance because of "the action of the elements on the human body, the diet and manners of men, are causes sufficient to account for that change in the organization of bodies which gives them a tendency to absorb the rays of light. A difference in these can make a distinction in the same latitude."[53] McLeod went on to argue the changes that occurred in groups over twenty to thirty centuries due to the climate and diet, but that these changes do not affect persons' intellectual capabilities, nor did it affect the dignity that is due to them for simply being human and bearing the *imago dei*.

McLeod went on to anticipate the argument that many southern theologians, most notably including Robert L. Dabney in the 1840s and 1850s, offered as a reason for the biblical justification for the enslavement of Africans and African Americans. Many southern, as well as some northern, theologians claimed that the curse of Noah in Genesis 9:25–27 was the reason for the Africans' subservient state. Those who would later be opposed to McLeod would claim that the African race was Ham's posterity. McLeod virtually dismembered this argument on four grounds.

> In order to justify Negro slavery from this prophecy, it will be necessary to prove four things. 1. That all the posterity of Canaan were devoted to suffer slavery. 2. That African negroes are really descended of Canaan. 3. That each of the descendants of Shem and Japheth has a moral right to reduce any of them to servitude. 4. That every slave-holder is really descended from Shem or Japheth. Want of proof in any of these particulars will invalidate the whole objection.[54]

McLeod continued to show in the subsequent pages how ridiculous and false this argument was for the justification of the American trade in enslaved persons since none of the particulars above either historically or archeologically applied to American Whites or American African men or either's ancestry.

McLeod closed with a plea to those holders of enslaved persons in his church and in America. He wrote, may God, "enable you to maintain an honorable testimony against the abominable usurpation. Be merciful to them. Cultivate their understandings. Make them feel themselves to be men. Raise them to the rank, which God has assigned them. Teach them the doctrines of the gospel. Give them habits of industry."[55] McLeod then begged holders of enslaved persons to set their men and women free stating, "Sacrifice the property, which the civil law gives you in them, on the altar of religion."[56] McLeod concluded his discourse with this poignant indictment of America: "It must appear ridiculous to Europeans 'to hear an American patriot singing with one hand declarations of independency, and with the other brandishing a whip over an affrighted slave.' Can you be sincere friends to liberty and order, and tolerate this dreadful traffic?"[57]

It is important to fully understand McLeod's discourse before examining the events at Rocky Creek in 1802. Indeed the Rev. Thomas Donnelly would use McLeod's arguments with the RPC's holding of enslaved persons in South

Carolina as the document was central to the presbytery's decision. McLeod's discourse was also considerable in that it lent historical significance to the orthodox, biblical Christians who believed in the infallibility of the Bible, held to a traditional understanding of the Westminster Standards, and consequently saw the American enslavement trade as an aberration of the sacred scriptures. The example of McLeod, the RPC, and Rocky Creek are important examples of American Christians in the US South who pushed back against the transatlantic enslavement trade and the domestic institution of enslavement. McLeod's thinking and arguments, buttressed by the presbytery's decision to remove holders of enslaved persons from membership, made its way into the hands of Thomas Donnelly in South Carolina at the beginning of the nineteenth century. To be sure the incident at Rocky Creek added to the impact that McLeod's discourse had on American Reformed Presbyterianism and South Carolina ecclesiastical life.

Rocky Creek Church in South Carolina's Chester District was located on Little Rocky Creek in the northeastern portion of the state near the border with North Carolina. The history of the church dated back to 1750 with the arrival of immigrants from Pennsylvania and Virginia.[58] It was the first Presbyterian church settled near this creek just five miles from the Catholic church. One of the early families of the area was John McDonald and his wife, who were killed by the "Cherokee Indians in 1761 and their seven children carried off."[59] The settlement grew considerably over the years and the Reverend William Richardson of Waxhaw was the only minister within a hundred miles. In 1772, the Reverend William Martin came from Ireland and became the first covenanting preacher among the people of Rocky Creek.[60]

The first church building was a log facility, which the British burned down during the 1780 American Revolution. Lord Cornwallis took the Reverend William Martin prisoner and released him at Winnsboro. Because of the "disturbed state of the country," Martin went to Mecklenburg, North Carolina. Martin ended up coming back to Rocky Creek after the war, but the church sent him away after a short spell due to his "intemperance." The Reverend William King along with the Committee of Scotch Reformed Presbyterians joined Reverend Martin in 1792. In the 1790s "the majority of the members of the (Reformed Presbyterian) church in North America" in the US South "were at this time in South Carolina."[61]

However, the people in Rocky Creek Presbyterian's demeanor and disposition toward McLeod's position must be somewhat attributed to Reverend James McKinney's work and preaching; he was the same man mentioned earlier as

McLeod's theological mentor. The Reverend D. S. Faris, in his history of the RPC in South Carolina, noted that McKinney was "very magnanimous. They flocked to his preaching from all quarters." In 1801, sixteen elders at Rocky Creek are listed, a number that would most likely represent a rather sizable community. Reverend Thomas Donnelly was "ordained and installed pastor of Rocky Creek and vicinity, March 3, 1801."[62] Reverend McKinney died in August 1803, and the brunt of responsibility for ministry of the RPC in South Carolina fell to Mckinney's fellow pastor, Reverend Thomas Donnelly.

Thomas Donnelly received his education in Glasgow, Scotland, and finished training in Carlisle, Pennsylvania. He then studied theology under the Reverend William King and was among McLeod, Black, and Wylie when they were going through ordination in 1799 at Coldenham. Donnelly was noted as the "divine" of the group, while McLeod was known as the "orator."[63] His contemporaries knew him as a "true and superior theologian." After the famous declaration of the Coldenham Presbytery of 1801 regarding enslavement, the presbytery sent a note to every member of the congregation in South Carolina involved in the enslavement trade. The note included the following:

> Sir, you are hereby informed, that none can have communion in this church who hold slaves. You must therefore immediately have it registered, that your slaves are freed, before the sacrament (communion). If any difficulty arises to you in the manner of doing it, then you are desired to apply to the Committee of Presbytery, who will give directions in any circumstances of a doubtful nature in which you may be involved, in carrying this injunction into execution.[64]

As the communion season was coming soon in South Carolina, Donnelly and the church of Rocky Creek decided that they needed to figure out how to emancipate their enslaved persons before the sacrament was dispensed. Faris noted that "said bonds be in the meantime delivered into the hands of Rev. Thomas Donnelly and that Thomas Donnelly, John McNinch, and Robert Hemphill be appointed to a committee to inquire into the peculiar circumstances of each of the slaves to be liberated, as also into the true legal forms of emancipation."[65] One significant issue was that the men and women of the church did not question the presbytery's decision even though they likely would have been the victims of derision in South Carolina. In addition the economic loss would occur, which would have come with manumission as enslaved people were kept as both property and investments. Their children were an investment in future property and potential for economic growth.

It would have been relatively easy for the church members to attend another Presbyterian church such as the Associate Reformed or even another RPC church that had split from Rocky Creek in 1798 due to political dissent. Nevertheless the members and session at Rocky Creek decided, "the intentions of the Reformed Presbytery in purging out the accursed thing from among them may be carried into the most speedy effect."[66] Samuel Wylie noted that a committee from the RPC Presbytery was commissioned to go south on a rather hazardous journey from the northeast traveling through Pennsylvania, Kentucky, Tennessee, and into South Carolina. They made it to Rocky Creek where Wylie mentioned that they were "kindly received and hospitably entertained" by a covenanter, Mr. Quinn.[67]

Before the next communion, the committee reported to the church at Rocky Creek that the last meeting of the Coldenham Presbytery decided "respecting slaveholders, declaring that such must either immediately emancipate their slaves, or be refused admission to the Lord's Table."[68] Wylie stated that the committee was "no less surprised than delighted, to find with what alacrity those concerned came forward and complied with the decree of the Presbytery. In one day, it is believed, that in the small community of the Reformed Presbyterian Church in South Carolina, not less than three thousand guineas were sacrificed on the altar of principle."[69]

Faris's history of the RPC Church in South Carolina noted that the committee representing the presbytery was "given orders on this matter" and "empowered by Presbytery to abolish enslavement in the church."[70] Wylie declared, "a nobler, more generous and magnanimous people, than these South Carolinians, are seldom met with in any community" and he went on to name a few of the church members including, "the Mcmillan's, the Kell's, the Cooper's, the Orr's, and the Neil's."[71] Howe's history of Presbyterians in South Carolina also mentioned the Kell family, who "owned a negro at that time and freed her."[72]

One result was that the enslaved African Americans who received their freedom were invited to join the church as ecclesiastical equals. Faris noted that "some of the slaves then freed also became members of the church. Three children of Will and his wife, the former set free by James Hunter, and the latter by John McDill, are now members of Church Hill congregation in Illinois."[73] The Carolina Covenanters continued in the belief that enslavement was an inhuman abomination in society and claimed some notoriety for their aiding and abetting fugitive enslaved persons in South Carolina. Faris mentioned that "the underground railroad found its most daring conductors and station agents among the Carolina Covenanters" of South Carolina's Chester District. Later Faris noted that "having abolished slavery among themselves, they were not ashamed to be called abolitionists; and they were not afraid to incur the wrath of citizens and civil officers by helping the fugitives. It was part of their religion."[74] However, a few members, according to Howe, "refused to submit to the regulations, believing that the scriptures justified the possession of the heathen, whom they as teachers, were civilizing and Christianizing. It would be, they thought, as cruel to free them as to turn a child out to buffet with the world."[75]

Donnelly continued in his fervent disdain of the institution of enslavement throughout his life. Some of Donnelly's contemporaries heard that "he had always consistently opposed the iniquitous institution, his severe denunciations and arguments were overlooked, with some such remark as, 'Oh, it is only old Donnelly, let it go;' while if a Northern man has said the same thing it would have secured him a coat of tar and feathers."[76] Donnelly's son would later become a Presbyterian minister, not in the RPC tradition, and a holder of enslaved persons. The two would argue the points of biblical holding of enslaved persons as well as the precedents set by Christians who were holders of enslaved persons, and the father replied, "It may be so, but a slaveholder amongst Christians is like a black swan in the flock."[77]

Because of the Carolina Covenanters' views on enslavement, many were forced, whether it was pressure from their neighbors or by the civil authorities, to leave their native state and flee South Carolina. Faris noted that his father, "The Rev. James Faris used to say that he would have made the south his home, had it not been for the danger to his family through the temptations held out by the peculiar institution."[78] In 1847, Thomas Donnelly died and was buried by the few remaining covenanters near Rocky Creek Church beside his wife as well as beside the men who labored as pastors before him, McKinney and King.[79]

It is possible that this "redemption at Rocky Creek" might be overemphasized as a triumphalist anti-enslavement success of just a few southern abolitionists, when in all actuality members of a church were simply submitting to the decisions of their superiors. While there is some truth to this objection, the situation is certainly more complex than at first glance. If the Carolina Covenanters were simply submitting to the presbytery, then why were there members of the church who left? They either objected to the presbytery's ruling or were not willing to face the social ostracism and public disdain that the faithful at Rocky Creek faced because of their decisions. We must then believe that these Carolina Covenanters were convinced by biblically orthodox principles and Donnelly's preaching on the matter that enslavement was wrong. If this is the case then the emancipation of slaves at Rocky Creek complicates the historical understanding of how Presbyterians in South Carolina responded to enslavement, at least in one mission church in the Upstate of South Carolina.

A second area of importance is Rocky Creek's place in historical research considering orthodox Christians and anti-enslavement. Many historians, such as Mitchell Snay, Eugene Genovese, and Larry Tise, have noted Christian clergy who took a biblical pro-enslavement stance. However few historians have taken up the charge of presenting biblical, orthodox, Christians in the US South who were involved in the anti-enslavement movement and were successful in promoting slave manumissions from members in their congregations. John Christie and Dwight Dumond have given us the example of the Virginian pastor George Bourne, who presented an overture to the Presbyterian General Assembly of 1815 denouncing holding of enslaved persons.[80] Lawrence Thomas Lesick has provided us with the case of the Lane Rebels, the Lane Seminary students who risked suspension from school on the grounds of their anti-enslavement sentiments and actions. Gilbert Hobbes Barnes's *The Antislavery Impulse, 1830–1844* also provided "a corrective to the overemphasis that had been placed on the role of William Llyod Garrison"[81] and consequently a shift back to revivalism as a motivator for anti-enslavement. Bertram Wyatt-Brown's *Lewis Tappan and the Evangelical War against Slavery* provided the story of evangelical men fighting against enslavement, but it shed little light upon the biblical reasoning for either of Mr. Tappan's motivations. Ann C. Loveland's article, "Evangelicalism and the 'Immediate Emancipation' in American Antislavery Thought," "was the first attempt to develop the idea that abolitionists 'derived the doctrines and methods of immediatism from evangelicalism and . . . prosecuted the antislavery movement as a religious and moral enterprise.'"[82]

There is still much work to be done on the role of the orthodox, reformed, biblical inerrancy-believing confessors to the Westminster Standards who opposed enslavement in the nineteenth century South. These Rocky Creek "rebels" add to the historical scholarship done on the role of evangelicalism, southern religion, and social reform in the US South. The example of the Carolina Covenanters showed that the Bible and Christian theology might contribute to civil rights, justice, liberation, anti-enslavement, and social transformation. The Rocky Creek Covenanters may provide historians with an example of the success, motivations, and tactics of some southern abolitionists in South Carolina. These incidents of abolitionists swaying the opinions of southerners toward their positions are rare, but the success of Alexander McLeod and Thomas Donnelly, while small, is noteworthy.

This incident set a precedent for how one could achieve anti-enslavement success in a Presbyterian mission church in South Carolina and the broader US South. The Reformed Presbyterian Church sent missionaries into South Carolina to live among holders of enslaved persons and to proclaim a biblically orthodox position on enslavement. Donnelly was ordained in New York State, lived among his neighbors, ministered to them, preached in their churches on Sundays, conducted their weddings and funerals, and became a leader in their community. Slowly through preaching and ministering he convinced his congregants of the biblical rejection for human enslavement as it existed in the American South. When it came time for the presbytery to abolish enslavement in the churches, most of the Rocky Creek members adhered to their decision without dissent or protest. In addition when Donnelly was publicly vocal about his abolitionist tendencies, he would only elicit the response, "It's only old Donnelly; leave him alone." This pastor, shepherd, and flock provided an example and a historical precedent for future Presbyterian South Carolinians that this pathway was possible. A shepherd did not have to always let wolves in to ravage the flock. He could stand at the door and protect them.

By the 1830s abolitionist movement's high-water mark the system of enslavement was much more entrenched in South Carolina. The proliferation and production of cotton due to Eli Whitney's invention would have made it close to impossible to achieve a similar result in Charleston or the Lowcountry. However perhaps these Carolina Covenanters provided an example that could have been followed or at least a precedent that would make later pro-enslavement persons at least question their stance. The Redeemers at Rocky Creek are men and women who fought for the rights of the enslaved in their own ecclesiastical contexts in South Carolina in 1802. The larger flock was against slavery, the shepherd preached against slavery, the sheep listened, and the wolves were kept at bay.

Many shepherds ministered to South Carolina White immigrant, Native American, and African American communities. Because of the RPC's strong stance and McLeod's arguments, which won the day in the presbytery, Donnelly and other shepherds were able to keep the savage wolves at bay for a time. They could have simply offered the wolves a preference in their church body amenable to a South Carolina population that preferred gaining wealth on the total enslavement of African Americans. By doing this they possibly could have grown the flock and achieved "success" by the standards of how some shepherds measure church "success."

However McLeod and Donnelly challenged these ideas and the Chester Covenanters of South Carolina, stand as an example of what can happen when a church lives out the principles it claims to follow.

The Rocky Creek mission kept the same categories for membership whether someone was White or African American. Further Donnelly and McLeod set a precedent for other Presbyterians in South Carolina to follow. They created a road map for other missionaries so that a church might exist as a representative in the deep South to disturb and disrupt the institution of enslavement. For these missionaries the savage wolves at the door were rabid, but the shepherds provided protection to the sheep under their care at great cost. Sadly even with this precedent future missionaries in South Carolina would allow savage wolves to come into their flocks and feast upon their sheep. They would not be willing to sacrifice economic growth and entrenched views on race to make room in the flock for all the sheep. Some Presbyterian missionaries in South Carolina would stay home and minister directly to enslaved African Americans. Others would move out to the western regions of South Carolina to minister to Native Americans.

Chapter 2

"The Father of Native American Missions in Western South Carolina"

T. C. Stuart and the Chickasaw Mission in Western South Carolina before Removal, 1819–34

In his transformative work on the missionary Charles Colcock Jones, historian Donald Mathews discussed writing about missions in the nineteenth-century South: "Awareness of class interest, religious self-delusion, and racial fears, however, should not prevent historians from considering the ironies and almost hopeless contradictions that bemired southern evangelicals . . ."[1] While no doubt "bemired" Presbyterian missions to the Chickasaw in western South Carolina and what would later become north Mississippi present many historical issues concerning the missionaries themselves, the Chickasaw, enslaved African Americans belonging to the Chickasaw, and the multiethnic nature of the early nineteenth-century church mission experience. Internal and sometimes external contradictions "bemired southern evangelicals," and the life and work of Presbyterian missionary T. C. Stuart, among others, bears witness to the complexity of those contradictions.[2]

The missions' existence among Native Americans in western South Carolina (now northern Mississippi) displayed unique ecclesiastical and theological nuances in the Presbyterian mission's goals and approach.[3] Before the removal of the Chickasaw peoples, Christian missionary men and women worked alongside and worshipped with Indigenous people. Historians have examined missions among the Cherokee,[4] but historians have not spent a great deal of time on the missions to the Chickasaw, particularly the Monroe Mission, with the exception of a few publications. One cannot separate the Monroe Mission from the overall development of Native American religion in America, in the US South, and specifically on the South Carolina frontier.[5] Yet Monroe and the work of Stuart are unique and worthy of their own historical analysis.

Historians have traced the role of enslavement within Native American nations. Many were struggling to survive where human chattel enslavement became normative.[6] Given the prevalence of enslavement in western South Carolina the mission activity in what would become Mississippi included a variety of ethnicities who participated in Presbyterianism. Missions' multiethnic activity in frontier South Carolina lends complexity to any understanding of T. C. Stuart, the Monroe church, Presbyterian domestic missions, and religion in western South Carolina. Multiethnicity was rooted in centuries of European incursion and tied as much to European ideas of property, race, and enslavement as it was to indigenous, Native American cultural practices.[7] Enslavement,[8] blood ideology,[9] and multiethnic Native American ancestry history[10] have a tremendous impact on any understanding of Presbyterian missions among the Chickasaw.

Like the Cherokees, identity, race, and the impact of a White supremacist culture played significant roles in shaping the domestic Presbyterian mission. White missionaries' preremoval efforts worked alongside federal policy and were unapologetically Christian and assimilationist in their intent. John C. Calhoun and Thomas McKenney, as well as other early agents of the US government, sought to use "Christian missionaries to mold Indians into the models of American society."[11] Early missionary attempts at "molding" the Chickasaw gave way to the power and influence of leaders who wanted their "children to read and write and do mathematics."[12] Indeed, missionaries soon realized that the Chickasaw had their own views and uses for missionaries. Chickasaw "leaders saw missionaries as a means of gaining an education in the White man's ways so that they could learn to deal with the forces infringing on their lives."[13]

Enslaved African Americans, Native Americans, Native Americans with European ancestry, Native Americans who intermarried with African Americans, along with White settlers from South Carolina created a multiethnic space in which an interracial religious community developed. Mission churches became spaces for reciprocal, multiethnic interaction, which produced complex racial communities, all experiencing the Presbyterian mission space through their own lens. However these spaces also served to reinforce White hegemony and control to shape the Southwestern South Carolina, specifically South Carolina Presbyterians.

This meant making sure the mission church to the Chickasaw and those who attended a Christian worship service reflected an acceptable White Protestant vision within South Carolina Presbyterianism. Missionaries often found themselves at the very center of these interactions. Given the fiercely racialized southern religious hierarchy of the early nineteenth century, missionaries to the Chickasaw would find themselves supporting a vision and agenda larger than their own. The enslaved African Americans, Native Americans, and individuals of mixed ancestry also found themselves forced to choose a variety of ways to practice religion, which often combined elements of indigenous practices, African religion, and White Protestant methods. These racial complexities help us further understand the nature of the early nineteenth-century South, missions in South Carolina, and how religion played a pivotal role in providing a space for interracial interaction and pluralistic religious expression.

Presbyterians in South Carolina, both White and Black, often used the language of Zion, "a phrase commonly used by Southern Presbyterians to speak of the church, especially their church, in an idealized, often triumphalistic way."[14] Milton Winter has argued that if South Carolina was the true "Zion" of Presbyterianism, then mission churches in western South Carolina (Mississippi) in the early nineteenth century were "outposts of Zion." Winter argued that many Presbyterians in Mississippi came from South Carolina and the seminary in Columbia, South Carolina and the Southern Presbyterian Review. The capital of the Presbyterian Church United States (or southern branch of Presbyterianism) found its home in South Carolina.[15]

Licensed to preach by the South Carolina Presbytery on April 19, 1819, the Reverend Thomas C. Stuart, otherwise known as "Father" Stuart, was one of the earliest Presbyterian missionaries in western South Carolina. Sent by the Synod of South Carolina in 1820, Stuart established the Monroe Mission in northeastern Mississippi and was a missionary among the Chickasaw. The Monroe Mission, or the old Monroe Church, is just six miles south of the town of Pontotoc. In 1823, Stuart organized the church and by 1830 had a membership of over one hundred members. E. T. Winston, biographer and editor of Stuart's published papers, mentioned that Stuart's mission to the Chickasaw was the beginning of "religion and education for all of North Mississippi."[16]

For much of the eighteenth-century Presbyterian missions among Native Americans were in the North, but by the beginning of the nineteenth century the work in the South was growing. With the advent of the Second Great Awakening, a religious revival of the early nineteenth century beginning in Cane Ridge, Kentucky in 1804, came a renewed interest in domestic missions in the US South. Southern Presbyterians were among those who shared in this interest. However instead of totally turning their focus toward foreign missions,

Presbyterians sent missionaries within domestic spaces neighboring their churches. On June 29, 1810, the American Board of Commissioners for Foreign Missions (ABCFM) was established. It took only a decade to establish several mission stations among Native American populations. The five main tribes that Presbyterians mostly sent missionaries among were the Cherokee, Choctaw, Chickasaw, Creek, and Seminole.

The Chickasaw of western South Carolina had a long-standing relationship with Whites in America in what has been referred to by Thompson as "friendly relations."[17] Indeed one White minister recalled, "In spite of the fact that the same pressure was brought to bear against them by the aggressive white pioneers that the Indians experienced everywhere they (Chickasaws) yielded to the inevitable with good grace."[18] However Thompson's description hints at historians' lack of understanding of the early twentieth century concerning pre-contact Chickasaw history. Further it did not consider the reasons why the Chickasaw might have "yielded to the inevitable with good grace."

By the time the Presbyterians arrived the Chickasaw nation was in the last stage of slow decline. The nation suffered tremendous loss of life through de Soto's introduction of smallpox and other European diseases. From 1770 to 1812, English and Scottish settlers brought even more diseases that took their toll on the Chickasaw. By 1820, the last remnants of the Chickasaw nation were using the missionaries as a mode of protection against what they saw as an inevitable federal land grab and further White incursion on their lands. Perhaps if the Chickasaw gave the appearance of being Christian, agricultural, and therefore "civilized" to federal agents in the East, then perhaps they would be permitted to remain on their ancestral lands. In contrast to the work of early twentieth-century historians like Thompson Native Americans' and enslaved African Americans' agency will be displayed throughout this book when examining Stuart's presence among the Chickasaw.

The first Presbyterian synod organized in America in 1717 established a "fund for pious uses" that was "designed for the relief of widows and orphans of deceased ministers, but also to support missionaries on the frontier and to assist in the organization of congregations there."[19] Some of the first missionaries Presbyterians sent, such as David and John Brainerd, were ministers to Native Americans. "[Their] writings inspired missionaries who later came to Mississippi."[20] After the French and Indian War England offered land to settlers willing to come to Natchez and what was considered West Florida. In 1772, "Captain Ogden sold 19,800 acres to his tract to Richard and the Rev. Samuel Swayze, also of New Jersey." They established a community in Adams County and "established a community known as the Jersey Settlement."[21] Swazye was the first Protestant minister, along with John Bolls, an ordained elder from the Hopewell Church in South Carolina on the land formerly belonging to General Andrew Pickens. Pickens, who served in the American Revolution, was also a ruling elder in the Presbyterian Church (known in Clemson, SC as Old Stone Presbyterian Church) and George Washington chose Pickens to serve as the chief negotiator between the Federal Government and the Cherokee, Chickasaw and Choctaw in the Treaties of Hopewell, the location now being in Pickens Co. South Carolina on the campus of Clemson University. Swayze continued to meet and hold a church community together under the governorship of Manuel Gayoso de Lomos and the Spanish. Swayze died in 1784.

The Treaty of Hopewell, signed on the Pickens Plantation on January 10, 1786, provided "American protection" for the Chickasaw. The boundary line of the nation was also moved below the thirty-first parallel, and much of the land where the Chickasaw lived became territory added to the United States. In 1789, the First General Assembly of the Presbyterian Church of the United States met, and missionaries played a major role. Presbyterians thus became "the first American denomination to make regular and systematic effort to reach the burgeoning population of the West."[22] They resolved:

> That each of the Synods be, and they are hereby requested to recommend to the General Assembly, at their next meeting, two members, well qualified to be employed in missions on our frontiers; for the purpose of organizing churches, administering ordinances, ordaining elders, collecting information concerning the religious state of those parts, and proposing the best means of establishing gospel ministry among the people.[23]

In 1797, both Georgia and South Carolina argued that their states extended into the Mississippi territory. On April 7, 1798, the US Congress passed a piece of legislation creating the Mississippi Territory, and signed by President John Adams.

The first Presbyterians baptized in Mississippi were likely not White. The first work among Native Americans was in 1799, when the Reverend Joseph Bullen came to the Chickasaw village of Big Town. Presbyterian "labor among the Chickasaw Indians began in 1799 by the New York Missionary Society."[24] Vermonter Joseph Bullen labored among the Chickasaw by visiting with Native families, preaching to them, teaching the Bible, conducting baptisms, conducting funerals, and his son even learned Chickasaw so he could teach Native American children to read. Bullen made "considerable progress among the Chickasaws" especially regarding "religious instruction, husbandry," and other late eighteenth-century notions of "civilized" behavior.[25] The Chickasaw allowed Bullen to live and work in their community for almost four years. Bullen's extensive diary points to his headquarters, the Chickasaw people's culture in the early nineteenth century, and the "extent to which white settlers had already come among the Native Americans, for even then, pressure was mounting to have the Indians moved west, so that the fertile area could be opened up to white settlement."[26]

Bullen's time with the Chickasaw provided a small glimpse into the world into which South Carolina Presbyterians would later enter. Bullen was surrounded by sickness, could not speak the Chickasaw language, depended on an enslaved African American interpreter, and spent time with many White settlers who had moved to the region after the American Revolution and married Chickasaw women.[27] Bullen preached his first sermon on June 2, 1799, and he taught reading, writing, and catechisms using the Bible. Bullen and his son translated the Lord's Prayer and the Decalogue into Chickasaw. Bullen also preached to enslaved African Americans owned by the Chickasaw, describing "the character and great love of Christ, that he loves poor blacks as well as others; told them how we should love Christ, and how a poor woman washed his feet with her tears."[28]

Bullen met with the chief of the nation, preached to several audiences, performed marriage ceremonies as well as baptisms and funerals, and constantly complained of the dangers of alcohol and drunkenness caused by rum sent via trade routes. In Bullen's time the Chickasaw would also see the coming of federal post roads via the Natchez Trace, which would eventually run across two hundred miles of Chickasaw land. Indeed "on June 18, 1800, Congress appropriated $20,000.00 for negotiations with the Chickasaws and Choctaws for rights-of-way through their lands and improvements on the Natchez Trace."[29] Bullen and his son taught woodworking, blacksmithing, reading, and writing as well as modern agricultural practices. However by 1803 Bullen closed the mission and left to work in Natchez. But his labors would be an important foundation for the work of later Presbyterian Missionaries from South Carolina.

Thomas Jefferson negotiated safe passage rights for travelers along the Natchez Trace and later gained about 2.6 million acres surrounding Natchez. The territorial Governor W. C. C. Clairborne and federal agents in the territory regarded Native Americans as uncivilized "savages" and attempted to "civilize" them using a variety of different accommodationist tactics. As the practices of spinning, weaving, wheelwrighting, blacksmithing, and modern forms of agriculture made their way into the territory, more Chickasaw farms and families began implementing log houses, plows, and wagons, and raised cattle, grew cotton, and became enslavers of African Americans.[30]

After the Louisiana Purchase, the War of 1812, and Andrew Jackson's battles with the Creek, politicians began to publicly advocate for the removal of the Chickasaw into lands to the southwest. Land cessions had begun in 1801 with the Treaty of Fort Adams and continued as the population of White settlers doubled in Mississippi. President James Monroe and his secretary of war, John C. Calhoun, believed that the peaceful removal of the Choctaw would encourage the Chickasaw to act accordingly.[31] Often the goals of the missions and the federal government were one and the same. Missionaries coming to work with the Chickasaw often cited their heavenly father as well as their earthly fathers, John Adams, and James Monroe, for the reasons they were present among the Chickasaw. Promoting education and an acceptance of western and European-based labor systems throughout the early nineteenth century would be advantageous both to the missionaries looking to Christianize as well as their government leaders looking for Indigenous assimilation.

In 1819, the federal government passed the Civilization Act, which urged churches to cooperate with federal and state governments in teaching agriculture and other "civilizing" techniques to Native Americans. A "conscious acculturation" settled in among the Chickasaw, and White missionaries often became agents working on behalf of the federal government as well as their denominations, synods, and mission boards. Perhaps based on Bullen's early contact, Presbyterians, particularly from the South Carolina Synod, continued to discuss a continued missionary presence among Native Americans in their western borders. Later that year, the South Carolina Synod resolved "that it is expedient to form a society for the purpose of sending the Gospel to the destitute within our bounds in South Carolina and Georgia, and for promoting the civilization and religious instruction of our aborigines in our southwestern border."[32] In spring 1819, the Missionary Society of the Synod of South Carolina appointed Thomas C. Stuart and the Reverend David Humphries to go on a fact-finding mission to gain information regarding a suitable location for a mission.[33]

The South Carolina and Georgia Synod's autumn 1819 session resolved to send a missionary to the "Southern Indians just east of the Mississippi River."[34] That spring Stuart and Humphries left Reverend John Harrison's house in Georgia. Just a young licentiate Thomas C. Stuart was an assistant to the elder

Humphries on the voyage to find suitable environs from which to conduct the mission. They traveled over 180 miles before reaching Chickasaw territory. On their journey Stuart and Humphries stopped and preached in several places in Alabama and Mississippi. Armed with documents from the War Department, as well as a congressional appropriation of $10,000, Humphries and Stuart's first encounter with a Native American nation was with the Creek. According to Stuart's letter of June 17, 1820, "the documents for the War Department, among which was a letter of introduction" from Secretary of War John C. Calhoun contained a letter "to the agents of the different tribes we might visit."[35] The missionaries "addressed them (Creek) in their town house stating our purpose in coming among them. We held forth to them that we desired to preach the gospel among them and also establish schools for the education of their children without any cost to them." Stuart recalled that "they listened attentively, but after short consultation they rejected our proposal."[36] Not surprisingly this rather quick refusal among the Creeks was likely grounded in previous experience with missionaries, interactions with the US Army, combined with a prescient knowledge of the intentions of the US government.

The Creek were justified in their apprehension. According to Stuart's recollection, the War Department required Native Americans to "teach their children agriculture and the various arts of domestic life, believing that they never could be civilized without this."[37] The federal government appointed funds that could be given to missionaries who brought a civilization plan to Native American nations through educational institutions, which taught agriculture and the "importance of domesticity." The Creeks rejected Humphries's and Stuart's offer responding "that if they wanted their children to work, they could teach them themselves."[38] Further the lack of immunity to European bacteria and germs had decimated populations of Native Americans for centuries. To many Native American groups, including the Creek, the coming of a White missionary was more the deed of a demon than of a benevolent god.[39]

Undaunted in their attempt to settle among a population of Native Americans and conduct a mission, Humphries and Stuart kept pushing west. Their arrival among the Chickasaw nation in 1820 was on the eve of a council to elect a new leader, Ishtohotopah.[40] The Chickasaw nation of northern Mississippi numbered about six thousand at the time of Stuart's arrival.[41] Presbyterian historian C. W. Grafton mentioned that "here they found a very different feeling between the races and especially between these races and the whites."[42] According to Grafton the Chickasaws had fought with the English against the French in 1715 and considered the English historic allies. Grafton mentioned that the Chickasaw "had a great hatred for the Spaniard and for the French."[43] Winter confirms this association mentioning "British traders came to the Chickasaw nation, and the number of whites residing there increased," and "whites entered the area to farm, and a substantial number of intermarriages with Chickasaw persons occurred. The resulting biracial population was more proficient in English than the natives, and a new ruling class emerged."[44] The Chickasaw would continue to support the British in the American Revolution up to the Treaty of Paris in 1783.

Stuart's original biographer E. T. Winston, writing in the mid-1920s, said of this sentiment, "Though having an inveterate hatred of the Spaniards, through their contact with Hernando Desoto, . . . they held the English, who had long taken 'pot-luck' with them, intermarried with them, fought their battles etc., in the highest esteem, and they were staunch friends and allies in their joint enterprises."[45] Winston then asserted, "the King, we may add, was Ish-to-hoto-pah, the last king of the Chickasaws. As a ruler, he was at this period a mere figurehead in the government of the tribe. The real rulers were the Colbert family, the eldest of whom, and perhaps the most influential, resided in the neighborhood."[46]

Chickasaw with European ancestry, like the Colbert family, played a tremendous role in the early admittance of the missionaries into the Chickasaw nation. Likely this was the result of the long intermarriage and relationship of the Chickasaw people with the Colbert family. According to Winston the Colbert "brothers—William, George, Levi and James—were descended from Logan Colbert, a Scotchman or Englishman who came from Georgia and settled among the Chickasaws early in the eighteenth century."[47] Winston placed a great deal of importance on James Logan Colbert, known among the Chickasaw for his leadership during wars with the French. Winston noted that "Logan Colbert's celebrity was so great that the French writers of that period conferred his name upon the Mississippi river or 'Father of Waters,' calling it the Rivere de Colvert."[48] Colbert was a Scotch-Irish trader who had married a Chickasaw woman and become very wealthy. Despite his prominent place in Chickasaw history, Colbert apparently did not live among the Chickasaw for long. However Winston is careful to mention that "he perpetuated his name through a most honorable lineage of distinguished Chickasaw."[49]

The Chickasaw through the Colbert family had a long tradition of interaction with the US federal government and were cognizant of America's intentions toward Native American peoples. Indeed Winston recalled the story of one Chickasaw leader who visited General Washington in Philadelphia in the late eighteenth century. This individual brought back "a small shovel plough, which was presented to him by Washington, and was carefully preserved by him in his house until he died. It was a great pleasure to the venerable chief to relate its history to his white guests."[50] Winston described how the man would repeat Washington's words to visitors in his home:

> When you go home, tell your people that if they attempt in this age to live as their fathers did, by war and by hunting, they will perish and pass away from the earth like the many tribes who have died where the white men live. But if they will quit war and hunting, and make corn with the plough, and use the tools of the white men in clearing their land, building houses and cultivating the earth; and if they will raise horses, cattle and hogs, and adopt the religion and customs of the civilized and Christian nations, they will live long and prosper as a people.[51]

Washington's words lived on in Chickasaw oral history and folklore regarding the US government's expectations of Indigenous peoples.

The long relationship between the US government, Colbert leaders, and the early acceptance of Stuart by Colbert descendants among the Chickasaw was the most likely reason for the establishment of a mission church. The Chickasaw realized, based on their history of interactions with Whites as well as George Washington's warning, that if they were going to keep their land they would have to adopt or "seem to adopt" the methods, religious practices, and culture of their White neighbors to the east. Likely it was William Colbert who "was no doubt instrumental in securing the Monroe mission for his people. Later his name, with that of his wife Mimey, together with several of their children, appears on the church rolls at old Monroe, and he was one of 'Father' Stuart's elders."[52] Winter noted that in late May 1820 "Stuart and Humphrey traveled further west and arrived at the home of Levis Colbert near Cottin Gin Port on the Tombigbee."[53] Levi Colbert also "informed his visitors that a ball-play and election of a kind would soon be held at his brother George Colbert's," which would be "an opportunity for Stuart and Humphrey to present the proposal for a mission school to leaders of the Chickasaw Nation."[54]

Marriages between Europeans and Native Americans were somewhat common among the Chickasaw. This unique aspect of Chickasaw heredity, which, in some ways, would serve to influence a religious framework buttressed by Stuart, helps to explain the reasoning behind admittance of Stuart and Humphries among the Chickasaw. Chickasaw with European ancestry seemed eager to bring in a missionary who might "legitimize" their nation in the eyes of the federal government. In his thesis on missions to the Choctaw and Chickasaw in Mississippi, William Hiemstra confirms this sentiment and desire to "legitimize" claiming that "the missionary deputation was more favorably received by the Chickasaws." His reasoning was that "they had become envious of the missions obtained by the Cherokees and Choctaws. The Chickasaw also believed that they must adopt the white man's civilization or become extinct." The Chickasaw's early reception of missionaries, and the desire to "adopt civilization or become extinct" were tremendous influences on the Chickasaw. It is possible that the Chickasaw allowed a missionary station for a multitude of reasons. Some within the nation legitimately wanted a mission school, families like the Colbert's seemed interested in religious instruction, while others might have wanted to use the missionaries as a tool to stave off White incursion and removal.[55]

The Chickasaw council, held on June 22, 1820, granted the missionaries permission to stay, and the council chose a site for the future mission. Humphries, Stuart, Ishtohotopah, and several Chickasaw representatives signed a formal agreement for the missionaries' presence. The fact-finding team of Humphries and Stuart had found a future home and returned to South Carolina. A council of the Synod of South Carolina and Georgia met later in 1820, and the members of the council reached a decision that Humphries and Stuart should establish a mission among the Chickasaw. The synod most likely decided on the Chickasaw establishment after communicating with Humphries and Stuart, who no doubt insinuated that meetings with the Chickasaws were hospitable in nature and successful. Further a letter from the Chickasaw nation to the corresponding secretary later that July no doubt cemented their decision. The letter read:

> Chickasaw Nation, July 8, 1820
>
> Friends and Brother Missionary,
> My head men address themselves a few lines to you to inform you that we had the Pleasure of seeing our brothers, Mr. D. Humphries and Mr. Thomas C. Stuart, which our head men are much pleased with their conduct, and wish strongly for them to return and educate their children. It is the request of my head men in general. Now we shall look for them in the course of the winter. Friends and brothers.[56]

However Humphries later received a call to be the pastor of the Roberts and Good Hope churches in South Carolina, which he accepted rather than moving west as a missionary. According to Winston Humphries "had a family and no resources. The probabilities are that it was never his purpose to become an

Indian missionary, and having discharged the duty imposed upon him as exploring agent, he doubtless felt justified in accepting work at home."[57] However this left the still young and largely untested Stuart as the best-qualified missionary candidate to the Chickasaw people. He and Humphries made contact, signed the agreement, and knew the landscape. The synod accepted Stuart's service, and he made preparations to move west into the Mississippi territory to begin his work as a missionary to the Chickasaw people.

Arriving on January 27, 1821, Stuart and his family reached the site mutually agreed upon to be the residence of the Presbyterian mission in Mississippi. One historian recalled that the Stuarts were "received by the Indians with expressions of gratitude and joy."[58] Whether this gratitude was sincere or part of the agenda toward cultivating a relationship with a future intermediary, the community accepted Stuart.

Later a few families from South Carolina, including a "farmer named Pickens and a mechanic named Vernon," joined Stuart and helped build the original mission site in fall 1821. The families built houses, started self-sustaining farms, and preached to the Chickasaw using an interpreter, Malcolm McGee, who came later. The mission was named Monroe, after James Monroe, then president of the United States and "under whose administration schools for Native Americans had been encouraged and financed."[59] It took Stuart and company just over eighteen months to clear the land, erect homes, and build a church. In April the small clan of Carolinians were joined by "Messrs. Hamilton V. Turner and James Wilson, the former a mechanic and the latter a farmer and teacher," along with their wives and families. Within a month, a school opened and was home to sixteen new students from among the Chickasaw nation.[60] Winter noted that "youngsters from six to sixteen took part. The school initially enrolled seventeen Chickasaws, but the number soon increased to twenty-five. By 1828, 100 acres had been cleared and eighty-one pupils were enrolled."[61]

Stuart and his colleagues received little if any compensation from the Missionary Society. The annual report of the Board of Managers of the Missionary Society of the Synod of South Carolina read, "As in the instance of Mr. Stuart, they receive no other compensation for their laborious service than food and raiment." The Board pronounced, "Theirs is to be a life of self-denial, their only reward in this world is to be the approbation of conscience in the discharge of their duty. To them we fully believe it will be no meager return for their toil and their multiplied care."[62] This would put a great deal of pressure on Stuart to receive support from the federal government and the Chickasaw nation. It displayed an unreasonable notion that somehow missionaries should be made to suffer financially to accomplish their labor on behalf of an ecclesiastical body. Certainly had the board of missions provided more financial care for the missionaries they would not have been as dependent upon the federal government as well as to ask for support from among the Chickasaw, which likely would have increased their prominence and positive impact on the community.

This put Stuart in a precarious position. In one sense, Stuart and the missionaries were to provide education, provide a Christian church, and acculturate the Chickasaw in the ways of their White neighbors both socially and economically. Stuart was not in a position of either economic or social autonomy. He was dependent upon the Chickasaw for his survival. Stuart was also a product of nineteenth-century notions of race in South Carolina, believing that Whites were superior to persons of color. In reality he could not apply that worldview in a space in which he was wholly dependent upon a people whom he considered inferior, and also to live, work, and be successful. What further complicated this position were enslaved African Americans among the Chickasaw. As we will see, many more African Americans ended up worshipping in the mission churches and becoming members of Monroe Mission than did Native Americans. Enslaved African Americans and Native Americans in mission schools and mission churches ministered autonomously in their own communities. Stuart's absolute dependence upon these communities highlights the absurd notion of any Native American or African American inferiority.

Part of the reason for the mission's unique racial ecclesiastical makeup was the space itself: the frontier. Historian Ursula Smith has argued that "patriarchal patterns were less firmly established in a region that was defining itself as it went along."[63] While there was some adoption by White missionaries and Native American landholders of nineteenth-century southern hierarchies inherent in the institution of enslavement, there were also more expanded opportunities in a mission church on the frontier than in a particularized congregation in the southeastern coastal cities like Charleston, Savannah, or Norfolk.[64] This multiethnic community in the space of a southwestern frontier complicates our understanding of the nineteenth-century southern religious landscape. While segregation in worship became the overwhelming historical narrative of southern religious history during the late nineteenth century and into the twentieth century, southern churches also had stories of multiethnic worship and ecclesiastical interactions across racial lines in an antebellum context in a frontier space that is distinct from interracial worship on plantation missions or urban settings.[65] Indeed the interracial interaction in a frontier mission space in the US South complicates our understanding of southern religion.

There were certainly motivating factors beyond religious sentiment that caused Stuart to move hundreds of miles from home with little to no remuneration. Because Stuart and his family were dependent upon the Chickasaw for survival the missions work forced Stuart and his colleagues to reconsider nineteenth-century notions of race and White superiority more closely. The Monroe Mission was a multiethnic religious community in the US South in the nineteenth century in which African Americans as well as Native Americans were considered savage, subhuman, and undeserving of equal status to that of Whites. One example of this sentiment existing in South Carolina can be found in Ben Robertson's memoir of the Upcountry of South Carolina entitled *Red Hills and Cotton*. Discussing his great-great-aunt Narcissa, who lived in the early Republic period as the ABCFM was discussing missions to the Chickasaw, Roberston recalled "she told the children to keep the Ten Commandments, to believe in God and to love their neighbors." One of her great-grandsons asked "are the savages our neighbors?" to which Narcissa replied, "No, the savages have no souls."[66]

However Stuart's view was different. Through working intimately with Native American and African American populations the missionaries at Monroe grew to possess a view of human beings in the church that allowed for a broader sense of ecclesiastical rights, which were nonexistent in many particularized southern congregations in more urbanized southeastern towns and cities.[67] Given the time period the prevalence of racism among southern Whites and the entrenched status of enslavement within southern culture, it is surprising that the Monroe church did not more clearly reflect accepted racial hierarchies in church membership, leadership, and educational opportunities. Perhaps this had something to do with Stuart. As Thompson remembered Stuart was called "Father" among the Chickasaw, possessing the "tenderest and gentlest spirit that touched and transformed the Indians of the Southwest."[68]

Perhaps the brutal existence of frontier life and his dependence upon Native American communities for survival forced Stuart to wrestle with and confront preconceived racial categories. Perhaps the Chickasaws' exposure to the English and Scots for many decades gave the Chickasaw a certain respectability in Stuart's estimation. His acceptance of a role in a patriarchal framework could have allowed him to view the Chickasaw as children. Finally it is possible that Stuart's exegesis of the parable of the good Samaritan and of the Ten Commandments was different from great Aunt Narcissa's. Perhaps he believed the Chickasaw were his neighbors, possessed souls, and were made in the *imago dei.*

There are many missionaries in American history with a troubling past: spreading disease, buttressing racism inherent within the institution of enslavement, disregarding Native American culture in their practices, and caring nothing for the condition of Native Americans through removal. Others were concerned with the "condition of men," both spiritual and physical. Presbyterian historian E. T. Thompson touched on an interesting facet and an intriguing question of nineteenth-century domestic missionaries' work in the South. He mentioned that some missionaries "renounced titles and estates to engage in the work; most of them were of finished scholarship and refined habits." "They faced all manner of privation merely for the sake of making some portion of the world a better place in which to live, or to improve the condition of a fellow mortal, no matter how unworthy the latter may have been considered in the esteem of mankind."[69] Why did these southern Whites of relative influence and impressive education desire to spend their lives to labor for spiritual and physical support of men and women who were considered of "unworthy esteem" in this particular time in a largely unknown wilderness?

While the direct answer to this question remains unknown, as we cannot see into the hearts and minds of men and women two hundred years ago, it is certain that missionaries to Native Americans sacrificed worldly interests for what they viewed as eternal kingdom work. Not only was Stuart not paid, but he and his wife were virtually cut off from extended family. Increasing "isolation promoted depression and loneliness, a shortage of personnel caused the small staff to be over-worked," and the missionaries performed other duties outside of their expertise such as "food administrators, physicians, registrars of vital statistics," teachers, and school administrators.[70] Presbyterian missions' unique contribution arose out of the latter two vocations as Presbyterians were typically valued education and possessed theological training. It is also possible that the Chickasaw nation saw some value in the schools as the "tribe allocated $5,000.00 in 1824 for additional schools."[71] The *Missionary Herald*, a publication that reached a variety of Christian churches mentioned that the Chickasaw "are more and more convinced of the importance of education," and their growing dependence upon agriculture given the lack of game to hunt "facilitates our communication with them, and gives us a more full opportunity of instructing them in the agricultural and mechanical arts."[72]

Unique especially in their attitudes toward Whites, the Chickasaw displayed an interesting and cautious "openness" to Stuart. Perhaps this was due to their history with the English, or maybe it was the intermarriages and subsequent "rule" of the Colbert brothers. However in reconstructing the source material from the viewpoint of and a reexamination of the behavioral attitudes of the Chickasaw, perhaps something even more complex is revealed. Throughout Chickasaw history, before removal, the Chickasaw interacted in methods of positive exchange with English settlers. Perhaps instead of the missionary using the Chickasaw for evangelical and "civilizing" purposes, it was the Chickasaw using the missionary as a future intermediary to what they foresaw as eventual removal by the federal government.

It is possible that this foresight extended to recognizing that a connection with the religion of eastern Whites might gain favor or good opinion of the Chickasaw as "civilized" for later negotiating purposes with the federal government. The Chickasaw nation was no doubt aware of the missionaries' possession of letters from the War Department. It would also be naive to assume that the Chickasaw were unaware of the military technology, that the US Army possessed or interests that Western settlers had in Chickasaw land. If a successful relationship with the missionary might be cultivated, maintained, and used then perhaps the Chickasaw could present a model of being a "civilized" tribe to an ever-westward-expanding government, and Washington's recommendation would come to fulfillment. This adaptation of seemingly adopting western culture and "legitimization" might even help the Chickasaw from eventual removal.

The Monroe Mission church itself was small and was where religious services occurred. Mrs. Julia Daggett Harris, a resident who lived close to the old Monroe Church, reported that it "was an interesting sight. It was a diminutive room 16 x 16, built of small poles" and had a "dirt and stick chimney and a large open fireplace, where, in the winter, the worshipers warmed their frostbitten fingers."[73] There was only one window in the church, which was "a hole cut through logs and closed with a clapboard."[74] The Monroe Mission was an accessible location as it was centrally located within various travel routes for Native American traders. From the north and south, the "Cotton Gin Road" passed through Monroe as well as the Natchez Trace, which came from the northeast and went south.[75] Winter mentioned that "at times Stuart preached to as many as 250 at this location."[76]

For education, the first order of business for the new mission was to build a boarding school for Chickasaw children. Stuart wrote, "Early in the spring of 1823 the school was opened with fifty scholars, most of whom were boarded with the family." Men of influence, such as Samuel Seely, in the Chickasaw district where Monroe was located, came and spoke to the school often. Seely eventually sent his son to be a student at Monroe. Stuart recalled, "From this time until the Chickasaws ceded away their country and agreed to remove to their distant home in the West, the school was kept up, with some interruptions, under the trials and difficulties that always attend a similar enterprise amongst an unenlightened and uncivilized people."[77] It is clear in this statement that Stuart's recognition of the Chickasaw as "uncivilized and unenlightened" reflects his views moving onto the frontier from southeastern South Carolina. Stuart established a school to "enlighten" the Chickasaw, but the Chickasaw people used their resources to start two more. Many within the Chickasaw nation saw schooling for children as important if their children were going to survive and even thrive in a changing landscape where, more and more, White settlers marginalized Native Americans economically, socially, culturally, and politically.

In 1824, "the chiefs of the council appropriated $5,000 to establish two more schools, and $2,500 per annum for their support."[78] The schools were open to both boys and girls and they learned to speak, read, and write in English. However according to Stuart "the number who obtained anything like a good English education was comparatively small." Among others, one reason might possibly have been the school's strict regulations regarding attendance. Indeed "the requirements of the station imposed such a restraint on their former roving habits that many of them ran off and never returned." Stuart made sure to note that "this was often a matter of deep regret and a cause of great annoyance to us; but it was one of those discouragements with which missionaries amongst an ignorant and heathen people have always had to contend."[79]

This student truancy is not surprising given the level of independence and autonomy that Chickasaw children were accustomed to in educational settings. Despite boarding school obstacles throughout the mid to late 1820s, the church grew from 8 missionaries at the outset of 1820 to almost fifteen times its original size just before removal with 123 individuals. Distinctions of one's cultural or ecclesiastical status stemming from ethnic and cultural differences seemed to be present but ambiguous with regard to function in Stuart's missionary model. One acquaintance recalled, "He earned the appreciation of all, regardless of color or condition or creed." Mission records showed a heterogeneous membership with twenty-nine Whites, sixty-nine African Americans, and twenty-five Indians in the late 1820s.[80] The heterogeneous makeup of the Chickasaw nation added complexity to this ecclesiastical and educational space because of intermarriage of the Chickasaw with Whites, the presence of enslaved African Americans, and with the presence of White South Carolinians as well as Chickasaw who had intermarried with African Americans. Each played a significant role in the churches and schools. Enslaved African American people played an outsized role in the mission church leadership structure and greatly assisted Stuart as translators, prayer meeting attendees, prayer leaders, and members.

In 1823, the Monroe Mission made the transition from mission to formalized or particularized church. On June 7, 1823, the Reverend Hugh Dickson, representing the Presbytery of South Carolina, was "commissioned by the Missionary Society of the Synod of South Carolina and Georgia to visit the Chickasaw missions in Mississippi."[81] Seven charter members were listed on the roll and Reverend Thomas Stuart was "nominated as stated supply, with other ministerial members of the mission serving as the church's session.[82] It was not until the next December that the first Native American made a profession of faith."[83] The Reverend Hugh Dickson was sent from South Carolina to examine if "the mission family having a desire to be united in a church capacity, that they may regularly enjoy the privileges of the sealing ordinances of the gospel." On June 7, 1823, the church was "organized with the following members, viz: Hamilton V. Turner, James Wilson, Nancy Turner, Mary Ann Wilson, Ethalinda Wilson, Prudence Wilson and Susan Stuart."[84]

The register listed no Chickasaw or Chickasaw names as founding members. This may have been the result of historically strict standards regarding Presbyterian Church membership. Admission as a member in good standing of a Presbyterian church in the nineteenth century was a laborious task compared to other denominations. This would especially be true for some members of society that White Presbyterians deemed inferior, "heathenish," or "uncivilized." A candidate would have to appear before the session, where he or she would be questioned and would have to provide a satisfactory description of his or her faith. Another reason for low numbers among the Chickasaw may have been the product of an existing cautiousness among the Chickasaw toward their new White neighbors and their hesitancy to abandon their own religious practices. Stuart and his colleagues had been with the Chickasaw for almost two years by the time the mission became an official church. However while the Chickasaw were cautious to join early on, records display an eagerness for membership among the enslaved African Americans in their midst.

After the opening services the first session or ruling body of the church met in what was considered the "prayer hall." Church session records showed that "a black woman named Dinah, belonging to Mr. James Gunn, applied to be received into the newly-organized church." The Carolina Presbyterians in Mississippi were indeed supporters of and participants in the institution of enslavement. It also indicates that enslaved African Americans were a part of what was becoming a racially diverse ecclesiastical community. However records also indicated that the Chickasaw were cautious of membership. If an enslaved African American woman in Mississippi in 1823 were deemed examinable for church membership, then surely a leader like Ishtohotopah, or a member of the Chickasaw nation, would have been considered. In allowing Dinah to become a member Stuart provided places of ecclesiastical membership for early non-White members. Indeed some enslaved members possessed prominent ministerial roles, on which Stuart relied heavily.

Services at Monroe were unique. Indeed "Stuart and the other ministers of Monroe Mission preached with the help of interpreters. The evangelistic program consisted of divine service on Sunday and prayer meetings twice a week and on the first Monday of each month, when prayers were offered for the missionary cause." When the preaching happened "the missionary would give a sermon in English, after which an interpreter would explain informally 'the free way of salvation through the Gospel.' This was followed by hymns in Chickasaw, and the service ended with prayers and exhortation."[85]

Monroe was certainly unique for a nineteenth-century southern Presbyterian mission church. Its nonsubscription to nineteenth-century cultural expectations concerning race and interracial interaction was evident on numerous occasions. One instance displaying unique multiethnic interchange was the prominence in leadership positions for some enslaved African Americans at Monroe. One such individual was the aforementioned Dinah, "a black woman, the first fruit of the Chickasaw Mission," who "being a native of the country, spoke the Chickasaw language fluently; and having the confidence of the Indians, I (Stuart) employed her as my interpreter, for several years in preaching the gospel to them."[86] For Stuart to employ an African American woman in a place of such prominence was unusual in nineteenth-century Presbyterian churches even among domestic missions. She was put in a powerful position of translating Stuart's preaching to the Chickasaw. This must have communicated something to both the White, African American, and Chickasaw attendees that only a human, with a soul, made in the *imago dei*, with ecclesiastical membership, rights, and responsibilities in the church would be given such a position of responsibility.

Slave mission churches on the frontier and even in some urban spaces in the South[87] were places in which ecclesiastical leadership opportunity and education for African American members occurred. Some enslaved African Americans became members at Monroe and their children even experienced ecclesiastical rights and opportunities. The church records of August 3, 1823, show that Stuart baptized Dinah's children Chloe, William, and Lucy. Indeed "Dinah, having previously expressed desire to have her children baptized, and having given us satisfactory evidence of her knowledge of this holy ordinance, presented her three children . . . to God in baptism."[88] Covenantal baptism is an important ceremony to Presbyterians as it brings in and recognizes the children of believing Christians as communing members of the household of faith. Other members take vows to support believers' children. To be a member and to have her children baptized was communicating something about Dinah's ecclesiastical service and the way that the leadership and membership viewed her presence as something positive in the community.

However sometimes the drastic nature of mission work allowed missionaries the freedom to maneuver even some of their own myopic notions concerning race. The session admitted Dinah and "after a careful examination the session felt satisfied with her Christian experience, and accordingly admitted her to the privileges of the household of faith."[89] Admittance was not a mere symbolic ceremony like modern church standards. As one became a member there were certain commitments and vows to which a member would be expected to agree. Further membership was something that a session continued to evaluate based on one's attendance, behavior, and level of engagement. It was something a person could lose easily if the individual was not conforming to the accepted standards and vows taken. There were individuals not accepted at Monroe. According to the session minutes recorded on July 1, 1827, the "session convened, and proceeded to examine several persons, who were not received" for membership. Furthermore church membership meant that Dinah was a member with equal ecclesiastical standing with her fellow Whites, with all the "privileges of the household of faith." This meant that she had equal voting rights within the church, an equal place at the communion table, and could receive benefits such as support if she were sick.[90] Stuart used the enslaved persons' relationship with their Native American owners and their knowledge of the Chickasaw language almost as autonomous missionaries to convince their Chickasaw enslavers to attend church. This nuance of Native American missions was how Esther (an enslaved African American) could have persuaded Mrs. Colbert, the second Chickasaw to become a member of the church, to attend Monroe.[91]

Dinah was not the only person of African American ethnicity present at Monroe.[92] The records of May 15, 1824, indicate that the church excluded Rindah, "a black woman belonging to Mr. Turner," due to improper behavior. However Rindah "made application to be restored" and "on professing sorrow for her offense, and promising amendment, was reinstated." Also on May 15 Abraham, "a black man belonging to an Indian, and husband to the woman received at our last communion, applied for church privileges."[93] These individuals further represented the heterogeneous and ethnically diverse makeup of Monroe Church.

Many walked several miles to attend service. Winter, historian of Presbyterianism in Mississippi, recorded the example of Cornelia Pelham, a member at Monroe, and wrote that African American members at Monroe Church taught within their own communities and even had their own missions to the Chickasaw. According to Winter some "effective mission to the Chickasaw at Monroe" were "conducted wholly by the slave."[94] Pelham recorded:

> A black man member of the mission church opened his little cabin for prayer on every Wednesday evening, which was usually attended by half a dozen colored persons. In 1830 that number increased to more than 50, many of whom were full Indians. The meetings were conducted whole by Christian slaves, in the Chickasaw language. One of their number can read fluently in the Bible, and many of the others can sing hymns, which they have committed to memory from hearing them sung and recited. The chiefs began to manifest increasing regard for the school and religious instruction.

Enslaved African American members of Monroe took it upon themselves to conduct missions among Native Americans, which seemed even more successful than their ordained White counterparts at prompting Native Americans to attend. These opportunities for African American-led worship were not as common in White-led mission churches on plantations in the southeast, or in particularized congregations and were therefore indicative of the fluidity of the frontier and opportunities that African Americans claimed through multiethnic mission churches in this frontier space.

Abraham, an enslaved African American attended Monroe and his owner was apparently present at the ceremony of membership induction. This could have been his owner's gesture to politely attend. Another possibility is that the owner was cautiously trying to detect what Stuart and his followers were doing.

It is possible Abraham attended of his own volition, or perhaps he came because of his wife's request. Finally it could be a combination of the three as human beings, their motivating factors, and religious worldviews are complex and can come from different motivations at different times.

It is possible that this attendance is indicative of the caution with which the Chickasaw approached early missionaries at Monroe. The Chickasaw, familiar with western European ideology concerning land, economics, and trade practices, allowed a missionary church to exist within their nation. However far more enslaved African Americans whom the Chickasaw owned attended Monroe than did members of the Chickasaw nation. Perhaps this had to do with African American familiarity with Christianity in the southeastern United States, in the Caribbean "West Indies," and perhaps even in Africa. Likely the Chickasaw allowed the missionaries to live among them and held them at arm's length in an attempt to appear legitimate in the eyes of the federal government, which also funded the work in hopes of "civilizing" the Chickasaw.[95]

The first Native American to become a member of the Monroe Church was a woman, Tennessee Bynum, on December 4, 1824. Described in the session records as "a native," Bynum joined along with Esther, "a black woman belonging to Mrs. Colbert."[96] Following Bynum a few years later on May 7, 1826, was Molly Colbert, "a native," of the influential Colbert family. The late arrival of individuals from the Chickasaw nation as members of Monroe is telling. The hesitancy on behalf of the Chickasaw to gain membership reveals the Chickasaw cautious approach to Stuart and the Monroe Mission, which had been accepting members for over a year in 1824. In that time only two Chickasaw joined, the aforementioned women, one of whom was from European and Native American ancestry. On September 29, 1827, William Colbert, also a Chickasaw with European ancestry, was the first male Chickasaw admitted to membership. He decided to join some six years after Stuart and his family arrived in northern Mississippi. According to Howe, Colbert was "a scholar in the school and on the 5th of April, 1834 was elected and ordained a ruling elder in our Church."[97]

This was significant in terms of Stuart's racial categories and leadership opportunities. A ruling elder not only had shepherding rule over the congregation but could rule over White members through church discipline cases. This was a major reason why there were seldom African American elders in Presbyterian churches throughout particularized congregations in the southeast until after the Civil War. A "native," albeit with European ancestry, having such a prominent role in the Monroe Church displayed Stuart's notions of ecclesiastical leadership opportunities for those with a multiethnic backgrounds in contrast with accepted notions of racial distinctions throughout the Southeast. Colbert was from a prominent family among the Chickasaw and this, as well as the family's wealth and influence and his experiences as a student of Stuart's in the Chickasaw school, surely played a role in his nomination, selection, election, and ordination.

Hiemstra, a historian who studied missionaries among the Chickasaw, found that "attendance at the services was considered excellent. In addition to the regular Sunday worship the missionaries conducted 'protracted meetings' and prayer services. Funerals and temperance meetings presented the missionaries with additional opportunities for preaching."[98] Many Chickasaw could have come in and out of church services without Stuart recording them. Not always having an interpreter on hand could also have played a vital role in this lack of membership since the session needed one for examination. The December 29, 1827, session minutes mentioned that "Mrs. Colbert, a native, also applied for admission. There being no good interpreter present, it was resolved to keep the session open and meet Mrs. Colbert at the house of Mrs. John Bynum on the next Monday morning with a suitable interpreter."[99] Regardless the Chickasaw hesitancy to become members en masse displayed the concern and sense of caution to invest fully in Stuart's work. Ultimately Stuart regretted that "comparatively few of our scholars embraced religion and united with our church."[100]

While the Monroe Church admitted enslaved African Americans as full members their surnames do not appear in the church records. Some Presbyterian mission churches in the South chose to display surnames so there was some precedent.[101] Native American surnames do however appear in the records. While this might seem like a small detail, it speaks volumes about the White record keeper's (probably Stuart himself) perception of enslaved African Americans and Native Americans. Acknowledgement of a surname in a church roll book was a public declaration that ran counter to the southern ideology behind the institution of enslavement: that enslaved African Americans were property and could not possess lineages and an identity beyond their property holders. Surnames declared that enslaved African Americans were more than property; they were human beings with everlasting souls and individuals with a family bloodline that superseded their status as property.

What does this indicate about the White membership's perceptions of enslaved African Americans and Native Americans? First, enslaved African Americans were full members, but their surnames were absent. Instead of listing a first name followed by a surname, it was "Abraham, belonging to" and "Dinah, owned by." Therefore it was more likely that missionaries saw membership as a necessity rather than an outright expression of ecclesiastical equality. Second, it is likely that enslavers were comfortable with church membership because it gave an extra layer of White oversight of African American behavior and movement. However it was still significant that enslaved African Americans were full members since this was seldom the case in particularized churches in the southeast. Third, membership was something prized highly by the missionaries, session members, and something the congregation took seriously. To admit someone to full membership status in the church who did not possess any kind of civic status beyond being chattel property spoke to the value that the church placed on the enslaved people's humanity.

In contrast, the recording of the last names of the Chickasaw displayed that Stuart and his session did see the Native Americans as human beings equal in full status (at least ecclesiastically speaking) to Whites. It also exhibited that White missionaries made a conscious distinction between African Americans and Native Americans. This distinction was so important that it compelled Stuart to note it in the records. This is supported by Hiemstra's research; he concluded that "it is evident that the missionaries never considered the Choctaws and Chickasaws to be members of an inferior race. The curriculum maintained by the various schools reveals that the Indian was regarded as one who had not received opportunities for cultural advancement; in no case was the Indian believed to have been born with inferior mentality."[102] Indeed racial categories and distinctions were prevalent among the mission churches between Whites, Native Americans, and African Americans. Stuart was a shepherd who let the "savage wolves" of this time come into the flock and created artificial distinctions, categories, and hierarchies, which should not have existed and did not exist in traditional ecclesiastical polity over previous centuries. While frontier mission spaces afforded the most possible fluidity to test accepted racial hierarchies, it seems that Stuart's mission reinforced those categories rather than test them with a biblical picture of community laid out in the book of Revelation chapter seven verses nine and following.

After its organization and particularization, "the Monroe congregation was under the care of the North Alabama Presbytery. This presbytery was, after 1826, part of the synod of West Tennessee."[103] On May 4, 1826, all the Presbyterian missionaries who served the Choctaw, Chickasaw, and Cherokee met at Monroe. In that meeting the missionaries organized the Association of Missionaries in the Choctaw and Chickasaw Nations. These individuals later formed the bulk of what became the Tombigbee Presbytery, which they later established on June 5, 1829.[104] By 1830, the membership was flourishing. The church numbered 110 members in the fall of 1830, "of these about one-half were natives, a few Whites, and the balance blacks, of whom there were a considerable number in the neighborhood of the station."[105] In 1832, "after the Presbytery of Tombeckbee was organized, the Monroe Church was transferred to its jurisdiction. The congregation achieved its largest membership in 1836, with 127 on the roll."[106]

More Chickasaw members, as well as a few Creek women, joined the Monroe Church after particularization, which is the formal process leading a mission church to an autonomous congregation able to function and rule on its own with a local session administering. Indeed a very interesting aspect of the church's racial heterogeneity struck Stuart. The African American members "generally spoke the Indian language; and being on an equality with their owners, and having more intercourse with them than is usual among white people, through their instrumentality a knowledge of the gospel was extended among the Indians." Therefore Stuart was able to use the Chickasaw model of enslavement to encourage his enslaved African American members to convince their Native American owners to visit the church. Further "the change, too, in their deportment had a tendency to convince them of the reality and excellence of religion, and to eradicate their (Native American) prejudices against it."[107]

In 1827, the Monroe Mission became part of the American Missionary Board, which supported similar missionaries to the Cherokee and the Choctaw. Stuart's letters suggest this as a welcome connection declaring, "To this we did not object, because it brought us into more immediate contact with the missionaries of the Choctaws, to whom we were much attached."[108] As the church moved into the 1830s, session records indicate that growth continued. With this growth, church discipline cases became more and more frequent. For example, Ishtimayi, "a native member of our church, having for a long time absented herself from the means of grace, and giving sad evidence that she is yet in a state of sin and heathenish darkness, was excommunicated."[109] Ishtimayi was brought up on discipline charges for not displaying regular attendance as a member. Given knowledge of Native American practices, it seems harsh to apply Western standards of attendance to a recent Chickasaw member, who might not have known fully the Western Christian standards and expectations associated with regular attendance and membership.

Indeed applying racial categories to church discipline cases in a way that negatively affected people of color occurred within the few church discipline cases mentioned in the session records in 1827–28. Regarding church discipline church membership included a responsibility to live in accordance with the tenets of Christianity and under the authority of the session, which possessed "spiritual oversight" over the flock. In the two discipline cases one was a White man named Mr. Cheadle and the other an African American woman named Mila. Both were guilty of a "heinous sin," and a meeting of the session examined the "circumstance of the offense." Both made full confessions of the crime, promised amendment, and expressed contrition. Mila was "suspended from the communion of the church until she gave evidence by her deportment that she is truly penitent," and she was "publicly suspended in the presence of the congregation." The church session felt that Mr. Cheadle "ought not be excluded from the privileges of the church." Mila's case had become public, while Mr. Cheadle's case seemed to be between him and the session. The session records read, "Since her offense has become public, she is publicly suspended in the presence of the congregation."[110] This also displayed a distinction of how women in church discipline cases at Monroe might have been treated differently than male members. Potentially certain sins could be treated and "disciplined" differently based on the gender of the offender. Mr. Cheadle's sin was dealt with privately while Mila's became public. One was brought back into the congregation while another was suspended.

While both acts were "heinous" Mila's case had become public knowledge to the church membership and the Chickasaw nation, likely influencing the session's decision. This unequal treatment was indicative of the session's racial and even gendered handling of discipline cases of male and female members. On January 3, 1829, the session restored Mila's membership because of her "having given satisfactory evidence of sincerity of her repentance, and having obtained a good report of her." However Mila left the Monroe Church the following July and joined another church within the Choctaw nation.[111] It is significant that Mila had the autonomy to make this decision and essentially decide for herself on her own church membership by leaving for another church.

Others who were disciplined included Dinah, who was considered an "adulteress"; Primus, "who has been living in adultery (having taken a woman who was put away by her husband)"; and Frances, "a black woman," who was "also excommunicated for the sin of fornication." The church excommunicated for a time and in some cases indefinitely all who confessed committing sins of a sexual nature. Many of those who expressed repentance, showed sincerity in their demeanor, and showed a change in their lifestyle could reapply for membership. The session often accepted them as new members. However some were under suspension "from the privileges of the church for a length of time and giving no evidence of repentance, but continued impenitent, were solemnly excommunicated." There was little chance of their readmittance. Such individuals included Molly Gunn, Nancy Colbert, Sally Fraser, James B. Allen, Benjamin Love, and Saiyo. Although two White men are included in this list before April 1834, seemingly every case of excommunication for adultery included either an African American or a Native American woman. Although displayed late in the record there was some consistency along gendered and even racial lines for excommunications and church discipline.[112] Rather than addressing the issues within the confines of the ecclesiastical body first the session chose to punish the woman publicly and to ostracize her from the ecclesiastical body. Mila would have had little to no power within the church or in Mississippi in 1827.

The session gave in to accepted cultural, social, and political pressures of how a southeastern church dealt with powerless women of color in the early nineteenth-century South. For example, Mr. Cheadle as a male possessed the same "heinous" sin, and he was not discharged from the congregation, nor was his case made public. The preference of the session here seems to give more respect, dignity, advocacy, and support to a man who already possessed some measure of power over a woman of color in the nineteenth-century South. As shepherds, these men could have advocated for the weak and powerless and at the very least treated the cases equally and showed that social norms dominating the landscape did not apply to the Monroe session. Instead the shepherds reflected patterns that were common and ruled in favor of Mr. Cheadle, thus reaffirming southern ecclesiastical patriarchy, which also seemed consistent with preexisting racial categories.

The session records also indicate a sense of concern among the elders of Monroe Church with both African American and Native American men practicing "experimental religion." For instance Edom, "a black man belonging to Mr. Wetherall, applied for admission" and "it being known that he is in good standing and the session having conversed with him on experimental religion, he was received." Also George, "a native man, was examined on experimental religion. His evidence of change appearing good, he was admitted to the privileges of the church."[113] By "experimental religion," Stuart was referring to both African American and Native American religious practices that often included seemingly non-Christian or un-Presbyterian practices.

Both African American and Native American religions possessed emotive and interactive components. Among African Americans, dancing, expressive singing, as well as collectively acting out historical religious events were common.[114] The Chickasaw incorporated dancing and much singing around fires through the evening, in some cases until dawn, performing medicinal treatments using "various roots and barks steeped in water."[115] Stuart alluded to this "experimental religion" in his letter to the *Southern Presbyterian* in June 1861. He lectured, "An Indian was seen slipping in, as if by stealth, with a large hand-gourd filled with tea, made of Yopon leaves, to which they attached a superstition of efficacy, believing that it enlightened their minds and led them to correct decisions."[116] Rather than incorporating, enveloping, or weaving these practices into a Christian experience at Monroe by using Yopon tea in social settings, the session disallowed "experimentation," which was considered "heathenish," rather than as sincere expressions of faith, religious zeal, or spiritual experience. The mission church seemed to be asking the new members to completely disregard and even discard cultural or historical religious practices and behavior in their new worship experience. In a sense they were asked to worship Christianity as White Europeans. This may be yet another reason why the Chickasaws remained cautious and why only a few dozen of the over six thousand members of the Chickasaw nation became members at Monroe.[117]

Historic Protestantism has included different kinds of wine, grape juice, and drinks in its communion or Lord's Supper celebrations for centuries. Wafers, crackers, and all manner of "breads" have replaced bread. Perhaps the church budget did not allow the congregation to purchase enough bread. Modern Presbyterian churches even carry gluten-free wafers to consider those who struggle with gluten allergies. It seems as if, instead of engaging in a process of trying to understand Chickasaw religion and incorporate aspects of it into ecclesiastical life, the missionaries forced the Chickasaw to completely abandon everything about their own religious culture and background.

Despite the early warm reception they gave the Presbyterians, the Chickasaw were cautious about Stuart and the Monroe Mission's progress. One historian noted, "Though Monroe Church was organized in 1823, it was December 1824, before the first Chickasaw made a profession of faith in Christ. Eventually, however, a number of the leaders of the nation were converted, and the mission began to make substantial progress."[118] The most prominent conversion, a personal friend of Stuart's, was Tishu Miko or Tishomingo, a leader of the Chickasaw where Monroe resided. Tishomingo and Stuart were friends throughout the existence of the mission until removal in 1839.

Another member was French Nancy. French Nancy was about five years old when she originally came to live with the Chickasaw. Her family was a member of D’Artaguette’s expedition from Illinois in the mid-1730s. After a major battle at Ogoula Tchetoka the Chickasaw destroyed D’Artaguette’s forces in 1736 and pushed back a French-led force of 150 French soldiers and several hundred more Native American militias. Hlikukhlo-hosh, a Chickasaw warrior, noticed Nancy while she was fleeing and captured the young fugitive. He spared her life and took her to live with the Chickasaw under the care of an elderly Chickasaw woman “to be reared and instructed in the most approved manner.” As she grew and became a woman, she and Hlikukhlo-hosh were married, and together they “reared a large family, and was honored and loved by the Chickasaw nation.” Indeed “she was regarded by the Chickasaws as a living monument of their victory over the inveterate enemies, the French.” French Nancy was in her mid- to late nineties when she joined the church. She would tell Stuart stories about “some of the circumstances of her capture” and that she “retained her European features, but in other respects was Chickasaw.”[119]

With French Nancy, the Colbert family, and a long tradition of interaction with both the British and the French, the Chickasaw people were well versed in European traditions, behavior, and culture. This also lends credence to the argument that the Chickasaw were using Monroe and Stuart as another interactive relationship to acquire legitimization.[120] In short the Chickasaw possessed their own agency and designs for the mission activity. In many ways the Chickasaw were directors of the mission, allowed it to function and practice, were financially supporting its presence, and controlled the mission’s limits or bounds.

Among the Chickasaw the heritage of intermarriage with English officers created a context steeped in knowledge of Western European culture and identity. Behind the scenes and from the time of Logan Colbert members of the influential Colbert family seemed to possess a great deal of power in the Chickasaw nation. The fluency with Western ideological frameworks and understanding of property seemed to put the Chickasaw mixed-heritage elite at some economic and political advantage when considering settler expansion. It also allowed the Chickasaw a unique avenue from which to pursue appeasement with a powerfully armed federal government. Pontotoc County land records show that William Colbert was intimately involved in the arrival of T. C. Stuart in Pontotoc. While Tishomingo served as leader and political facilitator, William Colbert donated the land on which Stuart built his home and the mission. “The property included Gen. Colbert’s allotment of three sections under the Chickasaw cession, and the section on which the missionary lived (S. 17, T. 11, R. 3).” Undoubtedly it was the influence of prominent Native Americans with European ancestry, such as William Colbert and his brothers, who helped persuade the Chickasaw to be more receptive to hosting Christian missionaries. One example of the Colberts's influence is found in Stuart's letter to the *Southern Presbyterian* in July 1861. He recalled his first meeting with the nation in 1820, noting that "there was a frolic on hand. Parties began to assemble, dressed out in their best, and instead of an Indian dance, such as I have witnessed many a time since, it turned out a regular ball, conducted with great propriety, and attended by the elite of the nation."[121]

Perhaps the Colberts were working to influence the Chickasaw nation to engage in greater levels of agricultural practices accepted in and Christian practices common in eastern states. Hence the Chickasaw would be perceived as more "civilized" and thus potentially exempt from removal. However, the strategy ultimately failed. Despite the Chickasaw accommodationist tactics and willingness to let Stuart bring Christian missions into their nation through the adoption of Christianity, education, and agricultural practices, these responses were unsuccessful. The federal government's highly racialized removal policies proved too strong for the Chickasaw legitimization plan. Federal removal policies did not account for adapted Chickasaw behavioral, religious, agricultural, and or economic shifts, but were consumed by the prospect of land speculation. In the end federal policy used race, culture, and religion to justify a land grab no matter how much the Chickasaw exhibited adaptation.[122] The Chickasaw were Native Americans and thus were dispensable to a United States federal government with notions of fulfilling the "manifest destiny" of filling every corner of their new land. In the minds of many land-hungry agents and speculators, Native American removal was a practical necessity. Many eastern would-be settlers sought Native American land with a ferocious greed, and the federal and state governments buttressed this greed with an intentional and thorough removal policy.[123] It is also likely that several of the new settlers would be Christians with no concern for their Christian brothers and sisters among the Chickasaw nation. They were only concerned with land for themselves.

Despite the mission's success in converting many and adding memberships along with the support of the Colbert family, Ishtohotopah, and Tishomingo, thousands more Chickasaw rejected membership. This indicated that the majority of the Chickasaw nation was either indifferent to Christianity or it was using Stuart as a buffer and as a future intermediary between itself and the impending removal policies of the federal government. The Monroe Mission grew exponentially in the nineteen years of its presence. The multiethnic mission can be seen as an example of interracial ecclesiastical activity in the nineteenth-century South that complicates the history of mission churches, which have been typically categorized as biracial spaces. At least in the frontier mission context there was far more interracial fluidity, multiethnic interaction, cultural reciprocity, interracial discourse, multiethnic ecclesiastical relationships, and complex cultural exchange. Despite the efforts of some Chickasaw to embrace Christianity and American acculturation throughout the first quarter of the nineteenth century the Chickasaw succumbed to the same fate as the surrounding Native American nations, and the federal government, fueled by land speculation, forced removal in 1834.[124]

The mission had the opportunity to reflect something different about race and gender to a watching world. It could have been a space that affirmed ecclesiastical equality and disregarded race and gender distinctions as membership distinctions and how cases were disciplined. Instead the Presbyterian missions to the Chickasaw, the enslaved African Americans, female members, and White male members had different levels of membership, discipline, and advocacy, or lack thereof, in the church based on one's race and gender. Rather than shepherding a congregation with a "kingdom" view or a view that took into account one's bearing the *imago dei*, or trying to achieve a heavenly view of human beings as Galatians 3:28 suggested, the Monroe Mission used American categories for race and gender, applying those categories to a functional ecclesiastical rule, membership, worship practices, and relationships. The mission largely reflected the culture in which it existed rather than challenge the culture with a higher view of human relationship. By doing this, the church sanctioned these categories, distinctions, and hierarchies based on race and gender, which worked to prevent African Americans and Native Americans from achieving full civic rights over the next century.

Stuart's missions to the Chickasaw "received the equivalent of a death blow when removal to the West became a reality."[125] However various acquaintances of "Father" Stuart recalled his animated and affable stories about interactions with Native Americans. These stories have led to the memory of Stuart as a paternalistic figure and as "father" of the Chickasaw Mission. Julia Daggett Harris left her remembrances of "Father" Stuart and the Monroe Church in the *Minutes of the Presbyterian Historical Society of the Mississippi Synod* in 1907. She recalled, "I first saw Mr. Stuart at my father's home near the old Monroe Church in 1854. At this time of course the last of the Chickasaws had long since left the red hills of their Mississippi home for the wild west." She particularly noted that "a never-failing theme of conversation with Mr. Stuart was his early Indian work."[126]

Education seemed to be a concern and focus behind Stuart's conversations. Harris noted, "An interesting phase of their conversation was that the Christian education of the Chickasaws in Pontotoc county was the basis of their Indian Territory civilization."[127] Others mentioned that Stuart "never lost interest in his Indian converts, and frequently visited them in their western home." After removal Stuart would ford rivers and travel across country with his daughter, Mary Jane Stuart, to visit his old Chickasaw flock. He was remembered as a "genial, kindhearted man." Reminiscences of Stuart's life reflected his passion and desire for missions work among the Chickasaw. Some remembered him as "a typical educated South Carolinian" who "radiated an air of culture and refinement."[128]

However Stuart's own letters indicate a sense of failure about his life's work. He wrote, "I often feel ashamed and deeply humbled that so little was accomplished." Yet he took solace in his faith saying, "It would be wrong not to render thanks to God that He was pleased to give any degree of success to the means employed." Stuart further justified his work noting "a large number of youth of both sexes were educated; much useful instruction was communicated, and a foundation laid for a degree of civilization and refinement which never could have been attained without it."[129] The number of Chickasaw who continued in Christian faith and practice also encouraged him. He wrote, "I visited the Chickasaws in their new home, and found a few of my old church members still living, and walking by faith."[130] Ultimately while Stuart felt that he failed he was consoled as a Presbyterian that God had foreordained him for this work and had brought him to this people. Expressing his own feelings on this matter, he wrote, "I would render thanks to God, that he counted me worthy to be employed in such a blessed work."[131]

While many affluent South Carolinians would have found this frontier lifestyle odious, Stuart counted himself blessed to be in such a position. While his imperialist-minded, racially prejudiced, and Western view of the Chickasaws was undoubtedly flawed, there is something to be acknowledged about his level of commitment and the personal sacrifices he made to leave his family and home for frontier missionary work. Stuart attempted to provide for the physical as well as spiritual estate of those around him and worked to alleviate the pain of the sick and bring literacy to those who could not read. He served his part within the Chickasaw legitimization plan to potentially assuage the fears of government officials in civilizing the Chickasaw. While this plan ultimately failed the relationships he cultivated and maintained with the Chickasaw persisted.

Forms of education common in the east, as a direct result of Presbyterian efforts, continued to be a tool of interest among the Chickasaw after removal.[132]

The Presbyterian Board of Foreign Missions continued to provide educational opportunities to the Chickasaw after removal to Oklahoma. The 1852 annual report for the board showed that the Chickasaw's interest in education was not fleeting. Indeed, parents discouraged truancy, students filled the schools to capacity, and "they (parents) sacrificed the services of the children at home in order that they might attend Spencer Academy or another boarding school. It was not uncommon for hundreds of parents and friends to be present at commencement exercises in May of each year." To be sure, much of this sustained enthusiasm about education was begun in Stuart's work in the schoolhouses of the Monroe Mission in Mississippi. This legacy of education may not have been as intentional as spreading the gospel but nevertheless became an important facet of Chickasaw culture after removal.[133] After removal Stuart continued to meet with his Chickasaw friends until his death. A favorite acquaintance was James Gamble. Gamble, educated at Monroe, continued his education in Mesopotamia, Alabama. As Stuart noted Gamble became a "great man of his nation-is a senator in their legislature- national interpreter and translator, and is their commissioner to Washington City to transact their business with the Federal Government." Stuart later remarked in 1861 that Gamble was a "standing refutation of the oft-repeated slander that an Indian cannot be civilized."[134]

Stuart's devotion, as well as a reflection of his role in assimilation, to his former members was also apparent in his recollections of trips to Oklahoma. He wrote, "I was delighted with the advances made in civilization which were everywhere apparent." Due to the lack of game in their new territory the Chickasaw had given up hunting and relied fully on agricultural practices for sustenance. The Chickasaw built homes out of logs with chimneys and by 1840 had abandoned "the office of chiefs and councils for the government of the people, and have organized a regular state government, with a written constitution, after the model of our sovereign states." Indeed many of the nominated candidates to rule over the legislature and the Chickasaw nation were educated at Monroe.[135]

After the removal of the Chickasaw Stuart continued to dwell in Pontotoc for thirty-seven more years. He preached to a growing community of new arrivals and "buried the dead, performed marriage ceremonies, and taught at intervals." Stuart's wife died on September 23, 1851, and Stuart had one living child, a daughter named Mary Jane. Mary Jane "became his companion and comforter in his old age." Mary Jane would also travel with her father to visit the remnant of the Chickasaw nation in Oklahoma.[136]

During the Civil War Stuart served as an instructor at Chickasaw Female College in Pontotoc, Mississippi. According to Winston, "He sought the place that he could do the most good, and readily found it. The war having disrupted the entire educational system of the South, and it was a rare opportunity that was offered to this section by keeping the school going through the troublous times." Stuart stayed on at Chickasaw Female College and taught throughout the tumultuous period of Reconstruction in Mississippi. The college was used as a hospital by both Union and Confederate soldiers. After the war, with Stuart's help, the college became a "respectable" academic institution, and by the end of the nineteenth century Chickasaw Female College was one of the oldest and most renowned coeducational colleges in the state. The school closed in 1936 due to financial nonviability.[137]

In the latter half of the 1870s Stuart and his daughter moved to Tupelo. Stuart died in Tupelo at the home of his daughter in 1883. He was buried in the Pontotoc cemetery, and it "probably appealed to him as a place of sepulcher" undoubtedly because "in 1852, a government deed conveyed the ground to the 'Chickasaws and their white friends forever as public burying ground.'" The Reverend T. C. Stuart's epitaph appropriately reads "For many years a missionary to the Chickasaw Indians."[138]

Some wounds in American history simply cut too deep. The difficult and tumultuous relationship between the United States and the Chickasaw nation is certainly one of those wounds. But perhaps some hope for future healing can be drawn from a deeper understanding of the injustices in our past. Today in an era in which attempts at multiethnic religious interaction seem rooted only in recent history, it is important to see how such attempts at multiethnic ecclesiastical interaction can be found further back in our shared history. These historic communities included Whites, Native Americans with European ancestry, African Americans, and Native Americans. "What these churches reveal are human beings from various racial, cultural, and religious backgrounds struggling to communicate, to know one another, and to make some sense of their changing worlds. In many ways, it was not unlike our twenty-first-century efforts to overcome divisions of race, religion, and culture. Studying the experiences of these mission communities can help us navigate the multiethnic dimensions of our national identity."[139]

These shepherds ministered to both Native American and African American communities. However rather than letting an orthodox, historical, and biblically informed perspective drive the work of the mission, Stuart and others let the savage wolves of racial categories ravage their flock. They gave way and provided preference in the church to a southern landscape bent on the greed of land ownership, which preferred gaining wealth on the total enslavement of African Americans. Rather than challenge these ideas the mission supported them. The mission created different categories for membership and applied discipline in different ways based on race and gender. The agenda and interests of the federal government, along with the interest in land by speculators and individuals interested in land holding, which required removal of Native American brothers and sisters in Christ, became normal and accepted within the Monroe Mission and among missionaries to the Chickasaw. For these missionaries the savage wolves were especially hungry for land, the labor of the enslaved, and were allowed in to feast upon the sheep under their care.

Chapter 3

"To and Fro Like a Forest in a Storm"

Antebellum Missionary Activity in the Lowcountry of South Carolina, 1829–47

By 1850, many recognized Reverend Charles Colcock Jones for his work regarding the religious instruction of enslaved African Americans. Historian Donald Mathews once linked him with northern abolitionist William Lloyd Garrison noting, "Both devoted their lives to the problem of black- white relationships. They developed, however, in different ways. Garrison personified the northern abolitionist movement; Jones represented the southern Christian mission to the slaves."[1] Missions to enslaved persons and especially mission work in the Tidewater regions of the South Carolina Lowcountry must begin with an understanding of Charles Colcock Jones and his work along the Georgia coast.

Jones was exposed to the philosophy of anti-enslavement and emancipation while attending Andover Seminary in Massachusetts and later at Princeton. Jones's experiences as an impressionable youth in a northern, free society, along with his Presbyterian roots informed his style of "slave missions" work. Indeed Mathews noted that Jones's ideology of missions to enslaved persons gave rise to "a long controversy about the emancipationist implications of Evangelicalism" in the surrounding lowlands of Georgia and South Carolina.[2] In this space while the emancipationist implications of missions to the enslaved were, in any civic sense, nonexistent, there were examples of ecclesiastical opportunities that served as a impactful force in enslaved African American communities toward expanded freedoms. However what could have served as a liberating force to enslaved African Americans, the Jones model would be used to continue to monitor, observe, and control African American communities, limiting the verbiage on freedom, and emphasizing the language on submission and obedience to white masters. It would be yet another symptom of a disease that had infected Christendom across the US South. Southern Christian missionaries were willing to allow enslaved

African Americans to be free spiritually, but they were never willing to grant any kind of cultural, social, political, economic or ultimately even ecclesiastical equality.

This makes the idea of a "slave mission" church, biblically and confessionally speaking, an unorthodox appendage to American Christianity in the US South. In a sense what Jones and other missionaries argued was that enslaved people are humans and have souls. They can be admitted into the church as members and brothers and sisters in Christ. However because of their race and their status as property, they can never have any kind of freedom or autonomy outside of their bondage to their earthly master. This would run headlong into Jesus's admonition that one cannot serve two masters. For missionaries to the enslaved, the ultimate allegiance for the enslaved in this life was to their earthly master. An enslaved person could give their soul to God, but not anything else. According to proslavery Christianity, after the church service, the soul, to the enslaved, became almost an appendage one might detach and disconnect from anything connected to the world. This also ran counter to historic Christianity and its teachings. If anything of the soul picked up at the mission ran counter to the institution of slavery than it was to be swiftly cut down.

Therefore southern missionary shepherds had let the wolves of economic, political, cultural, and social practice prey upon their flock and inform, as well as undergird, their exegesis and its exposition. Rather than protect and defend the flock these shepherds gave their sheep over to have their marriages torn apart, their children sold away, and their members dehumanized. The savage wolves who promoted the institution of enslavement by purchasing, selling, and expanding enslavement used these shepherds to better control their prey, and the shepherds led their sheep like lambs to the slaughter.

Southern Presbyterians were aware of northern abolitionism and the arguments made by northern pastors on the issues of enslavement. Mathews described Jones's experiences at Andover noting, "insurrection and abolitionism joined with a national impulse for reform to provide an audience for a man who hoped to save his country and soul by persuading his fellow southerners to create a biracial community based upon Christian precepts."[3] By 1845, Liberty County, Georgia, contained "5,493 slaves, 24 free blacks, and 1,854 whites," the enslaved Africans outnumbering the Whites almost three to one.[4] Liberty County, a coastal portion of southeast Georgia, consisted mostly of rice plantations. This meant seasons of malaria and White planter absence for extended periods to escape disease and to partake of social activities closer to cities.

While biracial congregations did exist, they were a different kind of mission church than the two in the South Carolina Backcountry and western frontier.

Those in power in the mission churches recognized a kind of functional Docetism, which was the idea that Jesus only appeared to have a human body. The repercussions of this teaching, which was considered heresy in the early church, was that the body was not spiritual and the things of the world were not holy, on the things of the spirit. Within the church, the souls of enslaved African Americans were sacred, but not their bodies. For Jones and others following in his footsteps, "slave missions" would serve as a kind of experiment in both justifying enslavement and attempting to evangelize the enslaved. These missions would simultaneously salve the conscience of the holder of enslaved persons by pursuing the owner's eternal obligation while justifying the inhuman treatment of the enslaved' s finite existence. Liberty Country therefore would not so much serve as a "biracial community based in Christian precepts" as much as it was an experiment in control, the exertion of power, and spiritual dominance using Christianity as a vehicle to provide a veneer of evangelism while furthering the economic goals of the master class. Jones's community would use nineteenth-century racial categories to inform ecclesiastical polity, membership, and roles of Whites and African Americans in the church. The institution of enslavement in the US South controlled how southern White Christians and the mission church thought about, preached on, and justified American enslavement and how only African Americans were uniquely situated for such a system.

Born in 1804, Jones began interacting with coastal enslaved African American populations at a young age, raised in "a slaveholding family whose religious inheritance was the stern moral discipline of Presbyterianism."[5] After Jones converted to Christianity in his teenage years he became increasingly concerned with the enslaved African American's condition and determined to work in some way to address that condition.[6] However as one Liberty County citizen wrote regarding the sentiment among planters, "Here generally speaking, it really appears as if to 'make cotton to buy Negroes, and buy Negroes to make cotton' is the dearest wish of their hearts, the sole employment of their noblest faculties. But this is human nature!"[7] Raised in this context Jones would go to seminary but also recognize that the context of holding of enslaved persons and the grip that the institution of enslavement had on the people of Liberty County would require some finesse as he would move home and begin his ministry. Jones's family owned 941 acres on a plantation called Montevideo, which included rice and a coastal cotton plantation employing over one hundred enslaved African Americans.[8]

This was an important aspect of Jones's missions work. The owners of enslaved persons of Liberty County saw him as one of their own. Indeed he could move in separate spheres of influence and gain the trust of owners of enslaved persons, while simultaneously having access to enslaved populations for ministerial purposes. This would prove important to his work as planters were especially cautious of northern abolitionism and interpretations of the Bible deeming enslavement as sinful. In the minds of Liberty County planters, Jones would be undoing his own livelihood by interpreting the Bible with such a hermeneutic. However Jones's ministry was also allowing the weight of the institution of enslavement to push his biblical and confessional commitment to his "flock." The concerns of the peculiar institution and the financial concerns of planters would override the concerns of the enslaved. Finally the concerns and preferences of a enslaved-person-owning society would drive the ways in which Christian missions functioned in Liberty County. It would cause Jones to be creative with ecclesiology and biblical passages on the *imago dei*, which would lead to imbibing of a kind of modern American form of functional Docetism in its Christian practice.[9] This kind of view would have been necessary for instance if Jones taught his congregants that their spirits or their souls were free, but nothing within their human existence could ever experience freedom or autonomy. For Jones and other missionaries to enslaved persons enslaved people's obedience and loyalty were to their earthly masters before their church or their vows as church members. In short the church played a secondary role to the institution of enslavement and followed its lead.

Because enslavement was so engrained in the landscape and the mental calculus of men and women at this time Jones and other missionaries could twist the scriptures in an acceptable manner to meet the needs of the "peculiar institution" and those who controlled it, making sure Christianity did not disrupt the driving power structure. This kind of manipulation of scriptures would certainly not have been allowed by a nineteenth-century presbytery in teaching the Ten Commandments or the Trinity. However when it came to passages like Exodus 21:16 ("Whoever steals a man and sells him, and anyone found in possession of him, shall be put to death") missionaries to enslaved persons could gloss over these passages, negate them, dismiss them, or do the theological gymnastics necessary to display how verses like this supported the system. If the distortion of scripture served the purposes of the owners of enslaved persons, then the contortions were acceptable. If exegesis of biblical texts challenged the power structure or the wealth of enslavers, then such notions were swiftly cut down.

While studying at seminary Jones's letters home showed an individual wrestling with much conflict over the peculiar institution.[10] Mathews has described these letters as "contrapuntal themes, the divine imperative of moral self-discipline, and the 'curse' of slavery. The first theme was common among young southern clergymen in the nineteenth century, but the second was quite uncommon, seldom appearing except as an anguished prayer of confession."[11] For instance Jones seemed embarrassed by his home state in comparison to the North, a place he had come to admire. He mentioned this sentiment in a letter to his fiancée, "Were you my dear to reside a few months only in a free community you would see more clearly than you now do the evil of slavery. There is calmness, an order, a morality, a general sentiment of right and wrong which is not to be looked for in ours."[12]

Later, Jones founded the "'Society of Enquiry Concerning Africans,' before which he delivered a paper urging the establishment of missions to the slaves in Georgia."[13] It was perhaps at this point that missions for enslaved persons for Jones became something distinct from what a contemporary southern holder of enslaved persons might have imagined. If enslavers allowed missions for enslaved persons to occur, then it was only to better control the enslaved or as a justification to northern abolitionists of benevolent treatment of enslaved persons. There could be genuine concern over the spiritual station of the enslaved, but that spiritual station should never work to challenge the institution of enslavement, only enforce it. In letters from seminary, it seems that Jones had given much thought to the missionizing of enslaved persons, far beyond the rationale. Indeed, "for some time he (Jones) had been struggling with this issue [enslavement] and an appropriate Christian response to it."[14] Jones seemed to be testing the waters of his thought process in letters to loved ones. Writing again to his fiancée, Jones was careful to note that enslavement "is a violation of all the laws of God and man at once. A complete annihilation of justice. An inhuman abuse of power."[15]

How truly did these letters to his fiancée reflect Jones's position? Mathews argued, "Brave words from a pious young man to his fiancée are a special kind of expression. In the early nineteenth century, they were often the exaggerated manifestation of romantic yearnings and were designed to demonstrate the moral sensitivity of the writer." Mathews went on to display how this argument did not convince him regarding Jones's expressions. "The austere and intense Jones, however, was not posturing for his lady, whom he had known since they were children. He was genuinely disturbed by the differences between the two sections and their citizens."[16] Supporting this claim Jones later wrote that "northerners ask favors, southerners demand service," which Jones accredited to the existence of enslavement.[17] It is clear that Jones was thinking and discerning the appropriateness of the institution of enslavement and the Christian response to it in distinct ways, which were informed by an abolitionist culture and a context removed from the institution.

Jones was torn between a variety of competing ideologies. His newfound sense of the benefits of freedom, his conscience, southern order, a love for his home and family, and his understanding of the state of enslaved African Americans all weighed on him. Indeed Jones would later boldly declare, "What I would not give if our family were not freed of this property and removed beyond its influence."[18] He even resolved in a letter to his fiancée that he would "postpone their marriage until he could make a living without depending on slave labor."[19] Further in an ideological departure from the southern planter class he penned these words in 1830:

> It is high time that our country was taking some measures of some sort, whose ultimate tendency shall be the emancipation of nearly three millions of men, women & children, who are held in the grossest bondage, and with the highest injustice. And where are the men to devise and execute these measures? No where.[20]

After completing seminary, Jones decided to come back and live in Liberty County, Georgia. He was drawn to minister among the enslaved populations in the South of whom he believed "are held in the grossest bondage, and with the highest injustice." By 1830, Jones had decided not only to minister to the enslaved, but to do something to alleviate the horrific conditions of the institution. He again wrote to Mary conflicted that he was not sure about this return to Georgia. However he finally concluded that he would "endeavor to do what I can for [blacks] there . . . or devote myself at once to them, in some special efforts in connection with the colonization society."[21] Jones contemplated emancipating his own enslaved persons, but realized this would ruin his ability to minister among enslaved populations and would likely bring financial ruin. In the end Jones felt that he could do more for the enslaved populations in Liberty County by submitting to the acceptable societal norms concerning the institution while attempting to mollify the effect on enslaved African Americans within his spheres of influence. He wrote, "There have been many ministers who have ruined their influence and usefulness in the southern states, by injudicious speech and conduct in regard to the slaves and the general subject of slavery."[22]

However after going home to Georgia, he would find a system so entrenched that even the slightest challenge to it would bring swift retribution. Missionaries to enslaved persons before Jones only asserted enslaved persons' submission to their masters. One example of missionaries in Georgia was the prominent Bryan family. As John Boles asserted this family "undertook to promote Christianity among their own and neighboring slaves, but they did so in such a way as to support the institution of slavery." Indeed one abolitionist who lived among missionaries to enslaved persons in the South for several decades, avowed, "I solemnly affirm that during the forty years of my residence [in the South] . . . I never heard a sermon to slaves but what made obedience to masters by the slaves the fundamental and supreme law of religion." Jones warned "that the slaves saw through and resented these lectures. He advised preachers to the Negroes to concentrate on parables, historical events, biographies, and expositions of the more important biblical verses."[23] Jones's idea was not simply to buttress the "peculiar institution" through preaching on texts with the theme "Slaves, obey your masters" but to teach from other passages in the Bible.

This context reflects the early to mid-nineteenth century coastal Lowlands of Georgia and South Carolina regarding the region's views on enslavement. The fact that a young seminarian was convinced of the truth of American enslavement being unacceptable to a Christian but was unable to ever utter such a phrase publicly, as it would have "ruined" his influence is telling with regard to the strong grip that the institution of enslavement had in this region. Further it displayed the variety of ways in which missionaries to enslaved persons accommodated the culture in order to make enslavement fit within a biblical worldview that could be applied to the southern, slaveholding landscape. Here we see that the shepherds not only allowed the savage wolves of greed and racism to come in and ravage the flock, but they also looked to an exposition of scripture that would justify their system and emphasized texts like Ephesians 6:5 in order to do so. Therefore missionaries to enslaved persons like Jones and those who would follow in his wake were in a dangerous position of being influenced so tremendously by the cultural, political, and economic sway of the region that they freely gave over orthodox teaching, biblical fidelity, and their own consciences on American enslavement to be accepted.

It is likely that if Jones had come back to Georgia, emancipated his enslaved persons, and spoken as an advocate for abolitionism, arguing that southern enslavement was human stealing and thus sinful he might have been imprisoned or perhaps killed. Survival would have been difficult in Georgia for the Andover-trained Jones, and he would have suffered the same fate as other idealistic southern ministers who "had tried emancipating their slaves with unfortunate results."[24] Jones therefore resolved to keep his private beliefs from becoming public, and he would work within the institution of enslavement without challenging enslavement outright. Jones would minister to enslaved people and to their enslavers.

In taking this route Jones and other missionaries moving into the middle of the nineteenth century would teach a religion that allowed one part of his flock to ravage the other. The Christians in the US South who were pro-enslavement and used the Bible to defend enslavement were ravaging their own flocks like wolves. In Matthew chapter 7:15, right after teaching about the Golden Rule, Jesus warns his disciples to "beware of false prophets, who come to you in sheep's clothing but inwardly are ravenous wolves."[25] It seems that wolves in sheep's clothing were prominent in the Presbyterian landscape of the nineteenth-century Georgia and South Carolina Lowlands. The pro-enslavement wolves came into the church and destroyed flock after flock, and the southern shepherds allowed it to happen. Rather than defending slave marriages the shepherds were overwhelmed by wolves who sought to divide families and sell husbands and wives away for profit. Rather than defending enslaved children, which should have been the shepherd's highest calling, they allowed them to be sold away from their parents. Time and time again southern shepherds allowed greed-filled ravenous wolves to come among their flocks and devour.

As a minister with a long career ahead of him Jones moved cautiously. Those who were planning on successful careers in ministry, especially to enslaved African Americans, throughout the antebellum South had to be extremely careful in order to, in Janet Cornelius's words, preserve "the best interests of the colored population and the approbations of the whites."[26] Hence upon Jones's arrival home, he endeavored to become the model prototypical southern, planter-class owner of enslaved persons, and lived the life of a planter's son while simultaneously earning the trust of his neighbors who owned enslaved persons. After moving South Jones was careful not to use the same language he had used in letters while living in New England. To be sure he must have recognized immediately that the views of enslavement's positive good in Lowcountry Georgia would have been overwhelming. Certainly like many shepherds he would have to make calculated decisions about which sins he would comment on and which sins would go unaddressed.

The fulfillment of Jones's plan came, as Mathews asserted, "at the end of a severe internal struggle, during which he put down on paper carefully and quite self-consciously a condemnation of slavery as an exploitative and dehumanizing system. He knew, therefore, that he must as a morally responsible person fight against it."[27] His "fight" was not always public and was not necessarily forthright. In many ways Jones worked from inside an immoral southern slavocracy, and in seeking to save the souls of enslaved African Americans he often overlooked their earthly suffering. He would robe himself in the codes of the slavocracy, its inner circles, its form of conduct and affectations. He himself would become a kind of wolf in wolves' clothing. He tried to find a way to shepherd a flock and seek opportunities to promote expanded ecclesiastical opportunities for the enslaved while the wolves would feast. His inward desires were never fully presented to the wolves and resigned to do what he could from within.

As Jones engaged southern society he seemed to fit into John Boles's model of southern missionaries operating within the framework of a "limited emancipationist impulse." This emancipationist impulse was not overtly public or political. This impulse would come from within an ecclesiastical context. Jones would have to show his southern neighbors that if enslaved African Americans were equal "in God's eyes" and "in the eyes of the church," then perhaps enhanced ecclesiastical opportunities would help display the humanity of enslaved people. As Eugene Genovese had written, "virtually all [slave-owners] insisted that freedom and moral progress had to be understood not simply as the product of recent political developments, but rooted in Christianity."[28] For Jones perhaps by working in the church the enslaved African American member could display to southern enslavers that Christian faith, membership in the household of faith, and moral progress could alleviate the ravaging.

Other historians have hinted at the seemingly controversial nature of Charles C. Jones's work to raise the ecclesiastical status among enslaved African Americans. Erskine Clarke, in his portrait of Charles Colcock Jones entitled *Wrestlin' Jacob*, argued, "If he were not to pursue his anti-slavery sentiments, he could take another path, he could turn to these black people in the hope of bringing them the gospel and elevating their conditions in the midst of slavery."[29] Janet Cornelius has described Charles C. Jones among other "genteel missionaries" as embracing "slave missions as a way to work through the contradictions in their lives and at the same time pursue their benevolent and spiritual goals."[30] Donald G. Mathews avowed:

> All these pieces were fitted by the diminutive young man into a mosaic of Christian responsibility, which in turn was laid into the framework of his own social and personal inheritance of slavery. Why he brooded so intently over the problem is impossible to say. But throughout his life there seemed to be a special relationship between himself and blacks—a sense of obligation which he never quite wished to be free of. Somehow he knew as a young man entering his lifework that he must fight against slavery to destroy it; that is what he said.[31]

Men like Charles C. Jones occupied a place within the range of individuals engaged in missions to enslaved persons that accommodated the culture of the landscape.[32] Jones was helping to perpetuate the institution of enslavement but also attempting to infuse measured ecclesiastical reform while simultaneously keeping his position in the slavocracy firmly intact. It was Jones's hope that over time these expanded ecclesiastical roles would produce change in the southern landscape perhaps destroying it slowly from within. Jones's fiancée Mary touched on this seemingly contradictory and difficult position in her description of Jones stating that she was "disturbed by Charles' outcries about slavery." Indeed, she displayed an attraction to Jones because of his ambivalence toward enslavement believing that he was different from all the men that she knew who only "made cotton to buy negroes and bought negroes to make cotton." "Mary realized that Charles used his letters to her as a sounding board for exploration of new ideas, but his emotional condemnation of slavery was different from his other reform enthusiasms," and "it revealed a deeply held emotion that was so dangerous that it could not have been expressed in Georgia."[33] Mary would likely have been concerned for her own, her husband's, and their children's well-being if Jones pushed too far.

Jones preached and ministered to the enslaved peoples of the Georgia Lowcountry for the next fifteen years of his life. Establishing the Association for the Religious Instruction of Slaves was his first task. This association became the first model for a consortium of missions to enslaved persons throughout the South and was at the time the only organization of its kind. Jones was invited to attend meetings and gatherings across the South to help instruct other missionaries and ministers in the finer points of Christianizing the enslaved. Jones's catechization and instruction of enslaved African Americans was mostly through oral repetition, voluntary from the community, and for the most part White-led. He encouraged masters to be more involved in the religious instruction of their enslaved persons, to improve their physical estate, and to treat their enslaved persons more humanely in accordance with biblical teaching. Jones even created a nondenominational catechism for enslaved persons entitled *Catechism of Scripture Doctrine and Practice*, which enslavers and missionaries across the South used in an oral call-and-response method.[34] Jones also authored *The Religious Instruction of the Negroes in the United States*, which gained wide circulation and remained the model on the subject until 1865.[35]

Jones also implemented a "station model" in missions to enslaved persons. These models became laboratories "in which he could test his theories about reshaping slaves according to a Christian view of human destiny."[36] He would attend various plantations or "stations" in Liberty County and at these "stations," with the permission of the planter or overseer, Jones would find a place where he could address the enslaved; give them religious instruction; preach to them from a sermon he had carefully constructed; and then conduct worship with hymns, prayers, and supplication.[37] One author noted, "Three separate houses of worship, located at convenient points, were built for their exclusive use. Every Sunday, at an early hour, Dr. Jones mounted his horse and rode to one of these churches. From all of the neighboring plantations the servants came in crowds, men, women and children."[38]

Although Jones performed much of the teaching and preaching, he also thought that having enslaved African American preachers was an important form of the mission work. This was a unique departure from the typical plantation experience described in Albert Raboteau's "Invisible Institution," in which enslaved preachers only taught under the cover of darkness and in hiding. Jones "vigorously championed the formal use of unlicensed, untrained Negro 'exhorters' as supplementary preachers," and he pointed out that "numerous black preachers serviced plantations and many of them did a good job."[39] Jones was aware of the important position these preachers already held in the enslaved community, and recognizing their skill and spiritual impact he provided important leadership roles within his own "stations" to more effectively serve the enslaved flock.

Jones's acknowledgment of enslaved pastor leadership abilities and gifts as preachers showed his belief that these individuals were not mere chattel property but human beings and human beings who were capable of literacy, teaching, spiritual oversight, and leadership. These African American shepherds certainly did not let savage wolves come in among them. They preached that the enslaved were "God's people" and they were God's children. These preachers refused to let the savage pro-enslavement wolves come in among the flock and say that African Americans occupied an inferior role in the church. These were the best of the southern missionaries, and like the African American preachers and exhorters at the Monroe Mission their very presence and work displayed the false premise undergirding the institution of enslavement: that enslaved people were chattel property. Property cannot preach.

Jones also employed what he called "watchmen" from among the enslaved African Americans to serve the various stations. It was the duty of the "watchmen" to "lead the assembly in prayer" and "made reports to the pastor with reference to the conduct of the church members on various plantations."[40] Thus enslaved African Americans were proving more and more to Jones that they were capable of leadership, teaching, and management and therefore were not meant for enslavement. This spiritual overseer was responsible for guiding the souls of the enslaved parishioners in Jones' absence. This construction, which also existed on the plantation apart from the church structure, might have served the same purpose as a "trusted" field worker given a special level of autonomy by enslavers in exchange for information or knowledge about the activities of the enslaved. However the "watchmen" in Jones's model seem to have been appointed or recommended by the enslaved African American membership and possessed spiritual qualities that provided them with a level of trust by the membership.

Further, Jones believed in preserving slave marriages and instructed the White planters in his community to keep enslaved families intact. However his words would accomplish nothing without action by enslavers. He wrote that "masters should guarantee the integrity of black families by requiring formal weddings and refusing to separate parents and children and also by counseling those with marital difficulties and providing separate accommodations for privacy." Additionally Jones was able to make great strides toward keeping slave families together and "came down especially hard against the disruption of family ties."[41] To support their families Jones "suggested that slaves be encouraged to grow their own crops."[42] Jones also performed many weddings for enslaved people on his own and neighboring plantation stations. An advocate for keeping enslaved families together Jones displayed his belief in the dignity of commitments that enslaved men and women made toward one another. This was yet another subtle assertion that human beings were not meant to be treated as property and were not fit for enslavement. However while Jones argued for this practice he was ultimately unable to prevent an owner of enslaved persons from selling away a wife from her husband or separating children from their parents. Moral suasion could only go so far. The shepherd could merely scream in the wolf's direction while he watched the wolf ravage his flock.

In a departure from Georgia slave codes and despite the legal and social prohibitions of teaching enslaved persons to read Jones made his preferences clear to some White church members that he wanted to teach enslaved African Americans to read. Later he remarked to a friend named John Cocke, who had trained an enslaved African American female to read the Bible, "it is not every owner who would feel either at liberty, or willing to adopt this plan; but it is said to work well, and to be productive of good results."[43] Jones's enslaved congregants appreciated these characteristics about the missionary as Genovese noted: "The slaves knew that many of these white preachers cared about them. The Reverend C.C. Jones wore himself out in pursuit of the religious instruction of the blacks, as he called it."[44] While there is evidence of private correspondence in the Jones record, it is hard to find any public exhortations that the enslaved should be taught to read.

When speaking to enslavers Jones emphasized the duties of the master to the enslaved persons rather than the enslaved persons' duties to the master. For instance in 1833 Jones wrote the following to the Synod of South Carolina: "Religion will tell the master that his servants are his fellow-creatures, and that he has a master in heaven to whom he shall account for his treatment of them."[45] These statements were no doubt unsettling in the sense that Jones implied a heavenly equality of the enslaved African American to the master. Jones also seemed to imply that poor treatment of enslaved African Americans would result in an "account" made to God, who viewed these men and women as made in the *imago dei*. This statement implied that owners of enslaved persons were eternally culpable in some way for their actions regarding the treatment of the enslaved.

Another example of Jones's perspective of missions to the enslaved can be found in the subjects of his sermons. Jones preferred to teach the entire biblical narrative as opposed to particular passages focusing on enslaved persons' duty to their master. He focused on texts relating to the salvation of the soul, spiritual freedom, and eternal liberation. He also preached to the enslaved in a context meant specifically for enslaved people, thus personalizing the message to his audience rather than preaching to White members with enslaved African Americans on the periphery. Jones also tended to stay away from "slaves obey your masters" passages except for once.[46] When he did preach on this text once it was to the immense displeasure of his audience who proclaimed, "that cannot be the gospel" and half the audience got up and left.[47] He recalled,

"Some solemnly declared that there was no such epistle in the Bible,' others 'that they did not care' if they ever heard me preach again."[48] Jones never forgot this incident, and he learned rather quickly that he could not preach this text to an enslaved African American audience. He realized that "these black slaves had a theological perspective to stand over against the whites." Jones's recognition of theological disagreement and his willingness to listen and understand why an African American audience would rebuke this preaching is telling. He was mindful of the theological acumen of his audience and even contemplated his approach to biblical exposition when preaching to the enslaved. Further his willingness to learn from the protest was a point of recognition that enslaved African American members of the flock possessed their own agency and could decipher which was the true gospel and which was not.[49]

Jones's enslaved congregants took their own theological positions and were encouraged to read, partake in leadership opportunities, and engage in ecclesiastical life. In addition Jones displayed to a wider southern audience that enslaved African Americans were human beings capable of spiritual and theological reflection as well as leadership. Enslavers, including Jones himself, were forced to contemplate how one could go on justifying a slave as inhuman and property if he or she possessed spiritual and theological acumen. Jones wrestled with this question and through his life and work brought it to the forefront of consideration for individuals throughout the South. However it must be acknowledged that Jones continued to let the pro-enslavement position drive the treatment of enslaved people and not this theological conviction.

What made Jones such an important figure in the history of missions to enslaved persons was the creation and implementation of a new system. Jones was able to create a vocational sphere that simultaneously eased his conscience about the horrors of the institution and allowed him to work within the institution of enslavement by offering measured ecclesiastical opportunities to enslaved African Americans while also perpetuating their dehumanization as enslaved chattel property. He did this while also maintaining social respectability and the support of enslavers. One scholar put it this way: "All the important people in Jones's life reinforced his decision to compromise his actions against the evils of slavery for what he had considered a greater benevolent good. Jones chose a path of lesser resistance." Indeed Cornelius made the argument that by "pledging his life to slave missions, he was able to advance his personal well-being."[50] Through this approach Jones was not only able to assuage his conscience and fulfill his seminarian ideals, but he was also able to carve out for himself status and honor in southern society while never really challenging the status quo. John Boles supported this line of reasoning with the assertion that missionaries to enslaved persons "understood the realities of the economic and social-control imperatives of the institution and occasionally stated explicitly that if they boldly attacked slavery, they would not be allowed to preach to the blacks, thereby–by their lights–causing the unfortunate bondspeople not to hear the gospel."[51]

Further as Mathews avowed, "Then the problem had been slavery and the solution, emancipation; but prudence and piety altered his goal. The missionary ideal was not to challenge social systems but to transform individuals." Indeed "the brave words and bold expectations of his younger years were tempered by the experience of multiplying responsibilities and subtle social interaction."[52] Jones chose the path of least resistance. By choosing this path he continued to allow wolves to ravage the flock of God. Unlike the Covenanter Presbyterians of the Upcountry of South Carolina Jones and the Lowcountry Georgia missionaries fully supported enslavement in America as an acceptable form of property ownership, labor, and means to profit.

This conflict in Jones's life displayed the complexity, varying interests, and disparate degrees to which missionaries to enslaved persons perceived their tasks. "He frequently spoke of affection between the two races and was sinfully proud of his special relationship with black parishioners."[53] His life exhibited the divergence that some southern missionaries felt toward enslavement, and it further displayed one missionary's attempt at something resembling Boles's notion of possessing a "limited emancipationist impulse." For Jones the world "limited" in "limited emancipationist impulse" became a reality as Mathews noted: "The institution that had to be destroyed became one that might be destroyed; it then became a perpetual apprenticeship in civilization for blacks." Yet still "in his letters, especially as he railed against the helplessness of pious young black women before their white seducers, he revealed that he understood personally what ideologically he could not admit."[54] Ultimately Jones chose accommodation, and the people he was called to shepherd suffered multiple attacks from the wolves in their midst.

Historians like John Boles and Donald Mathews have categorized Presbyterian missionaries to enslaved persons as significantly less successful than Baptist missionaries, William Capers's Methodists, and William Meade's Episcopalian counterparts, largely due to the numbers of participants in mission churches. They described Presbyterians as "disproportionately wealthy" and were said to have fewer African American congregants than other Protestant denominations. While Presbyterian numbers were lower across the board and located in a variety of settings "they tended to minister to blacks by providing them special ministers and separate accommodations."[55]

It may be a fallacy to categorize missionary "success" in terms of numbers of participants. Could there be anything resembling "success" in human enslavement? The content of the missionary's message might be as important as the numbers that listened. The impact of a missionary who was presenting a model of expanded ecclesiastical opportunity, as opposed to a missionary who reminded enslaved people to obey their enslavers might have possessed a broader impact in terms of preaching efficacy. It was the Presbyterians, through Jones, who started and produced this distinct type of "missions to the slaves" that created and defined a new category for attempting to understand southern domestic missions.

Presbyterians approached missions in a new way and it "motivated some [Presbyterian missionaries to enslaved persons] to devise ways to bring the gospel message to their blacks" and "the Presbyterian church was to remain relatively small but influential beyond its numbers."[56] What could have been influential beyond numbers was the way in which Presbyterians applied theological training to educational opportunities within missions to enslaved persons contexts. The use of catechisms, ecclesiological training, and the focus on learning Christianity in a systematic fashion were common. Whatever impact this might have had was corrupted through a synthetic weaving together of Christianity with national and regional interests in enslavement and the wealth it provided. Different catechisms existed for Whites and African Americans, different levels of memberships existed for Whites and African Americans, and White members were allowed to read while enslaved African Americans were largely prohibited from doing so. To truly be effective, the mission churches might have provided educational opportunities beyond recitation and preaching. However property holding trumped biblical conviction and overcame the bonds of a familial and spiritual membership tie. Missionaries to enslaved persons like Jones accommodated the southern way of life, the economic systems that supported it, and let enslavers ravage the flocks.

There are similarities in comparing Methodist, Episcopal, and Baptist missions to enslaved persons to the Presbyterian form, but there are also important distinctions, especially in the Lowcountry of Georgia and South Carolina. In Charleston, South Carolina, for instance, the Presbyterians not only enjoyed the largest congregation of enslaved African Americans in the state, but also remained influential in education, expanded ecclesiastical opportunities, and maintained a biracial religious community beyond the Civil War.[57] Given the attention historians have paid to the mission efforts of Methodists and Baptists it is telling that the "Father of Slave Missions" and "Apostle to the Negroes," the creator of the first organization and book outlining *Religious Instruction and Catechism for Slaves*, and the largest church building for enslaved African Africans (Zion Presbyterian Church in Charleston, South Carolina) were Presbyterian initiatives. Further it was Jones "who was the chief theorist of the entire movement; his book was its Bible, his catechism its guidebook, his country the ideal community, his theory the best articulated hope of evangelicals who wished to reshape their society." All of this while the "Methodist missions spread beyond the South Carolina conference which had spawned them, and as Baptists, Episcopalians wrote to him for advice."[58] However the Bible, the catechism, and systematic theological rigor could not shake the bedrock of the institution of enslavement in the southern ecclesiastical landscape.

As Jones was acutely aware "even good, Christian folk seemed to like the idea of the mission better than the work itself; the prejudices against the blacks were too great, the 'common sense' observations of black ignorance and perverseness too close to axioms to transform enough whites, let alone, blacks into people like Charles Colcock Jones."[59] The Presbyterian style of missions to enslaved persons through the Jones model engendered a unique brand of missionary. Jones pushed the envelope of southern culture regarding the priority of African Americans in missions to ways in which new missionaries tested innovative methods of missionizing enslaved African Americans along the coast of South Carolina.

Missions to enslaved persons allowed Jones and men like him to retreat from an anti-enslavement position. In many ways these missions were spaces for evangelical Protestants to deal with the guilty conscience of knowing enslavement was wrong, yet not wrong enough to denounce it publicly or become advocates for its abolition. Rather than attempting to change the status quo Jones was helping to absolve owners of enslaved persons and justify their actions. Southern Presbyterian missionaries convinced themselves that the salvation of the soul was their only duty, a kind of functional southern Docetism. They could not be engaged in changing any kind of civic or legal status. This position was undergirded by a doctrine known as the spirituality of the church. It became a dualist framework through which pastors and missionaries could excuse themselves from political engagement and advocacy for enslaved people and would allow them to pursue their vocation with theological cover. This doctrine would go on to have devastating effects in southern Presbyterianism during Jim Crow, the era of lynching, the Civil Rights movement, and even into modern concerns over racial injustice. Presbyterians simply told themselves, "Our only jobs are to deal with the spiritual realms" not the social, cultural, political, or economic realms. If the social, cultural, political, or economic realms included a position that Christians were for or that benefitted Christians, then it was acceptable to preach on the topic. Since so many Christians were invested in enslavement it became a position that most pastors were unwilling to challenge directly from the pulpit.

For Jones and others like him to defy enslavement would have been akin to defying the overwhelming membership, leadership of the church, and most important those who tithed generously. Such was the extent, power, and reach of enslavement. It forced Christians to dilute sound theology, biblical exegesis, ecclesiology, and principles of love and service of one's neighbors to fit with an entrenched institution based on supposed racial inferiority. The shepherd could not speak against such a behemoth evil and live or maintain a vocation in this space. Many of the church's members made vast fortunes on the backs of enslaved men and women, many livelihoods were directly dependent on the enslavement of human beings, many children were born through rape and abuse of African American women by White Christian men, and many a tithe came from money earned on the labor of the enslaved. Such a powerful force could not be undone without sacrifice and cost.[60]

If Jones's letters from Andover were ever made public, then it would surely have meant complete social ostracism and perhaps even death. Historians have touched on this dichotomy as Mathews mentioned: "The South's Protestantism is seen as something of a problem for its 'democratic' qualities, but its effect seems generally to have been to mold the 'paternalism' of the master class."[61] The distinctions and various levels of action between the pro-enslavement missionary, the abolitionist missionary, and the missionary leaning toward a "limited emancipationist impulse" or expanded ecclesiastical opportunities have not been thoroughly uncovered in the historiography of missionaries to enslaved persons. Like all movements whether it was abolitionism or civil rights there were always complexities, individualistic beliefs, various levels of fervency, and vicissitudes in ideologies given the context. Missionaries to enslaved persons and their varying principles of Christianization who attempted ecclesiastical reform or evangelization were no different. There were many shades of the southern domestic missionary, and when individuals are lumped into a generalization about the entire effort it robs us of a fuller understanding. Presbyterian domestic missions display men and women working in these spheres with deeply held personal convictions but without the ability to push back on a culture bent on oppression and brutal treatment of an entire race.

Despite his long labor, Jones never deceived himself into believing that he achieved a biracial ecclesiastical community with any sense of equity. Mathews argued that "had there been thirty thousand Charles Colcock Joneses instead of merely one, his ideas might have begun to change the South significantly, but the thought is pure fantasy." Instead "it reinforces the hopelessness of Jones's mission."[62] It would take individuals forged in the same fire as Jones to take up the "hopeless" work from the 1830s through the Civil War. While there were not hundreds of Joneses, there were Presbyterian missionaries to enslaved persons in Charleston, South Carolina, who were able to put Jones's vision, hopes, and dreams for the missionization of enslaved African Americans into further action.

Charles Colcock Jones, the "father of slave missions," had a tremendous influence on Charleston Presbyterians John Bailey Adger and John Lafayette Girardeau. Not only did Jones visit Charleston on numerous occasions to talk about his work in missions to enslaved persons, but John Adger translated and used Jones's catechism in his missionary work in Armenia.[63] The English model of missions had informed Adger's mission work and missionary perspective for the enslaved African Americans in Charleston. In England Thomas Chalmers worked with "the vilest portion of Edinburgh's low and filthy lanes, or Wynds." After visiting with Chalmers on a trip to England, Adger found the situation with enslaved African Americans in Charleston weighed heavily on his mind throughout 1846 and 1847. Distinct from Jones's work, in that the mission situation in Charleston was in a more urban context than the Liberty County model, Adger's idea for a mission to enslaved persons included a separate meeting place or church structure strictly for the use of enslaved African Americans. He found that there was not an appropriate amount of seating for the enslaved throughout churches in the city, and he believed that the members relegated enslaved African Americans to spectator status by forcing them to sit in the galleries.[64]

In 1844, the Reverend Thomas Smyth of Second Presbyterian complained about the gallery in which enslaved people sat during church services.[65] Later in 1846, about two hundred enslaved African Americans were attending or forced to attend the church. Smyth did recognize "the humanity of his black servants as possessors of the Imago Dei." He believed that "the Africans deserved humanitarian considerations. Against those insensitive to the needy, he pled for the improvement of the temporal and religious conditions of the slave."[66] Smyth was a staunch supporter of Adger, and in conjunction with creating a separate meetinghouse strictly for the purposes of enslaved African Americans, he oversaw the development of sabbath schools for the religious instruction of the enslaved at Second Presbyterian. In an important move toward realizing this vision Smyth asked Adger to outline his own concept for a mission for enslaved persons in Charleston.

Adger deployed his philosophy in a speech made to the congregation of Second Presbyterian in May 1847. He remarked, "Nowhere are the poor so closely and intimately connected with the higher classes as are our poor with us. They belong to us. We also belong to them." He went on to say that "they are our poor—our poor brethren; children of our God and Father; dear to our Savior; to the like of whom he preached; for the like of whom he died, and to the least of whom every act of Christian compassion and kindness which we show he will consider as shown also to himself." Erskine Clarke argued that this speech was "perhaps the clearest and most eloquent expression of the paternalism that characterized the Charleston churches in the work among blacks in the city."[67]

Adger was not saying that the enslaved members were equal in the church to White members for indeed their seating in the balcony displayed their inferior status. On the other hand, creating a separate mission church might do several things for Second Presbyterian Church. First it might remove the presence of enslaved African American people from the church for them to be "out of sight and out of mind" when worshipping. It might also work to the benefit of enslavers to have enslaved persons under the oversight of a White pastor, White session, and organizing structure rather than as mere attendees and spectators. However this might also be a kind of ecclesiastical separation or what was known as "organic separation" that would become fully realized in the highest ecclesiastical courts in 1874.

There also seemed to be a genuine concern for the condition of enslaved people that Adger was attempting to invoke in the consciences of the congregation. While paternalism was certainly a chief component of the speech, there was more going on. Adger and the largely enslaving membership of Second Presbyterian Church in Charleston, South Carolina, knew that they had a duty to care for enslaved people and their "poor brethren" among them as the Bible commanded. They also acknowledged that these were "children of God." Yet to Adger, Smythe, and the membership the enslaved were not full members of the church. Had that been the case then a full status of membership at Second Presbyterian Church would have been offered rather than at a separate "mission" church. The fellow children of God would have been brought into the life of Second Presbyterian Church with full ecclesiastical rights as other members and with duties and oaths that White members took. This was not offered, and the reason is that Adger, Smythe, and the membership never could have accepted an enslaved African American as a "fellow" member who would be equal in status in the life of the church.

For Adger and leading lights at Second Presbyterian church, there needed to be something to signify the spiritual and ecclesiastical worth of the enslaved yet also highlight difference and inferiority. With the church recognizing racial inferiority by seating, a nonmembership status, and a need to later be removed to a "mission church" Adger and Second Presbyterian were signaling to enslavers that the church supported an inferior status of enslaved people and that they should occupy their own spaces with paternalistic oversight. In creating a separate worship space with separate ministers missions to enslaved persons in cities were used to reinforce, rather than challenge, the denigrated ecclesiastical position that enslaved African Americans occupied. In creating these churches and not offering full ecclesiastical rights to enslaved people the church was sanctioning the destruction of the flock rather than advocating for the protection of the weak and vulnerable among them. In creating mission churches for the enslaved the southern Presbyterians took the lead in spiritually sanctioning American enslavement not just theologically but also in an ecclesiological way.

In 1846, the Second Presbyterian Session commissioned Adger to oversee the work of caring for the spiritual needs of the enslaved African Americans of Second Presbyterian.[68] Similar to how "Charles Jones was a missionary to the plantation slaves under the sponsorship of the Liberty County Association for the Religious Instruction of Negroes, Adger would be a missionary to city blacks under the sponsorship of the session of the Second Presbyterian Church."[69] Like Jones, Adger "received no financial support from the sponsor. What he would receive, like Jones, was the necessary approval and supervision from influential whites which would make his work appearing legitimate and acceptable to a suspicious white community."[70] Adger's work was "spiritual" only. To advocate in any way for ecclesiastical equality or full status as members in the church with voting rights or equality with White members would likely have brought destruction of this vision before it even took shape.

In August 1849, the *Minutes of Session of Second Presbyterian* noted that the "building committee of the Second Presbyterian Church, appointed to erect a building in which religious instruction may be afforded on a better plan than that formerly pursued by us." However despite some early support many Charleston community members rejected domestic missions work with enslaved African Americans. The Second Presbyterian Session seemed to be aware of this as it mentioned in the minutes "a missionary effort, which it is the duty of the church to enter, and though some difficulties still exist, these, it is hoped, will gradually be removed by Christian zeal, patience, prudence, and perseverance."[71]

One individual wrote letters to the *Charleston Mercury*'s editor under the pseudonym "Many Citizens."[72] The writer described the Anson Street work as a "dark and dangerous movement."[73] He argued that "the blacks would be joined together in an organized society with the right to consult and deliberate and be heard in matters of church government." He went onto say that "they would develop a spiritual allegiance to the church," that "they would learn that what they suffer for the church will be a proud distinction," and "to minds thus matured, what will be the language of the master or the owner."[74] The fear of large numbers of enslaved African Americans congregating in a church building was fresh in the minds of Charlestonians, including Adger, who only twenty-five years earlier witnessed the hanging of twenty-one enslaved African Americans, including Denmark Vesey who had been a member at Second Presbyterian Church, after an attempted slave revolt.[75]

Adger as shepherd promptly replied to the concerns that "blacks would always be under the supervision of whites and that the need for a new work was desperate." These new churches were not havens for biracial Christian community and ecclesiastical equality. They were meant to be spaces of further control, "supervision," and keeping the enslaved more closely under the eyes of Whites. A shepherd in this context was not a shepherd. His chief functions were watching and rigidly enforcing the will of the pro-enslavement wolves. However even these promises were not enough to cool the heated debate, which became more inflamed by the continued writings of "Many Citizens," among others.[76]

Charleston at this time was concerned about the possibility of continued slave insurrections. Uprisings of the enslaved, such as Charleston in 1822, Camden in 1816, and even the Stono Rebellion in 1739 were always on fearful enslavers' minds. Nat Turner's rebellion in 1831 added much anxiety to an already cautious Charleston community when it discovered that many involved in the Denmark Vesey plot meetings took place at Morris Brown AME Church, where Vesey was also a member. The 1850 census displayed why that caution existed in Charleston, which was 24,580 White, 3,849 free Black, and 44,375 enslaved. Another large church structure built specifically for the instruction of many enslaved African Americans, which could serve as a meeting space for potential insurrectionists, was not something that helped to allay White fears. The shepherds needed to show the wolves how these spaces were ones of control and not liberation.

The Second Presbyterian Session, as well as the Presbytery of Charleston, approved Adger's plan in May 1847. The plan was unique in that it called for building a separate church for African Americans themselves rather than Jones's method of visiting the plantation and preaching in modest churches located near the enslaved's quarters. It was also much different from the predominant slave missions' model, which allowed enslaved African Americans and free people of color to attend White churches but forced them to sit in the galleries or balconies. In Adger's mission work, enslaved African Americans were the priority and so were afforded the best seats. In contrast to slave codes and most southern enslavers' overwhelming belief, Adger favored teaching enslaved African Americans to read and worked to promote the repeal of the law against slave literacy.[77] While the intent of Adger's advocacy is debatable, the interest was most surely spiritual. There was no belief that enslaved people needed to read to attend school or to promote their own economic opportunities. This belief was purely for spiritual improvement and with the idea that enslaved people would only read the Bible, catechisms, and spiritual songs or hymns.

Later in June of 1847, what would eventually grow into the Anson Street Mission began first in the basement of a building on Society Street, which was known as the Presbyterian Lecture Hall or Presbyterian Lecture Room. The minutes of session noted that "this Lecture Room was in Society Street, South Side, a few doors from Meeting Street. Here the egg of the church was laid."[78] Very small numbers of individuals attended these meetings compared to the numbers of enslaved African Americans who would later attend Zion. Much of the reason for this was John Adger's failing health; the limited space of the building; and according to the minutes, "the morning being an inconvenient hour for many of the Blacks, that service was attended generally by only forty or fifty people."[79] An interesting omission in the session records is that the new mission church did not seem to advocate to the enslaver membership that it allow enslaved people the day off to attend worship. Surely a strictly Sabbatarian church, as many Southern Presbyterian churches were in the nineteenth-century South, would have made sure that the members would be in attendance regularly on Sundays. While the expectation of fulfilling the Fourth Commandment existed for White members, this advocacy was not extended to enslaved African American members, whose labor took priority. The wolves preferred worship and rest for some members of the flock but labor for others at all costs.

Other Charlestonians worried about the numbers of enslaved African Americans who were attending. As a direct result of the Vesey plot, slave codes were strictly enforced regarding the congregating of enslaved African Americans at a given space. Embodying Charlestonians' fears, a leading attorney in Charleston, Henry DeSaussure, contended that the education of enslaved African Americans should not be permitted, nor should there be separate Black churches.[80] This made Adger and Second Presbyterian proceed with caution, often writing to the *Charleston Mercury* to defend their work and assuage the fears of men like DeSaussure, "A Slaveholder," "Concerned," and "Many Citizens," who often wrote to the newspaper with concerns.[81] In easing the fears of Charleston Whites Adger was functioning as a shepherd of his flock. However rather than advocating from a biblical position as to the rights of Christians Adger chose to assuage enslavers' concerns. He promised observance, oversight, and limited opportunity for unsupervised interaction. In doing so the slave mission experiment was allowed to commence as long as it continued to serve the interests of enslavers.

The mission work on Society Street was similar to sabbath schools established at Second Presbyterian Church on Meeting Street. Adger would teach and preach to enslaved African Americans followed by oral question-and-response exercises directly from the Jones catechism. Several White members of Second Presbyterian, especially the women of the Church, helped with enslaved African Americans' religious instruction. The Society Street mission set apart a space for missionary work with enslaved African Americans in an urban context in contrast to the limited instruction received from balconies and instruction on plantations in the Jones model. Providing enslaved African Americans with their own place of worship, their own space, their own pastor, and their own community space was unique and set the Presbyterians in Charleston apart from other denominations.[82]

To be sure, provision of a worship space must have been something of a comfort to enslaved people and must have provided a welcome space for respite in the midst of unremitting toil. However one must wonder how the enslaved members of this mission church perceived their presence. Their attendance was not voluntary as their presence in Second Presbyterian balconies was not voluntary in the 1840s. These members were present at the behest of their owners, and certainly they would have preferred hearing from their own preachers and teachers who looked like them. Since there are few records of this early work other than session minutes we are only left to speculate.

In 1850, the work on Society Street soon moved to a Gothic structure, which was constructed by Second Presbyterian on 91 Anson Street. In 1861, it became St. Joseph's Roman Catholic Church and today is the home of St. John's Reformed Episcopal Church. The cost of this building "was seven thousand and seven hundred dollars, and this was paid by the congregation of the Second Church."[83] On May 26, 1850, the mission conducted the opening service in this new location on Anson Street. While in other churches enslaved African Americans were relegated to galleries, at Anson they now sat in front of the preacher in the pews, and they occupied the entire space. Lois Simms, the first historian of this mission church in Charleston, has called this occupancy "the main body—the place of honors—in the area."[84] To move from the balconies to the pews in front of the pulpit was an important shift in terms of how the enslavers and the enslaved perceived the mission.[85] This was also the first church for African American enslaved people south of Calhoun Street. All other churches for African Americans were north of Calhoun Street. South of Calhoun Street in 1850 was living and meeting space for Whites only. For African Americans to occupy this space was significant. This was yet another way in which the Presbyterian work was distinctive.

For the dedication service at the new Anson Street Mission "Thomas Smyth and John Adger were there to hear a sermon preached by James Henry Thornwell."[86] In his book on James Henry Thornwell entitled *The Metaphysical Confederacy*, James Farmer noted, "As sectional tensions were being inflamed by debate on California's petition for statehood, an event of little fanfare but substantial symbolic significance took place in Charleston. Zion Church, also called Anson Street Church, was dedicated." Thornwell preached, oddly, to a congregation of all Whites and "considering the opposition to this enterprise and the Northern attack on slavery, it was decided to combine the dedication with a presentation of the views of the South's religious community on Slavery." Thornwell preached on Colossians 4:1, which read, "Masters, give unto your servants that which is just and equal, knowing that ye also have a master in heaven." Farmer found that of all the verses Thornwell could have chosen to preach he chose the text "that focuses on the duties of masters." The Anson Street Mission, Thornwell maintained, "was a far better way of meeting the abolitionists than embracing the doctrine of separate creation and asserting that the black man is a fit subject for slavery because he is not human for 'We are not ashamed to call him our brother,' he insisted."[87]

The use of "brother" is very important here. Thornwell means that the enslaved African American is a brother "in Christ" in the family household of God. Since we can assume he did not mean literal brother then we are left with the assertion that Thornwell thought of the enslaved African American Christian as a brother "in Christ." This would mean that the brother was deserving of all the ecclesiastical rights and privileges that a White "brother" would have access to in the church: full membership status, voting rights, the ability to serve on committees, and being open for nomination as a deacon or elder. None of these were available to enslaved African Americans in Thornwell's own church. What Thornwell was suggesting was not a brotherhood, but a second-class ecclesiastical position based on the race of the enslaved. African Americans could be spiritual brothers and perhaps one day in heaven they could be equal, but Thornwell and many other Southern Presbyterians never openly advocated for African Americans' equal ecclesiastical rights. Therefore the similar dichotomy existed for Thornwell that existed for Jones. Spiritually the African American could be a brother or sister, but in no way was this equality a bodily reality in a real-world or even ecclesiastical perspective. In every other way, other than spiritually, the enslaved African American was inferior. This position is a radical departure from orthodox Christianity and a departure from what the scriptures of Christianity teach. This displays the grip of the institution of enslavement upon the shepherds. The shepherds could never acknowledge any kind of equality, other than spiritual, with their African American flock.

Thornwell continued, "'The slave has rights,' indeed 'all the rights which belong essentially to humanity, and without his nature could not be human or his conduct susceptible of praise or blame. In the enjoyment of these rights, religion demands he should be protected. The right which the master has is a right not to the man, but to his labor.'" Thornwell even noted that "this building is a public testimonial to our faith that the negro is of one blood with ourselves" and that "one of the highest and most solemn obligations which rest upon the masters of the South is to give their servants to the utmost of their ability, free access to the instructions and institutions of the gospel."[88] Thornwell insisted that enslaved African Americans were human and of "one blood" with Whites, that they had certain rights, and that the owner of enslaved persons had no right to the ownership of persons, but only of their labor. Masters were to give to their servants that which was "just and equal" concerning their opportunities to worship. To say that an enslaver had no ownership of persons but only of their labor would have certainly been startling to the largely White enslaver audience. Also in attendance was "C.C. Jones, who had preached to the enslaved African members" at Anson Street earlier that afternoon and participated in the service with the opening prayer. The White members sat on either side, to the left and right of the pulpit.[89] That Jones was present and participated in the mission's grand opening was indicative of how much influence he had in the new work. Further it displayed Adger's vision, which was informed by and similar to that of Jones's work in Liberty County.

Thornwell's presence and sermon were important but not because of a representation of any expanded rights offered to the enslaved by the church. Thornwell was there to justify that the kind of enslavement or master and servant relationship Paul discussed in Colossae was the same form of enslavement being practiced in Charleston, South Carolina almost two thousand years later. This sermon was one of many preached by pro-enslavement shepherds across the US South, who directly adopted the form of enslavement as it existed in the US South and compared it to Roman, Greek, or even enslavement as it existed in Israel in the times of the kings and, before that, the patriarchs like Abraham. This position justified Christian enslavers' rights as supported by an apostle in the bible, supported by Israel's example as a kingdom, if not supported Jesus himself. However there was no recognition or evidence provided that the enslaved experience in Greece or Rome was anything similar or akin to the African American experience of being kidnapped, stolen, and sold into a trans-Atlantic, market-driven system in which their labor was exploited in perpetuity because of their race.

Likewise there was also no discussion regarding treating enslaved people as equals in the church. Instead of advocating for the ecclesiastical rights and privileges of enslaved peoples as equal members of God's church, Thornwell took this opportunity to address larger national and political issues. He was speaking directly to abolitionists and anti-enslavement persons as if to say, "we in the South are biblical and do things appropriately." Rather than challenging the institution of enslavement, how it robbed humans of their worth and dignity, or how being a church member afforded African Americans rights due to their equal status as members of the kingdom of God, Thornwell was justifying southern enslavement over and against northern abolition as the biblical and therefore right position. The mission church to enslaved persons in Charleston provided him with merely an example to prove his point. The enslaved members of Anson Street would hear the Bible and the Gospel preached, but they would continue in enforced labor with no hope of freedom, and their full rights as church members would not be fulfilled to the same degree as the rights of

White members. Also, while Thornwell advocated in word that an enslaver had no right to the human, but only to his labor, there was no action that followed this. The church still created a second-class membership for the enslaved. White Presbyterian church members could have the facade of Christian charity and benevolence while maintaining, buttressing, and supporting unbiblical enslavement using the Bible, missions, and separate churches with separate forms of membership based on one's race to justify their true submissiveness: to the institution of enslavement and the power brokers behind it.

Further, the irony of Thornwell preaching this sermon must have been palpable. Thornwell had been a very strong proponent of the spirituality of the church doctrine that taught the church should only preach the gospel and not politics. One theologian has argued the doctrine of the spirituality of the church is that "there are limits to church power and this power must not be confused with the power of the state." The church is limited in how it can weigh in on political issues. "Through most of Reformed history, the spirituality of the church has not entailed a silence on all political matters, but rather a commitment to the uniqueness of the church's mission and a principled conviction that the concerns of the church should not be swallowed up by the concerns of the state."[90] Therefore the church should weigh in on political matters it deems necessary in terms of challenging biblical principles. However since enslavement was acceptable, biblically speaking, according to southern theologians, then Thornwell would have seen no reason to challenge enslavement, despite the fact that it violated the very tenet spoken of in his sermon: true brotherhood in Christ and equal ecclesiastical rights. Further since enslavement was legal according to federal, state, and municipal law in 1850 then there was no need for the theologian to engage in political statements from the pulpit.

The sermon was as much a response to abolitionism and the political context of the day as it was intended for religious instruction for the primary audience. It was a sermon with political overtones disguised as not being political, as many Southern Presbyterian ministers in the nineteenth century were adept at doing. Thornwell was engaging in a larger political struggle and national debate without specifically mentioning politics. The focus of the sermon could have the "look" of being about the gospel, but what he was also doing was showing abolitionists that southern Presbyterians had the proper biblical understanding of enslavement and were appropriately applying that understanding in a theological and ecclesiastical framework. Since enslavement, abolition, and a future vision for enslavement's expansion into Kansas were also an ongoing political debate in Washington, DC, and Thornwell accepted the southern vision as the appropriate and biblical form, he now had a mission church dedicated to enslaved persons to display the ways in which the southern Presbyterian vision was superior and more biblically grounded than the northern abolitionist vision. Hence the sermon was most certainly political.

While the spirituality of the church doctrine did include "a principled conviction that the concerns of the church should not be swallowed up by the concerns of the state,"[91] it also left it up to the church to decide which measures were considered "principled convictions." If the church had deemed enslavement a matter of principle and a biblical violation, as earlier Presbyterians had done, it would have certainly been costly to most southern Presbyterian congregations given the immense amount of wealth many members of Presbyterian churches in South Carolina accumulated through the institution. The church therefore made the decision that matters of principle that just so happened to benefit the membership financially were political issues that the church could not address or on which it could not preach. If the government or a political party was doing something to potentially tamper with the profits of the enslaving members of the church, then they no doubt saw it as a "principled conviction" to speak out on such a violation. The crux of the matter is that, historically speaking, southern Presbyterians were able to pick and choose which political issues to speak about and they typically chose the ones that benefitted them financially, politically or culturally. If the issues did not benefit them financially, politically or culturally, then a southern Presbyterian pastor would hide behind a spirituality of the church doctrine to prevent them from having to speak or put themselves in a difficult position.

The church decided which issues were and were not spiritual and could find or hide behind the appropriate biblical texts to justify this decision. For instance from 1890 to 1940, southern Presbyterians decided that both segregation and lynching were acceptable issues and not worth political engagement. Southern Presbyterians would also decide that from 1955–64 the civil rights movement was not something on which the church should comment. However when the political winds were blowing in a way that might affect White southerners' wealth, power, or status then they most assuredly would find that it would be a necessity to speak and act politically from the pulpit. Thornwell's presence at the mission and his sermon were strong symbolic connections to the southern pro-enslavement position, and the mission work among the enslaved was used to justify the institution of enslavement as the "biblically sanctioned" position. However this sermon was not meant for an African American audience, but a White one. The preaching to African American enslaved people was left to Adger.[92]

Many considered Adger's preaching at the church on Anson Street to be very basic, and it was meant to appeal "to the level of the illiterate and uneducated with hopes that they might understand the gospel in its rudimentary form."[93] This was not due to Adger's personal abilities as a minister. On the contrary he had served at Second Presbyterian for many years and was noted as a prominent teacher.[94] Instead it likely resulted from the elderly Adger's health problems. He knew that he needed a younger and more vibrant successor who shared his vision to carry on the mission work at Anson. It was Adger who laid the groundwork from 1846 to 1851, but he would turn to John Lafayette Girardeau to carry on the work.[95]

John Lafayette Girardeau, born in 1825, was a descendant of French Huguenots, the first College of Charleston honors graduate and cousin to the aforementioned "father of slave missions" Charles Colcock Jones. Girardeau was raised on James Island, was familiar with the Gullah language, and had displayed an interest early on to minister to enslaved African Americans. Girardeau had been doing similar work since graduation from seminary at Adam's Run and Wilton Presbyterian Churches by employing the Jones model of visiting plantation "stations" and preaching to enslaved African Americans where and when he could find a place and time. As W. F. Robertson noted, "he gave the best part of his life towards seeking the salvation of the Negroes of Charleston. One cannot study the work of this minister without realizing that his Soul's greatest passion—like that of Paul about the Jews—was that the Negro might be saved, and he realized that he was a 'man of like passions' with other men."[96] Throughout Girardeau's career it is indeed evident that his professional interests lay in ministering to those on the margins of southern society in the nineteenth century.

In 1852, disabling eye problems caused Adger's health to fail, and in December 1853, at the age of twenty-nine, John Lafayette Girardeau filled the pulpit at the Anson Street Mission Church. Reverend George Blackburn described Anson's ministry under Girardeau's guidance as experiencing "steady growth" and was "divided into classes, each under a proper leader and the sick, with a sick fund were regularly looked after. The energetic work of Dr. Girardeau, at the Bible weekly instruction, led the leading negroes of other churches to admit that the Anson Street work was 'of the Lord.'"[97] Girardeau's ministry and preaching attracted great numbers of enslaved African Americans, and the congregation soon outgrew the building on Anson Street as it "quickly became the most prominent gathering place for the African American community of the city."[98] The location of Anson, south of Calhoun Street, would have been attractive as well as a church in which enslaved African Americans occupied the pews and not the balconies. Because it had been established for the specific purpose of ministry to enslaved people in Charleston the Anson Street Mission was a space in which enslavers at Second Presbyterian church would send their enslaved people to worship on Sunday.

Blackburn described Girardeau as "a child of the sea islands, at home with the Gullah dialect and the African Americans of the city. A powerful preacher, a master of classical rhetoric and the techniques of folk preaching, he could deeply move a congregation of blacks or whites."[99] Girardeau used what he referred to as "key words" in his sermons and would emphasize these words with dramatic facial expressions and vocal inflection to emphasize the larger points that he was trying to communicate. For instance, "Holy God,' he said in a tone of awe and 'sin hateful' with a look of intense abhorrence."[100] Indeed, "he was a gifted speaker, writer and teacher . . . who was heard to pray 'Oh, Lord be merciful to Thy unworthy servant.' In fact, this phrase was used so frequently that an admiring member [at Zion] who was patterning his prayer life after Dr. Girardeau was heard to pray, 'Oh, Lord be merciful to Thy unworthy servant, the pastor of this church, and keep him in health to do Thy work.'"[101] It is evidence from his ministerial interests, preaching technique, prayer life, and the cultural context of his childhood that Girardeau was the appropriate choice for this position.

Girardeau's early life helped to shape his vision for missionary work among enslaved African Americans. He was born on November 14, 1825, on James Island, just slightly southwest of Charleston, South Carolina. The island consisted of White planters and enslavers as well as a large population of Sea Island enslaved African Americans. His childhood playmates included young African American children living on the surrounding plantations of James Island. Living in relatively close quarters with such a large population of enslaved African Americans afforded Girardeau the opportunity to learn the Gullah language and to experience that enslaved people were fellow human beings who suffered greatly. These experiences became a driving impetus in Girardeau's life pushing him into a career of ministering to enslaved African Americans. Indeed, "even as a young man he held prayer-meeting for the benefit of the colored people on his father's plantation" and "while teaching school in another place he visited a number of plantations one after another on certain afternoons during the week and gave religious instruction."[102] From an early age and into his schooling Girardeau was interested in ministering to enslaved African American communities. Adger and Girardeau's views were that a biracial religious community could be created in which enslaved African Americans and free Whites could worship together if the same racial hierarchies that existed outside the church were reinforced inside the church.

John Adger hinted at this biracial religious environment of Whites and Lowcountry enslaved people worshipping together and described the interactions being "divided out among us and mingled up with us, and we with them in a thousand ways. They live with us, eating from the same store-houses, drinking from the same fountains, dwelling from the same enclosures, forming parts of the same families."[103] The proximity to enslaved African Americans allowed many missionaries to enslaved persons a familiarity with the culture of enslaved African American communities that northern missionaries did not have access to. Familiarity with communities and the culture of those communities might have afforded the White missionaries to the enslaved a certain measure of enhanced knowledge regarding the focus of the mission. However that mission often served to reinforce the status quo. Familiarity did not breed advocacy for enhanced ecclesiastical rights.

Second Presbyterian Church's *Minutes of Session* noted this phenomenon: "Unacquainted with the nature of our institution—strangers to the prejudices, habits, and peculiarities of the Negro—incapable of appreciating his peculiar sympathies and associations—ministers from abroad, even if they were permitted to enter the field, could not be expected to cultivate it with the same success as our own men."[104] Perhaps an example of understanding the "habits and peculiarities" of the enslaved African American was that Girardeau spoke Gullah with proficiency, which was the language of Sea Island African Americans, and would later incorporate it into his conversations and dialogue with church members. He was also moved to care for the enslaved as children through his mother's example. Girardeau wrote, "The poor negroes of the Island were often the recipients of [his mother's] kindness. She was kind to all, but especially the sick and needy negroes."[105] Girardeau's childhood experiences and the ways in which he was introduced to African American culture and the African American experience certainly shaped his interests.

After college Girardeau attended Columbia Theological Seminary to train for the ministry. There he continued to care for the poor and socially disadvantaged until his graduation in 1848. During seminary Girardeau conducted mission services in abandoned warehouses in the poorest sections of Columbia for enslaved people, prostitutes, and other social outcasts.[106] Throughout his seminary career Girardeau expressed a strong interest in evangelism in combination with a desire to share the Gospels with enslaved African Americans in his native Lowcountry of South Carolina. In a letter dated Friday May 15, 1846, to his "Dear Sister" there is a glimpse of the young seminarian's evangelistic focus: "Sister dear Sister, when shall this be? Come oh come to Jesus and give yourself away. Why do you delay? 'My savior bids me come. Ah, why do I delay? He calls the weary sinner home and yet from him I stay.' Oh my constant prayer is that God would awake you and . . . to sit at Jesus' feet and weep and praise Him for His gracious love."[107] George A. Blackburn, Girardeau's son-in-law and original biographer, observed that "on his trips back to Charleston [from seminary] he would ordinarily stop at some plantation and preach to the negroes. His heart sought the salvation of their souls, and he threw the zeal of his great soul into the work of their salvation."[108] This fervor would not change for the rest of his life and career.

Girardeau described this himself in a partly autobiographical sketch found at the South Carolina Historical Society

> While at the Theological Seminary in Columbia, the questions agitated me whether I should devote myself to a Foreign Mission work, but the fact that slaves at the South could only be ministered to by Southern men, powerfully impressed my mind, and I felt called to preach the Gospel to them . . . I determined to accept an invitation to preach at the Wappetaw Church in Christ Church Parish, S.C., in the bounds of which were a large body of coloured people. In November, 1848, I began to preach there. An immense coloured congregation gathered from the two parishes of Christ Church and St. Thomas Sabbath after Sabbath at that church. they crowded in the building and used to saw to and fro like a forest in a storm. In April 1849, I accepted an invitation from the Wilton Church in St. Paul's Parish to preach to them. The parting with the coloured congregation at Wappetaw was most affecting. One poor little African woman followed me to the buggy crying, "O Massa, are you going to leave us? O Massa, are you going to leave us?"[109]

Girardeau was most certainly affected by this experience, and it was likely confirmed in his professional life.

Upon graduation from seminary, the Presbytery of Charleston ordained Girardeau and he began his work of ministering to the enslaved population.[110] One author noted that Girardeau even "refused a call to a larger and important church because he considered it to be his duty to preach to the mass of slaves on the seaboard of South Carolina."[111] Girardeau described this refusal saying, "The church was pleased to call me to be its pastor, but having learned that there were only five coloured members in connection with it" he decided to preach in the Wappetaw Church in Christ Church Parish, South Carolina, "in the bounds of which were a large body of coloured people" in November 1848.[112] To turn down what would have been a larger salary with a much more influential congregation than the people of Wappetaw Girardeau was prioritizing in his first vocational choice the people who he felt most needed his services and who had been a priority in his life since childhood. This decision is a unique departure from the thinking of seminary graduates in the mid-nineteenth century South who were often all too eager to have larger congregations with more wealth and influence as a sign of "the fruit" or success of one's ministry. In April 1849, while he was working at the Wilton Presbyterian Church in St. Paul's Parish, enslaved African Americans came in large crowds to hear Girardeau preach. He remarked, "They would pour in and throng the seats vacated by their masters—yes, crowding the building up to the pulpit. I have seen them rock to and fro under the influence of their feelings, like a wood in the storm. What singing! What hearty handshakings after the service. I have had my finger joints stripped of their skin in the consequence of them."[113]

Second Presbyterian Church in Charleston, South Carolina, had established a church, largely for enslaved African American Congregants. Stokes noted that Girardeau "like Smyth, shared the view expressed by John B. Adger that 'southern slavery was just a grand civilizing and Christianizing school, providentially prepared' and that, 'the two races were steadily and constantly marching onwards and upwards together' to eventual emancipation, when enslaved people were ready to 'graduate.'"[114] However, with Draconian literacy laws, limited educational opportunity, and no property rights, how were enslaved African Americans ever going to receive emancipation in a society in which freedom was connected to property ownership and the ability to buy and sell using documents, which required literacy. This statement was little more than a justification for the institution of enslavement and meant as a southern response to abolitionists and nothing more.

After the Second Presbyterian Church had established the Anson Street mission, and the work of Adger had taken root, Girardeau left in 1853 to take this call. He wrote:

> I commenced preaching to the Wilton Church in April of 1849, and was ordained to the Ministry and installed pastor of the at church in April

> of 1850. In November of 1853, I bade a reluctant farewell to take charge of the Anson Street Missionary work in Charleston. I found a small handful of coloured people. Sometimes only a dozen were present at prayer meetings. But the congregation increased in number until in 1858, the building became too strait for them, the fences around it being occupied by those who could not get in, and sometimes even the trees in the rear. In that year a most remarkable outpouring of the Holy Spirit was vouchsafed us and hundreds professed conversion. I have preserved a list of white persons who professed hope. They were about 120. How many more white persons experienced hope will not be known until the last day. Crowds of coloured peopled people were added to the church.[115]

It is interesting to note that while Girardeau's call was specifically to the "coloured people" of Charleston, it is the White converts who are deemed worthy of keeping a list and numbering. The enslaved African American congregants Girardeau described as "crowds" who were "added to the church."

As soon as Girardeau had taken over the helm at Anson Street he obtained permission from the Session at Second Presbyterian (which owned the Anson Street Church) to create a separate mission under his own control. He received permission from the session and then received the same from the presbytery on May 13, 1855. From then on Anson Street went from being a part of Second Presbyterian to "a Missionary Church, under the care of the Rev. John L. Girardeau."[116] Girardeau must have believed that if there were going to be a separate church for enslaved African Americans there also had to be a separate mission identity and that he must have autonomy to make decisions leading his own session, which removed it from under the control of the session at the Second Presbyterian Session. The work continued to grow, and "under his leadership the Anson Church was soon overflowing." Girardeau began with thirty-six members in 1854, and by 1860, there were over six hundred enrolled members with an attendance of over fifteen hundred in a regular Sabbath congregation.

In 1857, the six-hundred-seat Anson Street building was simply not large enough to accommodate the individuals attending, and it was decided that a new building was needed.[117] Later in 1857, Robert Adger, the brother or John Adger, approached Thomas Smyth with the idea of sending an all-White session to Anson so that the mission could be formally organized into a particularized church within the presbytery. Thomas Smyth gave his consent stating, "The cause was good and great, and Mr. Girardeau noble and devoted."[118] The presbytery determined that a larger church be erected, and "Robert Adger located a prime piece of property near the corner of Meeting Street and Calhoun Street–barely a block from Second Church-and bought it for $7,220."[119] The location on Meeting Street was near the old Citadel Military College as well as some very fine houses, business establishments, and churches in the city. Supporters raised more than $25,000 for a new building with the Adger family supplying most of the funding.[120]

One can only imagine the fear and concern from the Charleston White elite when at the close of service on Sunday the church opened its doors and almost two thousand enslaved African Americans poured onto Calhoun Street in Charleston.[121] Whether intentional or not Girardeau was sending a message to the White population of Charleston regarding his belief in the ecclesiastical work among enslaved African Americans. One historian, author of *Southern Presbyterianism and Racial Issues*, noted that "Presbyterian converts among the slaves were not permitted to form independent congregations. Instead, they attended white Presbyterian Churches but were generally barred from office-holding and were seated in separated areas of the sanctuary."[122] Displaying the complexity of the history of Presbyterian missions to the enslaved in South Carolina many enslaved African Americans came to Girardeau's church because he acknowledged their need to have an identity independent of the White congregations in Charleston.[123] Girardeau acknowledged that enslaved African Americans needed to be treated as valued congregants in the life of the church and not peripheral attendees. By providing this in his mission Girardeau endeared himself to his flock.

Stokes wrote that "having consecrated his life to his special calling, Girardeau turned down a number of offers from prominent churches in other cities, North and South, which would have afforded him a more lucrative position and prestigious position." Stokes also mentioned that Girardeau operated within and perpetuated a paternalistic framework but one that was "deeply compassionate toward slaves." As evidence Stokes noted that "he had an extraordinary ability to communicate the Gospel" to enslaved African Americans, and that he would even tailor his sermons "speaking in a simplified but emotionally powerful narrative style enhanced by his knowledge of Gullah" experiences and culture.[124]

Later, John Adger was careful to remark that "the negroes named it [the church] Zion."[125] The name Zion means a "glorious city" or "dwelling place" that God had given to his people. While this might seem insignificant at first the naming of the church carried tremendous significance for enslaved African

Americans. For the church to adopt a name selected from among the enslaved displayed the central role that the enslaved played in the mission and function of Zion. Further it provided some sense of dignity to the enslaved as naming, calling someone by name, and giving someone who is enslaved the right to name had meaning. Enslaved people were sometimes not even allowed to formally document the name of their own children, much less an institution like a church. To have the opportunity to decide the naming of the mission was symbolic of the mission's priorities. Naming displayed that the church was a real home, also pointing toward a spiritual home. The concept of "home" was important in this naming. As Katherine Dvorak has mentioned, "For an enslaved people stolen from African homes and too often torn from 'home' slave communities by sale, home became an eschatological symbol celebrated in slave songs as a new Jerusalem, as Canaan's shore, as promised land."[126]

Chapter 4

"We Are Marching to Zion"

Antebellum Missionaries in Charleston, South Carolina, 1847–60

Throughout the Bible, Zion is referred to as the glorious "city" or "dwelling place" that God had set apart for His own people.[1] Frequently in the Bible the term "Zion" connotes a holy place, God's kingdom, or the most holy place, while some biblical references also equate Zion to heaven.[2] The hymn "We are Marching to Zion" captures Zion as a place of beauty, freedom, and rest. Certainly these scriptural principles were among the enslaved membership's thoughts when it chose the name in 1858. This is yet another indication of how both the enslaved church members and Girardeau defined their contrasting yet shared identities. The enslaved African American congregation perceived Zion as its own space, a space built for it, that it named. For enslaved African Americans just like God had preserved the city of Zion for his liberated people from Egypt in North Africa to Israel so God perhaps preserved this church for his hopeful yet still enslaved people from Western Africa now in South Carolina. Little did the enslaved African American congregation know in 1858 that in seven years, by 1865, it would be attending a school in Zion Church as freed persons and voting in Zion Church as citizens. In the meantime Girardeau did not dispute the naming of the church and went on to minister in a way that instilled hope, expanded ecclesiastical freedoms, promoted spiritual liberation, but also made sure the mission upheld the racial and institutional status quo of enslavement in Charleston, South Carolina.

Erected in 1859 and said to be "gratuitously furnished," Zion had a seating capacity of around twenty-five hundred, which made it the largest church building in Charleston and one of the largest churches constructed for enslaved African Americans in the entire state.[3] The "architect of the building was Edward C. Jones, who was later an Elder at Zion, and the builder was David Lopez Jr. a leader in Charleston's Jewish community."[4] It was ironic that a member of

Charleston's Jewish community built the church. Jews were a people whose ancient history was one of enslavement and liberation from Egypt.

However not all saw Zion as a holy place. Local residents attempted to tear down the walls of the church upon its construction, and Girardeau's public reputation as well as his life was threatened on numerous occasions. Despite this vandalism and slander on June 12, 1859, the congregants entered the newly finished church building and took Holy Communion. Girardeau and his congregants endeavored together to form a unique mission's style. Never had a church in South Carolina like this been constructed. The very building itself was a testament to the seriousness of the work. Beatrice St. Julien Ravenel once described the building as a "barnlike structure, with . . . twin high arched porticos" and the facade took up close to half a city block.[5] In examining Girardeau's perspective on ministry, it is clear he was a traditional Presbyterian and a committed church member. There was also something distinct about Girardeau that separated him from his contemporaries. Perhaps it was the "compassionate ethos" of Girardeau, described in reminiscences, or the keen theological sense that something was awry in the ecclesiastical structure. Certainly a man of such theological rigor and rigid views on polity would have understood that something within the church membership itself was askew when his fellow Presbyterians created a separate church specifically for one race and largely to accommodate a system of enslavement. Whatever that "something" was caused Girardeau to approach antebellum missions work in a unique fashion.

Some Charleston citizens, particularly the more militant groups like the Charleston Minute Men, physically threatened Girardeau for his work in this mission. One incident occurred after the new structure on Meeting and Calhoun was completed, and the Charleston Minute Men, with loaded guns, entered Zion Church during a worship service. The Charleston Minute Men had "intended to kill the preacher if he said anything against the recent hanging of a black man. The black man was a member of Zion, and Girardeau did not think him guilty of the alleged crime."[6] M. F. Robertson recalled that after the hanging of an innocent African American, Girardeau "announced that he would preach on the Negro's death. Somehow a report got out that he was going to justify the Negro. An excited state of public feeling developed. A young member of the church heard that a crowd was talking about killing Dr. Girardeau." The young man then went to the mayor's office, and the mayor then "secured a strong secret guard to attend the service."[7] Unknown to Girardeau at the time "the Charleston Minute Men filled one gallery and an armed guard from the state filled the opposite gallery"[7]

Girardeau came into the church, and "when it came time for the sermon, Dr. Girardeau showed the awful consequences of sin and pointed to the dying form of the Son of God for atonement. The audience broke down and he exhorted them to repent. Those who had misjudged his intention apologized after the service."[8] This incident indicated that Girardeau's work was upsetting to some Charlestonians and that his style of missions to the enslaved might have been too radical for the tastes of his contemporaries. After the writings of "Many Citizens" appeared in the *Charleston Mercury* in May 1847, the Second Presbyterian Session recorded the interactions in the minutes. The records noted that "the scheme [to start the slave mission] was attacked by a writer in the Charleston Mercury, who misrepresented our plan and endeavored not without success, to rouse popular prejudice against it."[9]

Another incident occurred in 1859 just after John Brown's raid on Harper's Ferry. A letter to the editor appeared in the *Charleston Mercury* under the pseudonym "A Slaveholder." The author described Zion Church as a breeding ground for insurrection. The author also claimed that the pastor was teaching the enslaved persons doctrines that would incite insurrections and destroy the community. "A Slaveholder" also spoke of the marriage ceremonies conducted by Girardeau at Zion. "Where are we drifting to," he penned "when in a slaveholding community the 'nuptials of blacks' are celebrated in a spacious temple of the most high?"[10] These articles drew much support from the Charleston public in later issues. Girardeau's biographer, C. N. Willborn, even mentioned that "it appeared strategically while Girardeau was out of town and was designed to evoke public sentiment against the missionary-pastor and the African-Americans who constituted Zion Church."[11] Something in this mission church incited White Charlestonians' ire. Perhaps this work also added to a distrust of Girardeau and continued to stoke fear among a White population in Charleston concerned about what would happen if enslaved African Americans at Zion ever decided to revolt.

Southern Presbyterians, who were consumed with theological acumen, ecclesiastical order, biblical fidelity, and for things to be done by committee with a process, rules, and in good and decent order. It must have been strange for some to observe fellow church members in South Carolina essentially creating an entirely different ecclesiastical structure that made accommodations and distinction for new kinds of members, roles, instructional activities, weddings, funerals, seating in pews, and even services based on one's race and whether or not one was enslaved. Thinking back to Alexander McLeod one wonders if he would have created a fully equal structure for enslaved African Americans in Charleston if given the chance. Would advocacy for the ecclesiastical and civic rights of enslaved African Americans have been challenged in Charleston under McLeod's shepherding oversight? Even the scantiest reading of South Carolina and Charleston history would assuredly affirm that no, McLeod would not have been accepted. One is left to ponder then why these Presbyterians in South Carolina were willing to adjust the church to accommodate an economic system and social order when South Carolinian Presbyterians in Rocky Creek just fifty-six years before had openly challenged it.

Charleston had experienced slave uprisings and had a much larger population of enslaved African Americans compared to Chester district. African Americans in the Lowcountry of South Carolina had been in the majority since at least 1670. This created a heightened sense of fear and concern among Charlestonians compared to Chester, in which the number of enslaved was nowhere close to a majority. Further Charlestonians funding Presbyterian churches had made and possessed sizable fortunes using enslaved labor and in owning enslaved people. While the membership at Rocky Creek might have possessed a half dozen or so enslaved African Americans, members of Presbyterian churches in Charleston possessed hundreds if not thousands. It also took elites to make this slave mission work acceptable in Charleston.

Elite concern over the status of the mission church was mollified, not by the work itself or the assurances of White oversight, but by the willingness of the Adgers, a very prominent and wealthy Charleston family, to be advocates for its continuance. The critics' voices in the *Charleston Mercury* were loud, but the status of elite families like the Adgers, Smyths (who married into the Adger family), and other members of the prominent Second Presbyterian Church Session certainly helped to continue the work in the face of open hostility coming from other members of the White elite. Girardeau also was a Charlestonian, a White enslaver himself, who had attended seminary in Columbia, South Carolina and not Andover, Massachusetts. Certainly his privileged status, his prominence as an honor graduate of the College of Charleston, and his family's owning of enslaved persons helped calm White enslaver anxiety.

One historian, writing about the effort of missionaries to enslaved persons in Charleston, mentioned that South Carolina's religious leaders "thought that religious education would be the best way to refute the abolitionists. Underlying their strategy was the tenet that proper Christian instruction would reinforce the ideal of a paternalistic society in which the slaves were loyal and obedient servants to a benevolent master."[12] While this statement is no doubt true for many missionaries to enslaved persons and their work both Anson

Street and Zion offered something of a counterexample. Simply because the church was White led did not mean it should fall under a broad category of a church that only "reinforced obedience to the master." The Charleston public deemed many aspects of Girardeau's mission work at Anson Street and Zion as repulsive. A more complete examination of Girardeau's unique features, as well as the antebellum and postbellum work at Zion, allows for greater understanding of the complexity of enslaved person missions and the unique roles that South Carolina's shepherds played in how missionaries to the enslaved practiced their vocation.

One of the features unique to Zion was that Girardeau divided the church into "classes." This was common in other denominations, such as Methodism, but elements within the classes were distinct to Zion. The meaning of the classes was "to promote mutual acquaintance and brotherly love among the members; to apprise them of one another's sickness and need; to acquaint the leaders with the same; and to further the growth of the members in Christian knowledge and experimental religion."[13] Each class member and class leader had a particular role and purpose, and recognized each other as members of the church. This affirmation of membership in a community would contribute to the central role religious activities played in the lives of enslaved African American communities. Often enslaved African Americans forged religious communities away from White oversight. At Zion the church promoted community development and helped to strengthen the community in support of one another.

Each class had a "leader." A leader was someone that the all-White session recognized as a person of spiritual maturation with administrative abilities. Through these classes, leaders took up collections from their members for the sick or infirm. Distributions of these funds rested on the need of the one who was sick. A weekly stipend of fifty cents was offered to someone in the time of sickness.[14] The leaders' duties also included visiting members of their class and reporting on any sickness or discipline matters to the session. Through these leadership positions enslaved African Americans were encouraged to nurture one another. Boles saw this recognition of a White enslaver session as possessing enhanced responsibility in the church, which was "(recognized by whites to have) moral responsibility" or what Timothy L. Smith has called "moral earnestness."[15]

The class leaders also appeared at session meetings as well as church discipline cases, and the elders considered their testimony. It was significant that enslaved African Americans gave testimony in the church courts.

Historian Robert Hall has argued that in the church "slaves were allowed to give testimony–sometimes even conflicting with white testimony–and that on occasion their witness overrules the charges of whites."[16] This occurred in a society in which enslaved African Americans were not allowed to testify against Whites in civil courts. However, at Zion, enslaved African Americans frequently appeared as witnesses and gave testimony either for or against their fellow African Americans. Church cases included discipline or censures for a variety of behaviors including drunkenness, lying, and adultery. In some cases the church charged enslaved African Americans for the same actions as Whites. Boles mentioned that this form of ecclesiastical legal equality existed "nowhere else in southern society," in which "slaves and whites brought together in an arena where both were held responsible to a code of behavior sanctioned by a source outside the society–the Bible."[17] As enslaved African Americans were navigating these ecclesiastical spaces, it would be reasonable to assume that thoughts might have crossed their mind regarding leadership opportunities and access to courts. If they could be members of a church and engage in the courts of church, then why could they not be members of a society and engage in civic courts? If enslaved African Americans could serve as functional deacons in their classes as leaders, then why could they not serve in an official or ordained capacity? Indeed many questions might have arisen out of this system.

Girardeau's classes at Zion also had "exhorters." Exhorters could conduct funeral services and were able to teach and preach to other members of the church. Allowing enslaved African Americans to conduct funeral services, teach, preach, and perhaps even read to one another sent a clear message to participants in the classes.[18] One historian wrote about the importance of enslaved leaders to the congregation, arguing, "Slaves apparently had their image of being creatures of God strengthened by the sermons they heard—even when that was not the intention of the ministers—and the discipline they accepted. Their evident pleasure in occasionally hearing the black preachers speak to biracial congregations no doubt augmented their sense of racial pride."[19] Indeed enslaved African Americans were not reliant upon White-controlled institutions to foster their sense of self-worth but neither were they adverse to seizing opportunities wherever they found them and using them appropriately. Certainly "in a society that offered few opportunities for blacks to practice organizational and leadership skills or hear themselves addressed and see themselves evaluated morally on equal basis with whites, small matters could have large meanings."[20] While White ministers may have interpreted having class leaders, exhorters, and ecclesiastical testimony as small responsibilities, the enslaved African American derived hope, self-worth, racial pride, and a sense of identity as a human being with a spiritual and ecclesiastical equality from African American leaders and exhorters.

There is little to no evidence that Girardeau was teaching his congregants to read. South Carolina state literacy laws in place since 1834, outlawed teaching enslaved African Americans to read. But he did teach enslaved African Americans to memorize vast passages of the Bible, catechisms, and hymns. Further the educational curriculum of Second Presbyterian's sabbath school continued at Zion. Girardeau taught classes for applicants in church membership, Bible, and theology. He used C. C. Jones's catechism as well as one that he had written himself.[21] Girardeau taught many theological doctrines including the Trinity, God's law, the covenants, justification by faith, and the office of Christ. In addition an important distinction between Jones's catechism and Girardeau's was that Girardeau made no mention of domestic relationships or the relationship of master to slave. Perhaps this was a subtle recognition that Girardeau was not interested in teaching this doctrine to the enslaved members of his congregation. However the fact that an entirely different catechism for enslaved African Americans even existed is evidence that the education and curricular experiences of African Americans in the church was different from, set apart from, and a kind of second-tier educational practice and experience compared to that of White members. This is further evidence that different categories of ecclesiastical experiences were common for the enslaved and wholly distinct from the experiences of non-enslaved White members.

In 1860, 250 enslaved African American children enrolled in Girardeau's Sunday school program. According to Willborn, "The presence of Sunday School, an educational and evangelistic device, reveals Girardeau's commitment to educating the African-Americans, even though teaching them to read was illegal in his motherland from 1834."[22] After the Civil War "Girardeau told the Scotsman David Macrae that he had always wanted to teach the slaves to read but could not because of civil laws and the effect of the radical abolitionists' writings on Southern attitudes. He could have been arrested and charged with a crime. In his ideal world, slaves would have been taught to read, a view similar to his low country friend John B. Adger," as well as that of Jones.[23] This sentiment while privately espoused and timely in its presentation (after the war) no doubt was in Girardeau's mind throughout his work in antebellum Charleston. However it is likely that the tenets of southern legal codes regarding literacy of the enslaved would have kept Girardeau from making this hope a reality. Educating enslaved African Americans to read would also have been breaking South Carolina law. For Girardeau, if word of this had gotten out, not only would "Concerned Citizens" demand the mission to end, but Girardeau could have been arrested and charged with a crime.

As with Jones, the reach of slavey on missionaries to enslaved persons was long, and it severely limited whatever prophetic voice might have come from the church challenging the institution. Also the South's ruling elite, its government, and its institutions were bent on preserving enslavement. To speak, challenge, or act in any way contrary to the laws and mandates buttressing the institution would have meant complete ostracism, imprisonment, or perhaps even death for Girardeau.

Yet another distinction was that Girardeau conducted wedding ceremonies with large numbers in attendance and in the middle of a prominent social district of the city of Charleston. Typically enslaved persons' weddings were small ceremonies on the plantation outside of the public eye. As a Presbyterian Girardeau believed in the importance of the institution of marriage and that it was a display of a covenant that should be publicly celebrated. Further Girardeau, like his cousin Jones, tried to preserve families in his congregations from being separated or sold away. Girardeau likely used large wedding displays to affirm the sacredness of marriage between enslaved people and display to the broader Charleston community that marriage was a sacred institution that could not allow the separation of a family to make a profit in enslavement trading. However when a sale separated a marriage Girardeau was forced to accept the decision, and he could not do anything to appeal or to stop the enslaver from the sale or purchase. He could appeal to God's law, but it could not prevent an enslaver from selling a portion of his or her chattel property away for profit, which was protected under South Carolina and national law. There is also no evidence that he publicly ever tried to do so.

For many enslaved African Americans marriage was often a tenuous commitment based on the whims of the owner. Often the owner sold one or both partners regardless of whether they had been married. It was common to hear in marriages of enslaved people "'til death or distance do you part." In stark contrast to these accepted principles regarding enslavement Girardeau believed that enslaved African Americans were human beings made in the *imago dei*, they possessed a soul, and their marriages were valid before God. Further Girardeau taught that the marriages of enslaved Africans were legitimate institutions that ought to be preserved. This certainly showed the influence of previous missionary John Adger who had argued that "slaveholders should not separate, nor allow the separation of husband wife, unless for cause lawful before God."[24] Moral suasion under the weight of economic incentives driven by racism and supported by law had minimal effect.

Southern Presbyterians highly valued marriage. When ministers officiated at a wedding, it was an official act of the church and recognized by the state as legal. It is interesting that rather than fight for marriage as any Southern Presbyterian shepherd would do for a White family, the Presbyterian missionaries to enslaved African Americans simply gave in to the status quo and accepted that African American marriages had no civic meaning. Southern Presbyterians possessed a great deal of wealth, political influence, and power in the nineteenth-century South. If for some reason the state or economic system was invalidating or not accepting the marriages of White members then the shepherds would most certainly have gone to war to defend the right of their members to marry. Such was the zeal and passion for the institution of marriage. If the federal government would have sought to abridge or challenge the sacredness of marriage the pastors would not worry about violating the "spirituality of the church doctrine" in their preaching.

However, it was also clear that Girardeau regarded his enslaved membership as human beings with an identity separate from their enslavement. This was particularly apparent in Zion's church roll books. Girardeau wrote down all names of individuals who became members, whom he baptized, and those for whom he performed marriage ceremonies. Contrary to many record books of enslaved African Americans during his time, Girardeau wrote down their first or "given" names as well as their surnames in the roll books. In antebellum southern society, owners of enslaved persons typically did not record surnames of enslaved persons as this suggested a status as a human being with a lineage rather than as chattel property.[25] John Boles has noted the importance of such a demarcation: "This equality in terms of address may seem insignificant today, but in an age when whites were accorded the titles of Mr. and Mrs., and it was taboo for a white to so address a black, any form of address that smacked of equality was notable."[26] Indeed this small decision by Girardeau to record full names was an ecclesiastical action that led to some semblance of human equality for enslaved members. In a society that sought to destroy any semblance of equality, small matters could have large meanings.

This unique attribution separated the Presbyterian Zion mission church from other denominations in that "typical Baptist or Methodist churches included black members, who often signed (or put their 'X')" and "were not accorded genuine equality."[27] Enslaved African Americans were listed in most church roll books as, for example, "Sam, servant of John Dawson."[28] For decades, owners of enslaved persons throughout the South had denied their enslaved persons surnames to show that enslaved persons had no lasting family connections because of their status as property.[29] Church historian Erskine Clarke discussed this phenomenon further stating:

> Across the South, whites have refused to recognize that African Americans had surnames—blacks were simply Sam and Toney, Rose and Mingo, Tissey and Joe, with no surnames acknowledged–except that when needed, the name of the owner could be used. Such a practice was a powerful symbol, declaring that African Americans, within the world view of whites, had no lasting family connections of their own; they were rather the property of whites and belonged to their owners. Such a symbol allowed African Americans to be sold and to be separated from parents and children, from husbands and wives, without the appearance of any separation but only as a transfer of property.[30]

Zion members who claimed surnames were consciously making a bold display of independence. By encouraging this action, Girardeau made Zion Presbyterian Church a place where the enslaved could publicly declare that they too had a family history and they had an allegiance to people other than their owners.[31] Zion was distinct from other churches throughout the South. In many churches "such a worldview [enslaved African Americans only listing Christian and not surnames] and its accompanying ethos and social system were legitimated in the roll books of the churches."[32] Zion embodied a different practice, which suggested a measured ecclesiastical equality. Indeed the session clerk at Zion (E. C. Jones) as well as Girardeau himself "recorded not only the owners of the hundreds of slaves who joined Zion but also the surnames of the slaves."[33] Behind this subtle distinction was the idea Zion's leadership accepted: that all members, regardless of their race, enjoyed some measure of ecclesiastical equality or human equality through church membership in the church leadership's sight and in the eyes of God. However this advocacy never went beyond the walls of the church.

Further, the enslaved African Americans did not just pick the names of their owners but "by the late 1850's, more than 92 percent of the slaves who joined Zion gave as their own surnames names that were different from those of their owners. Moreover, in addition to claiming the name of their families of origin, wives gave the surnames of their husbands, affirming their slave marriages."[34] Encouraging members to choose a surname was indicative of a unique mind-set toward enslaved African Americans in antebellum Charleston. While at first glance this might be seen as a small detail of this particular slave mission, it was (along with the seating structure and classes) indicative of the larger philosophy behind Girardeau's experimental work. As indicated in the *Zion Presbyterian Minutes* the White leadership avowed, "We enter this church as white members of the same, with the fullest understanding that its primary design and chief purpose is to benefit the coloured and especially the slave population of this city."[35] The mission's focus was on the enslaved. Therefore the church's activities were focused on the benefit to the slave and not on the benefit to the White leadership. This simple refocus was both intentional and somewhat drastic. White individuals who attended a service at Zion would not be seated in front of the pulpit and the focus of the teaching and preaching was not directed at them. To many White southerners, whose churches and pulpits revolved around addressing their lives, this would have been jarring.

Augmenting this philosophy and affirmation of humanity at Zion was the place where enslaved Africans sat in the church or "the place of honors."[36] Unlike in many southern Presbyterian churches or churches in general of the time African Americans sat in the pews at Zion while Whites sat in the balconies and galleries. The environment that Girardeau created for African Americans in his church has been described as "their church, as no other church in Charleston had been theirs since Morris Brown and the African Methodist Church. It was a building, a place that had been built for them. Here they could gather, could claim a community and thus a humanity in the very midst of an alienating and dehumanizing bondage."[37] Southern Presbyterians believed in the primacy of "God's word" in worship: preaching the Bible was the most important portion of the worship service. Southern Presbyterians believed that the Bible was the word of God opened and taught alongside the power of the Holy Spirit to communicate his word to his people. Therefore pulpits in the nineteenth century were elevated above the congregation to communicate that the word of God was coming from a higher power or authority.

Further, the pulpit's place, facing the pews, was important. Presbyterian pulpits were typically centered in the middle of the pews to have the most commanding effect for the entire audience. For someone sitting in a balcony this effect would be lost. The listener's preference would have been to sit in front of the pew looking up at the preacher, not sitting in a balcony above the preacher looking down. This practice allowed the preacher to make eye contact with his listeners, which communicated to them that they were the primary audience.

In the US South and Charleston in particular heat rose to the balconies so sitting there was drastically more uncomfortable than sitting in the pews below. Thus the seating preference was given to enslaved African Americans at Zion and not to Whites.

One visitor, John Grimball, wrote home to his family on November 27, 1859, about this phenomenon, which he had never before witnessed. He steamed, "I waited until after J.L. Girardeau had performed the service for the Negroes. There were there unusually large numbers and occupied all of the pews of the church."[38] This practice was another not-so-subtle display of Girardeau's belief in his congregants' humanity. This seating arrangement sent a message to African American attendees regarding their spiritual value. It also sent a message to White participants that they were of secondary importance in Girardeau's mission. Visitors such as Grimball were undoubtedly shocked by Girardeau's failure to ascribe to the cultural milieu's societal as well as accepted ecclesiastical hierarchies. According to Grimball and many others offense was taken that Girardeau provided for the preferences of enslaved people over White visitors.

This was especially significant as Girardeau's contemporaries regarded him as one of the finest preachers in America. Many referred to him as the "Spurgeon of America" and made connections between the most prominent preacher in England (Charles Haddon Spurgeon, who was known as the prince of preachers) and Girardeau. Many had heard of the young preacher's renowned ability and visited Zion to catch a glimpse of his famed oratory. One such visitor was the eventual Union general Benjamin F. Butler of Massachusetts. During the National Democratic Convention of 1860 in Charleston Butler asked his friend Alfred Robb, "Where are you going?" Robb stated, "To hear a great white preacher whose life is consecrated to the salvation of negroes." Butler replied, "Well, as I have never heard of any such thing as that, I will go with you." When they entered the church, they had to sit in the galleries while the enslaved African Americans occupied the pews before the pulpit. Colonel Robb went on to describe the scene:

> The prayer of the preacher was earnest, simple and humble as of a man pleading with God. The singing was general, heartfelt and grand. The sermon was tender and spiritual, and though profound, was plain, delivered with fire and unction. After the preacher took his seat, deeply impressed, I was with closed eyes meditating on the wonderful sermon, when I heard someone sobbing. Looking around I saw General Butler's face bathed in tears. Just then the church officers came for the usual collection and at

> once General Butler drew from his pockets both hands full of silver coin (put there to tip the waiters), and cast it into the basket, with the audible remark, "Well, I have never heard such a man and have never heard such a sermon." In two years from that day Colonel Robb had died on the field of battle fighting for the South, Dr. Girardeau was a chaplain in the Confederate States Army, and General Butler was hated by the men and women of Dixie.[39]

Such was the impact that Girardeau's oratorical skill left on many. It was also the reason why Zion could expect anywhere from 2,500 to 3,000 attendees on a given Sunday. It was indeed rare that one as talented as Girardeau would reserve his skill for the most rejected and subjugated people of his time: enslaved African Americans.

Typically young pastors eventually hoped for a more affluent pastorate in an influential White church. Missionary work was good preparation for leading a more prominent congregation but it was not typically the most sought-after vocation among ministers. Churches and denominations reserved the best preaching for a majority White audience. In stark contrast Girardeau gave up prominent positions in Columbus, Atlanta, and the Northeast to continue his work with enslaved African Americans in Charleston. He often said, "I would rather accept $400.00 and a cabin in a country church in South Carolina than the $4000.00 and the splendid manse in the magnificent city of Atlanta."[40]

Girardeau also conducted ceremonies and services on the entire corpus of biblical literature that spoke to enslaved African Americans. Presbyterians believed in preaching through an entire book of the Bible at a time and were careful not to skip passages because they might be hard to preach. This style of preaching through the entirety of a book meant that enslaved African Americans were exposed to a variety of teachings. This makes Presbyterian missions to enslaved African Americans distinct from other denominations. John Blassingame saw that "an overwhelming majority of the slaves throughout the antebellum period attended church with their masters. Then, after the regular services ended, the ministers held special services for the slaves."[41] These special services, John Boles asserted, "were more typical of Episcopal and Presbyterian churches" whereas "Methodist and Baptist preachers would usually, sometimes toward the end of the service, call for something like 'a special word for our black brothers and sisters.'" The ministers would then "turn to them in the back pews or in the balcony and address them with a didactic sermon that often-stressed obedience to earthly masters."[42] At Zion not only were the enslaved African Americans seated in front of the pulpit, but they also received teaching on a variety of topics not related to issues surrounding obedience to one's master. It was a worship service that belonged to them and was intended for them. At Zion enslaved African Americans were no longer on the periphery or in the balconies; they were the core audience.

Girardeau's primary function was the salvation and liberation of the soul. He did not preach sermons that merely enforced the legal and cultural structure of the institution of enslavement, nor did he preach sermons about freedom or civic liberation. Indeed as John Boles has noted of the majority of missionaries to enslaved persons, "their paternalistic efforts towards the blacks under their control seemed a truncated version of Christianity."[43] Usually the primary function of the paternalistic slave missionary was to serve the White community by preaching about obedience and subservience to enslaved Africans in order that enslaved persons might learn to "obey their masters." One enslaved person recalled that the "White preacher he preach to de white fo'ks an' when he git thu' wid dem he preach some to de 'Niggers.' Tell'em to mind dere Marster an' b'have deyself an' dey'll go to Hebben when dey die."[44] Such was not the case in Girardeau's sermons, whose topics ranged from "The Last Judgment" and "Sanctification by Grace" to "the Efficacy of Prayer."[45] Girardeau preached the entire counsel of God's word and a variety of theological topics.

"Slaves saw through" and "felt contempt for the self-serving attention they received." As Boles discovered in many of the sermons offered by sincere ministers "slaves heard a more complete version of the gospel, and despite whatever social-control uses some ministers tried to put religion to in a portion of the Sunday service, most slaves found grounds for hope and a degree of spiritual liberation through their participation."[46] Girardeau worked within and was a part of the framework for southern Presbyterian theologians who argued that slave missions were a justification for the benevolence of the institution of enslavement. His mission work was not just to simply buttress enslavement, pacify a guilt-ridden conscience, or justify the institution to northern abolitionists. Missionaries to enslaved persons like Girardeau believed that their work would bring spiritual freedom and ecclesiastical reform. As noted previously it was a genuine affection for enslaved African Americans and a true calling to the ministry that undergirded Girardeau's work. Girardeau's mission work to enslaved African Americans was not rooted in professional advancement, notoriety, or prominence. This affection however was limited, and it was limited to the confines of the church structure.

Spiritual freedom became the backbone of the African American community in Charleston as it sought survival during enslavement and social justice, liberty, and civil equality throughout Reconstruction, Jim Crow, and into the civil rights periods. It was the church that provided African Americans a respite from a predominantly White, violent, and oppressive culture, as well as a base from which to draw its leadership. The church was a place in which spiritual fulfillment allowed for hope in the face of overwhelming odds, faith in the face of a history of enslavement, and the love and grace to recognize that any worthwhile protest activity be conducted without violence and would display forgiveness.

Other historians have hinted at this continuity, mentioning that postbellum Charleston churches "were largely formed out of the membership of several antebellum churches. All of these old but new African American congregations took with them into the postwar period histories and traditions, leaders and a sense of identity that had been nurtured and kept alive during the difficult days of slavery." Further "they indicated that African Americans, no less than whites, had a sense of loyalty to congregations and theological traditions."[47] The antebellum mission churches' interracial nature and the work to promote ecclesiastical freedoms must be factored into this historical record. The identity, sense of loyalty, and prolonged interaction in biracial churches had an affirming effect on the individualities of both Whites as enslavers and enslaved African Americans as human beings in the midst of a degrading bondage.

To be sure there were many instances within slave mission churches in which Whites belittled African Americans, created a second-class church membership, or supported a degradation of the human condition sharpened by harsh and unrelenting systemic oppression. However this is not the only story. The biracial slave mission churches, such as Zion, were also spaces for expanded spiritual and ecclesiastical freedoms. As John Boles has so eloquently noted:

> Slaves apparently had their image of being creatures of God strengthened by the sermons they heard—even when that was not the intention of the ministers—and the discipline they accepted. Their evident pleasure in occasionally hearing the black preachers speak to biracial congregations no doubt augmented their sense of racial pride. Taking communion together with whites, serving as deacons or Sunday school teachers, being baptized or confirmed in the same ceremonies, even contributing their mite to the temporal upkeep of the church, could surely have been

seen as symbolic ways of emphasizing their self-respect and equality before God.[48]

While Erskine Clarke argued that the White-led Zion was "strictly regulated" with "vigorous oversight," he admitted that there were distinctions between Zion and other slave mission churches. While Zion was White-led, "there was also a significant expansion of the freedom of African Americans, and an African American controlled structure was put into place with black leaders and teachers."[49] This same structure would become an important cornerstone for the building up of autonomous African American churches, schools, and organizations in the mid to late 1860s and early 1870s.[50] Under a different slave mission "leaders" and "exhorters" would have been watched at all times by a White overseer and never would have been allowed to read, preach, or show other enslaved Africans that they could read and preach in a public setting. Further Whites at Zion did not oversee all African American "leaders" and "exhorters," thus going against the very basic fundamental principles of a paternalistic, racist system such as enslavement, which would have enslaved African Americans rely on White oversight at every instance. Instead Girardeau promoted leadership from among the enslaved African American community in the church, African Americans pushed for expanded rights within the church, and this would continue to have ripple effects across the African American community in antebellum Charleston, throughout Reconstruction, and into the twentieth century.

In 1869 Zion ordained as elders many of the antebellum "class leaders" and "exhorters" such as Paul Trescot, John Warren, and William Price. Expanded ecclesiastical freedoms allowed enslaved African Americans to maintain positions of honor in an otherwise degrading environment. To be sure enslaved African Americans at Zion did not possess any civic equality, but they found ecclesiastical recognition, hope, and acknowledgment. As one historian has argued, "through the church slaves found a meaning for their lives that could give a touch of moral grandeur to the tragic dimension of their bondage." Indeed "participation in the biracial churches was one of the ways slaves found the moral and psychological strength to survive their bondage."[51]

However Girardeau rigidly affirmed the institution of enslavement, buttressed it in the church, and used the slave mission to display that enslavement was the preferred space for enslaved African Americans until Whites could decide when they were ready for emancipation. While helping to create a space for expanded ecclesiastical equalities Girardeau also created a space that openly supported American enslavement, aided and abetted enslavers, and provided theological, and ecclesiastical cover for enslavers as they sought to morally justify the institution of enslavement. On March 27, 1860, on the eve of Civil War, John Lafayette Girardeau gave a commencement address to the Society of Alumni at the College of Charleston that embodied secessionist sentiment and thus justifying South Carolina's eventual action. Girardeau said forcefully, "It sometimes happens when the fundamental law of the land is violated by the powers which administer the government. Here it is a conflict between the duty to adhere to constitutional law, and the duty to render obedience to those who are entrusted with the conduct of the government." He argued further, "The disobedience to the law of the land is really chargeable on the existing government, and not on the citizens to maintain their duty to obey the law and to resist all encroachments on the fundamental principles of the Constitution. Disobedience to government, in such a case, is obedience to constitutional law."[52]

Little did Girardeau realize the drastic repercussions of the actions South Carolina took in December 1860 and subsequent actions of the Confederate States of America on behalf of maintaining the state's right to preserve the institution of enslavement. The decision was put to the test through five years of war, death, suffering, and civil strife. The decision of his state, South Carolina, would also cost Girardeau. He left his beloved Zion to serve as a Confederate chaplain and thus sacrificed his great passion to service on the battlefield.[53] Throughout the war Girardeau would long to be back with the enslaved peoples of the South Carolina Lowcountry. It was a longing that would never be fulfilled, at least in the way that Girardeau experienced it in the antebellum context. The end of the war and the passage of the Thirteenth Amendment would forever change the institution of enslavement in South Carolina. However Girardeau still had a longing to pastor African Americans, and this did not leave him during Reconstruction. That desire had also not left some former enslaved members. John Boles once wrote, "The kinship between the white and black churches of today is readily apparent, and it points back to a time more that a century ago when the religious culture of the South was fundamentally biracial."[54] To be sure the Reconstruction era integrated churches built upon relationships forged in the antebellum context.

Despite this kinship, as the church accommodated owners of enslaved persons by making room in the house of God for the institution of enslavement, the church simultaneously was sullying the bride of Christ and tarnishing its ability to speak or act against racial injustice. Southern Presbyterians believed that the church was the "bride of Christ." It was the job of Southern Presbyterian Christians to care for that bride, steward her, and present her as a "spotless and stainless offering" back to the Lord Jesus upon his return. Therefore it would be very strange to see a Presbyterian going to such great lengths to make changes to this bride to force her to fit into and accommodate the systems of the world. By forcing the bride to accept worldly institutions (like American enslavement), southern shepherds contributed to a "sullying" of the white dress of the bride of Christ.

This "sullying" was also indicative of the ways in which human greed was brought into the life of the church. The nineteenth-century southern Presbyterian church acted as if this command to enslave based on one's race came from Jesus, the Bible, or church history. It did not. Jesus was also very clear about the "sullying" of his bride. Upon entering Jerusalem Jesus overturned the money changers' tables. In Matthew 21, verse 13 he said, "'It is written, My house shall be called a house of prayer,' but you make it a den of robbers."[55] A church filled with enslavers and enslaved people meant that enslavers purchased men and women who were stolen, which the Old Testament law had made illegal in Exodus 21:16: "Whoever steals a man and sells him, and anyone found in possession of him, shall be put to death." This meant that the church in Charleston was not a house of prayer but a den of robbers. The very nature of Zion itself, a church for the enslaved, who were stolen, and that was created by enslavers, was a violation of God's law and condemned by the Bible. In turning over the tables of the money changers Jesus was speaking directly to those who sought to make a profit and used the church as a space to expand those profits at the expense of his flock.

The racial ramifications of these Southern Presbyterian shepherds' decisions would be felt into Jim Crow segregation, the civil rights movement, and the twenty-first century. Southern Presbyterians sanctioned racial separation, White control, and White violence through lynching and continued to deny civic rights to African American citizens all in the name of protecting their own political power, profits, and status. They would use the "spirituality of the church" doctrine as theological cover. This began in the early nineteenth century with the argument for slave missions and the practical creation of slave missions' churches as a response to abolitionism. Southern Presbyterians argued that slave missions were the best way to justify American enslavement as a biblically sanctioned institution.

In doing this the church aligned, supported, and gave approval to the entire system of American enslavement and made room for it to exist as a sanctioned relationship within the church. The church created separate memberships, offices, church structures, catechisms, and processes specifically to accommodate enslavement. The church created a second-class membership status for enslaved African Americans that did not include all the privileges of White church members. The church bestowed a sense of holiness upon White members and pastors who participated in these missions thereby assuaging, rather than challenging, the consciences of their members toward the institution of enslavement in America. On the contrary those who challenged enslavement received an apostate's insignia.

However due to his antebellum ministry experience Girardeau was more adequately prepared to promote greater ecclesiastical equalities for freedmen after the Civil War and into Reconstruction. Not just Girardeau's antebellum work but also his postbellum work had a lasting impact on the African American ecclesiastical community in Charleston. While many of Girardeau's contemporary southerners fought integration, African American ecclesiastical leadership, and the rights of the newly freed people after the Civil War from 1866 to 1874, Girardeau was willing to work for the expanded ecclesiastical rights of African American freed persons in the confines of one of the last White-controlled institutions in South Carolina during Reconstruction: the church.

Chapter 5

"Still in Its Bud in Our Every Heart"

Postbellum Multiethnic Worship in Charleston, South Carolina, 1865–74

After the Civil War and during Reconstruction "freedpersons continued to find in their churches solace from the cares of the world and joy and a purpose for living in a society that continued to oppress black people."[1] This was certainly true of newly freed African American communities in Charleston, South Carolina, after the Civil War. While many African American congregants left their old antebellum churches, Zion continued to have African American members attend. John Boles argued that "Blacks in significant numbers—eventually all of them—began to move out of the biracial churches and join a variety of independent black denominations." Others have shown that many White church members of biracial antebellum churches applauded "the new segregated patterns of worship" during Reconstruction.[2]

What has not been told adequately are the stories of churches that remained integrated during Reconstruction and what this meant for the lives of White and African American congregants. In a somewhat surprising letter, given that many African American freed persons preferred having African American pastors, members of the old antebellum Zion Presbyterian Church asked Girardeau to come back and minister to them as during Reconstruction. Despite being offered the pastorate of Second Presbyterian Church in 1865, Girardeau agreed to the request and went on to become one of the leading advocates for integrated worship and improved ecclesiastical status for African Americans in the southern Presbyterian Church during Reconstruction. In 1869, he was the first and one of the only White southern Presbyterian to ordain African American elders.

This action was rooted in Girardeau's antebellum work and an example of his unique views of the ecclesiastical relationship between African American and White members during Reconstruction. As Reconstruction progressed from state-controlled to a congressional-controlled program fully integrated institutions that afforded mutual care and support across racial lines became harder and harder to locate. As African Americans began participating in state, local, and municipal elections as voters and officeholders and participating in meaningful citizenship exercises, White South Carolinians expressed a desire to exert more political influence through racial violence. South Carolina's state legislature had an African American majority, and to White southerners the church was one of the few spaces in which they still maintained control and authority. If once-enslaved African Americans were to experience more public and civic freedoms then White Charlestonians, as well as most White southerners sought segregated private institutions, especially the church.[3] However from 1865 to 1874 African American freed persons and White southerners worshipped together and in a congregation in which John Lafayette Girardeau served as pastor.

Charleston was in utter ruin by the end of the Civil War. Girardeau served as chaplain of the Twenty-Third South Carolina Volunteers, served in a number of battles, and was remembered by soldiers for how he was able to bring comfort to the troops even in the midst of combat. An example of this soothing sensibility was evident in a letter from a camp on Sullivan's Island that Girardeau penned on April 5, 1864. At the regimental meeting, he spoke on "the safety which even a sleeping Christ in the same boat guarantees the believer against the fiercest storm, even that which rages on the vast and shoreless ocean of eternity. Offered our evening sacrifice of prayer; pronounced the benediction and we separated . . . reminding us of the preciousness of mortal life, and suggesting, by contrast, the celestial 'city that hath foundations.'"[4] The same was true in the midst of battle.[5]

On April 6, 1865, Girardeau was captured at Sailor's Creek and "although a non-combatant and pursuing strictly his spiritual duties was taken prisoner along with other chaplains, surgeons, and non-combatants," was sent to Johnson's Island prisoner-of-war camp to spend the remaining days of the war.[6] In June 1865, the Union Army released Girardeau from prison. He sold his watch and was able to gather some support from friends in Philadelphia to make the long voyage home to South Carolina. He arrived in Charleston after spending time with his family in the Darlington District, South Carolina. It was not a time for jovial homecoming; he found Charleston in a state of turmoil and dismay.[7] South Carolina was impoverished, and the economic status of the state was bleak. Girardeau was determined to carry on his work and was delighted when he came home and found a large number of members awaiting his return to the Zion Church pastorate.[8] Girardeau wrote in an autobiographical account that

> I was sent to prison, first at the old Capital, Washington, afterwards to Johnson's Island, whence I was released in the latter part of June. Upon returning home to Darlington District, S.C. where my family was, I received several calls, but determined to accept an invitation by Presbyterian gentlemen in Charleston to preach to the scattered fragments of our churches there. At the close of the War the coloured membership of Zion Church was exactly 500. In January 1867, the church-building in Calhoun Street having, by military order, been recovered by the Corporation from the Northern Presbyterian Church, I collected those of the old coloured members who were willing to go with me, and began preaching to them regularly again, in connection with my pastoral labours for the white congregation in Glebe Street. Those who were re-enrolled were 116. We had great difficulties to contend with. The attendants upon our services were ridiculed and twitted with being still under the control of rebels. But the work went steadily on, and now the membership has risen to 460.[9]

Girardeau returned to Charleston to find the Zion building locked. The Zion Church structure on Calhoun Street was "held by the United States Bureau of Freedmen, Refugees and Abandoned Land," and the church operated "under the auspices of the Committee of Freedmen of the Old School General Assembly of the Northern Presbyterian Church in December of 1866."[10] As Girardeau's biographer and son-in-law noted, "Mr. Girardeau was absolutely shut out of his own church building, which had been taken possession of by a missionary of the Northern Presbyterian Church and held by the Freedmen's Bureau, under the authority of the United States Government, and its occupancy positively denied to its legal owners and regularly installed pastor."[11] It is telling that while Girardeau saw this church as the property of the Southern Presbyterian Church and as Zion Presbyterian Church, under his pastorate the African American community of Charleston, as well as members of the Freedmen's Bureau, considered this space as "theirs" and as belonging to the African American community of Charleston. Even though it was built, maintained, and largely supported by White Presbyterians the space was seen by freed persons and the freed persons' bureau as belonging to African Americans. This is consistent with the antebellum views of Zion from among the enslaved African American membership.

The missionary in control of the Zion building was the Reverend Jonathan C. Gibbs from Philadelphia, Pennsylvania. He came to Charleston with the specific duty to oversee the church as well as to provide education for the enslaved African Americans of Charleston. "Reverend Gibbs occupied Zion Church and later brought suit under the Civil Rights Act to retain possession. He unsuccessfully contested the legal title to the property, arguing that since the church had been built for blacks it should belong to the Northern Presbyterians." One historian argued that "the restoration of the church property to the Southern Presbyterians provided additional reasons for blacks to desert Zion for other congregations."[12] However a large number of freed persons remained committed to Girardeau despite the restoration. "A substantial congregation of blacks once again gathered at Zion under Girardeau's preaching."[13] Girardeau was eager to continue his work no matter the new circumstances, and many of his flock were eager to have him. On December 23, 1866, Girardeau once again oversaw church services in the old Zion building. He preached that evening from 2 Corinthians.[14]

After the war, Girardeau's "mind naturally turned to his beloved Zion Church in Charleston, and his heart yearned to be with that dear flock again."[15] Girardeau had returned to Charleston for a brief period in 1864 from service and found that many of the individuals who had been Zion members were anxiously awaiting his return to be their pastor. During Reconstruction northern missionaries, pastors, and freed persons were starting new churches for the recently freed African Americans, and many were fleeing their antebellum churches. Despite this mass exodus Girardeau continued to see some old members remain at Zion. One historian noted this phenomenon mentioning, "In contrast to the enthusiasm black Methodists and Baptists evinced for establishing separate churches, many of the [African American] Presbyterians were extremely reluctant to sever ties with their original churches."[16]

An example of this continued relationship was found in a letter dated July 27, 1865, from Paul Trescot, one of the African American class leaders from the antebellum Zion Church. This correspondence displayed the desire of many in the congregation for Girardeau to return to Zion. Girardeau said of this letter, "One of the first invitations, in writing, which I received . . . to resume labor, was from this colored membership, entreating me to come back and preach to them as of old."[17] The letter contained the following passage:

> Revd Sir & Pastor
> We the undersign members of Zion Presbyterian Church embrace this opportunity, as one among the many good ones we have engaged in the

> past and in doing so you have our best wishish for your health & that of your loveing family hopeing all are engaging that blessing of good health and realizing that fulfillment of god words those that put their truss in him shall never want. The past relations we have engaged together fro many years as pastor and people are still in its bud in our every heart. Therefore we would well come you still as our pastor. To inform you that you past congregation will be the same in future and Till death provide past relations with you are and considered the same.[18]

Based on this letter the numbers of individuals retaining their membership at Zion and the fact that Girardeau carried on his labors at Zion into the mid-1870s, highlights the interconnected racial activity in churches during Reconstruction in South Carolina. These examples display the complexity of biracial religious activities in South Carolina during Reconstruction. While much work exists on political and economic institutions and interracial activities during Reconstruction in South Carolina few scholars have focused on interracial religious activity. These examples complicate the long-held interpretation that only widespread withdrawal of African Americans from White-led churches characterized the African American Christian experience during Reconstruction.

Many African American members remained at Zion and wanted Girardeau to be their minister once again. However Girardeau mentioned, "we had great difficulties to contend with. The attendants upon our services were ridiculed and twitted with [by other freedmen for] being still under the control of rebels. Many African American Presbyterians left Second Presbyterian Church, First Scot's Presbyterian, Missions Presbyterian, and First Presbyterian churches due to the "white membership's 'deprecating spirit of exclusiveness' that kept blacks from the 'rights due to all church members in good standing regardless of majority or caste.'" These freed persons left the aforementioned churches and in 1867 and built their own Presbyterian church on George Street.[19] Certainly the African American members at Zion would have been familiar with this Presbyterian exodus. However a continued relationship existed between Girardeau and his antebellum flock, and that same "deprecating spirit of exclusiveness" did not exist at Zion.

In 1866, while serving as pastor of Zion Church after the war Girardeau became the leading Southern Presbyterian advocate for integration of the Presbyterian Church. The General Assembly, which is the national governing body of the entire denomination, appointed him to chair a committee called the Committee on the Religious Instruction of the Freed People. Girardeau considered the topic and drew up a plan for how the integration of newly freed persons into positions of the church hierarchy would work. He felt strongly that the church had to offer ecclesiastical emancipation and to elevate African Americans from their minority status in the church. His desire was "to maintain the unity of the black and white congregations."[20] Girardeau had pastored a church in an antebellum context in which White visitors profited from engaging in services meant for enslaved African Americans. Girardeau understood something of the benefits of a multiethnic congregation, and "he was convinced that blacks and whites ought to remain together."[21]

Girardeau desired to see both White and black members "continue in their spiritual relations as an integrated body."[22] Immediately following the Civil War factions within the Presbyterian Church of the United States (PCUS) began to debate what the ecclesiastical status of the newly freed African Americans would be. To resolve this matter the General Assembly of the PCUS called Girardeau to serve as chair on a committee "to consider the relations of the church to the freedmen and report on the whole subject."[23] He drafted a report to the General Assembly in 1866. Many of those at the assembly commended the report, and "the assembly adopted the committee's resolution and ordered that Girardeau's paper be published in the Southern Presbyterian Review."[24]

In the report Girardeau explained his fundamental beliefs in the equality of the freed persons in the church, and he cited several biblical texts supporting these views. First, he pointed to the scriptural doctrine of the specific unity of the human race. In support of this doctrine he cited several biblical examples to prove that "all mankind sprang from one original pair, are involved in the consequences of Adam's fall, and depend for their recovery solely upon the mediation of the Lord Jesus Christ. Therefore God hath made of one blood all nations of men to dwell on the face of the earth."[25] The newly freed persons were equal in their humanity, created status, sinful estate, and need of a savior. This was a position held by many White church pastors and theologians of the time; it was an important foundational principle for Girardeau's position on racial equality in the context of church membership.

Second, Girardeau claimed that all believers in Christ were united in goodwill, which distinctions of race, nationality, gender, culture, or civil status did not affect. He cited Galatians 3:28 in which Paul affirmed that there is neither slave nor free, Jew nor Gentile in Christ, dispelling any notion of a racial priority in salvation or in church status. For Girardeau with regard to one's ecclesiastical status and membership in the church, Christ had wiped away all barriers of race, ethnicity, or nationality, and Christians had always been those who received his promise by faith alone. Girardeau's opinions can be contrasted with those of Robert Lewis Dabney, who in his book *A Defense of Virginia* and later in the *Ecclesiastical Equality of Negroes*, referred to African Americans as a "subservient race; made to follow, and not to lead; that his temperament, idiosyncrasy and social relation make him untrustworthy."[26] Girardeau's affirmation of the spiritual equality of all regardless of race pushed his position toward spiritual and ecclesiastical equality.

Third, Girardeau suggested that the new civil climate of Reconstruction, in light of the Thirteenth Amendment, demanded a renewed consideration of African Americans' status in the church. In accordance with the emancipation of the enslaved Christians were now under civil obligation to grant equality to formerly enslaved African Americans. As Girardeau stated, "The ecclesiastical disabilities which attached to them, growing out of the state of slavery, are no longer in existence. It must be admitted that, technically speaking, their minority in the church must be removed."[27] He believed that southern Presbyterians could no longer use the "slave argument" to keep freed persons from serving as equals in the church. For Girardeau it was time for full ecclesiastical equality, which meant granting greater privileges and powers to the African Americans in the church because of their new civil status as citizens in the United States.

Fourth and finally Girardeau wrestled with the social differences of the two races. Pulling back from the earlier thrust of his report, Girardeau maintained that social distinctions do exist between White and Black and that these will most likely not change. He stated they "naturally spring from the memory of relations recently destroyed, and destroyed in opposition to the views and desires of the white people of the south."[28] Girardeau understood that decades of White southerners seeing African Americans as enslaved would create in their minds a view that African Americans were inferior people. It is also likely that Girardeau himself believed this and was hesitant to fully grant that new freed persons would be qualified to teach and preach. Little would he know that the memory of these "relations" would not be forgotten even into the twenty-first century as southern Presbyterians continued to contend that African Americans could not attend and become members of White churches. Girardeau understood that African Americans would soon have "a desire for social equality," which he argued, "whites will not be willing to concede."[29] While Girardeau was willing to concede ecclesiastical and spiritual equality he could not yet envision other Whites extending social equality outside of the church and even the right to preach or lead as a senior pastor over White congregants within it.

For Girardeau even the way toward ecclesiastical equality would be slowed by present difficulties. He believed that newly freed African Americans were not ready in their educational preparation to serve as ministers in the Presbyterian Church. Three times in his report he observed "the freedmen have not men who would be capable of sustaining the weighty responsibilities and discharging the difficult duties of spiritual teachers"; that "the colored people have not, at present, the men who are capable of adequately discharging the difficult and responsible functions of ministers of the gospel"; and they are "ecclesiastically speaking, but children still in the condition of growth, as the wisest of them admit."[30] For Girardeau ecclesiastical equality for African Americans depended on spiritual growth, adequate seminary education, and ministerial training. It is clear from Girardeau's words as well as the general context of his report that his decision to deny equal ecclesiastical status to potential leadership among the freed persons was based on a paternalistic framework and denied opportunities for freed persons to preach. Indeed many had already been preaching at the antebellum church as "exhorters." It seems as if Girardeau was using a lack of formal ministerial training to make the argument that African American freed persons were not ready for pastoral leadership positions. This is likely because Girardeau knew it would take time for White congregants to accept the authoritative role of an African American pastor over a White member.[31]

The Presbyterian Church's ordination standards, which were extremely high for ministers and pastors regardless of race, supported Girardeau's line of reasoning. To become a minister in the Presbyterian Church, one would need to first display a desire for ministry and then receive a call from leaders in the church who noticed these gifts. Next the candidate would have to gain some knowledge of language (usually Greek and Hebrew) as well as biblical and theological expertise through extensive seminary training. Finally the candidate would be tested with a series of written and oral examinations under the care of his presbytery and pass them competently. Being a traditional Presbyterian Girardeau likely wanted candidates to go through this process before he acknowledged them as candidates for ecclesiastical leadership. Apparently Girardeau did not see any African Americans in his congregation ready to take on this formal educational evaluation. However enslaved African Americans were never given an equitable opportunity for a seminary education in South Carolina before the Civil War. Even their educational opportunities in slave mission churches were limited to a second-class curriculum such as catechisms specifically designed for the enslaved and Bible classes where students were not even allowed to read but had to commit texts to memory.

To provide for their training and eventual equality Girardeau proposed that a "missionary congregation of colored people with the power of electing their own deacons would be a possibility for the worship of new freedmen. Under this system the election of deacons would be a step in the maturing process for the freedman and if the maturation process went as planned then there would be the possibility for the possession of the ruling eldership."[32] Girardeau also provided for theological education in his report. He recognized those in the African American community who possessed the spiritual gifts to become leaders and pastors in the church, but those individuals would need financial support and mentoring. Girardeau was asserting there were no African Americans who could be considered candidates for leadership as none had attained the proper qualifications. The church would have to provide leadership training, financial support, and encouragement for African Americans to hold their rightful place as pastors.

Girardeau argued publicly for the ecclesiastical equality of freed persons, and he desired to retain a church in which both White and Black worshipped together. He realized that these freed persons were "the poor in our communities, and we are only their neighbors, when, in accordance with the great principle inculcated by our Savior, we go to their assistance in their need."[33] He was also interested in preserving a close relationship between the two races in the church organization and was willing to grant, "It is impossible to deny them the greatest extension of their rights."[34] Girardeau sought ecclesiastical integration of the two races at a time and place in which many Whites sought complete separation from freed persons. Indeed the church was one of the few spaces during Reconstruction in South Carolina in which Whites and former enslavers still exerted some measure of spiritual authority and control over African American life. To yield this authority to African American leadership would have been unlikely.

It is noteworthy that while many White southerners were fighting for strict racial control of every single southern institution during the later years of Reconstruction, from government positions to economic opportunities, Girardeau was advancing integration in one of the last places that southern Whites still maintained a measure of control: the church. The church was one of the last strongholds for southern Whites to maintain antebellum spiritual roles, and it was one of the few places in which federal law could not intervene and force the church to grant ecclesiastical equality. Therefore many White southerners during Reconstruction used the church as a space to reenforce antebellum racial stratifications. However, Girardeau was advocating integration, education of freed persons with a gradual move toward leadership, and equality in ecclesiastical status. His forward-thinking proposals could not overcome many outright racist sentiments among his contemporaries.

In response to Girardeau's report, the PCUS General Assembly made several resolutions. Most of the responses were positive and seemingly agreed with much of what Girardeau recommended. One of the resolutions included "that it is highly inexpedient that there should be an ecclesiastical separation of the white and colored races."[35] Others provided for communities to set up educational and mission churches for the poor freed persons in their communities. Whatever good came from these resolutions toward the uniting of the two races would be challenged by Robert Lewis Dabney's separatist ideologies rooted in racism, White supremacy, and his ability to shape public opinion toward the fear of racial amalgamation in the church.

Historian and theologian Sean Lucas described Dabney as "outraged and desperate" in his 1867 response to Girardeau's recommendations. Dabney penned, "I knew that this racial amalgamation would ruin our church. I felt like it was a moment of life and death for the church. I resolved, therefore, to fight like a man striking for life or death, to drop every restraint, and to give full swing to every force of argument, emotion, will, and utterance" (against the idea of ecclesiastical equality).[36] Like Dabney many White southerners were not yet ready to grasp notions of ecclesiastical equality that Girardeau argued for in 1866, and early thoughts on Girardeau's report were positive. However in 1867, "outraged and desperate" Robert Lewis Dabney, pastor, theologian, and former Confederate chaplain provided a glimpse into the possibility of having ecclesiastical equality in the church for the newly freed African Americans.

Robert Lewis Dabney was born on March 5, 1820, in Louisa County, Virginia. Early in Dabney's life he developed a deep passion for the South and especially for his native Virginia. Dabney's love for the South and his limitless devotion to its ideals of gentility, paternalism, and piety became an influence throughout his life. This devotion shaped his biblical understanding in the defense of enslavement and for the subjugation of the African American race. Lucas, the most recent Dabney biographer, suggested that, "while Dabney held that his belief in hierarchy, patriarchy, and household relations was drawn from Scripture, his anti-egalitarianism was deeply influenced by his un-biblical antipathy toward African Americans."[37] Living in the very rural county of Louisa, Dabney was exposed to a limited number of African Americans compared with the southerners in the Lowcountry areas of tidewater Virginia or South Carolina. Southerners like Girardeau who grew up on the outskirts of a more urban city like Charleston, would have known many enslaved African American males, their wives, and children, and would have engaged with them regularly. Dabney's somewhat limited engagements with those of different ethnicities was a coercive force that served to shape his racial tendencies.

At the heart of Dabney's background perhaps is the Virginian as well as southern commitments to honor and masculinity. In antebellum southern culture honor was gained by social position maintained by one's actions and defended violently either in war or in a duel.[38] Dabney's commitment to honor most likely started to develop early in his life. When he was thirteen his father passed away, and he was left to manage his mother's household, farm, and enslaved African Americans. Later at the Hampden Sydney College, the University of Virginia, and Union Theological Seminary Dabney saw his academic studies as a way of maintaining his family name and thus securing his honor.

The root presupposition of southern gentility was that not everyone in society could be honorable. Dabney displayed a sense of this ideology when he stated that "the master slave relationship, while not an inherent positive good to either party, was the best possible social relation between white and black Americans."[39] There were those in southern society who were unable to attain honor due to their subjugated status. For Dabney this included African Americans, as well as poor Whites whom he saw as under his paternalistic care. Lucas insightfully noted that "this code of honor was pictured best in the Southerners' favorite novel, Sir Walter Scott's Ivanhoe. During battle, Ivanhoe was injured and was not able to participate in the battle. By being 'passive as a priest, or a woman,' while others were 'acting deeds of honor,' Ivanhoe felt especially dishonorable."[40] This southern system of honor and masculinity would certainly have been formative to Dabney's views of the status of African Americans, who were not honorable because they were enslaved.

Dabney's theological commitments shaped his worldview as well. Later in his life when Virginia was engaged in the Civil War In 1867, Dabney wrote his famous book, *A Defense of Virginia*. In this book Dabney attempted to provide biblical, social, and economic arguments for enslavement. While Dabney provided biblical bases for his arguments his work was filled with his hatred of the rationalistic abolitionists, the northern hordes who sought to "Yankee-ize" the biblical southerners, and the barbaric and pagan African race who did not deserve equality.[41] While many of Dabney's arguments for enslavement referenced biblical passages many of his references were either taken out of context or were chosen with the purpose of propagating his own agenda concerning enslavement and a racial hierarchy. Often it is hard to discern the areas in *A Defense of Virginia* in which he was trying to be faithful to the text and the areas that he was manipulating biblical passages for the protection of a southern economic system, an honor culture of the South, and the "good of the Lost Cause." Eugene Genovese, on the topic of segregation, mentioned this cultural pervasiveness into the lives of many southern divines: "Nothing is more disheartening than to see such firmly orthodox Christians as Dabney, who stood all of his life on sola scriptura and turned to the Bible for guidance on every subject, plunge into arguments from sheer prejudice that hardly pretended to be scripturally grounded."[42]

After Reconstruction, Dabney became embittered both by the South's loss and the pervasiveness of northern culture into the South. He eventually lost his teaching position at Union Theological Seminary in Virginia and moved to Texas where he accepted the chair of Mental and Moral Philosophy at the University of Texas in Austin. This move would have been seen as somewhat of an "exile" for the aging theologian who was so in love with his native Virginia. He threatened many times in letters to his friends (specifically Moses Hoge) to emigrate to Brazil where he claimed that a new South could be created, one that was not influenced by "Yankee-ized" culture and in which southern gentility could be preserved. While he never emigrated to Brazil Dabney sought to maintain a sense of "sectionalism in the reunited country. It was primarily in the Presbyterian Church, not in monuments or Confederate Day speeches that Dabney sought to preserve southern identity."[43] Dabney saw the PCUS as the last bastion of maintaining southern culture, and so he sought to keep the church sectional at all costs. It is in this time of Dabney's life that we begin to see him "outraged and desperate" at the prospect of having ecclesiastical equality with African Americans.

As historian H. Shelton Smith observed, "The old school Calvinist argued, to the very end of his life, that the Negro was an inferior member of the human race whom God appointed to play a subservient role in a white-ruled church and state."[44] For Dabney, African American ecclesiastical equality meant that the destruction of White civilization was imminent. Dabney and other White southerners feared that along with ecclesiastical equality would come social, political, and inevitable racial amalgamation or racial mixing. As a result, Dabney and many other southern Presbyterian clergy fought hard against any move toward equality in any ecclesiastical sphere for African Americans. It is not too much to claim that this "century of segregation" from the early 1860s to the mid-1960s and into the twenty-first century is the result of Dabney's and others' unbiblical justifications for race-based enslavement and racial segregation. It was these same ideas and references that theologically like-minded southerners used for decades to continue racial separatism in the church. It is only recently that those in southern Presbyterian traditions have begun to reevaluate what the scriptures teach concerning enslavement and race and have come to realize the implications of adhering to the arguments of nineteenth-century southern theologians on these topics.

The PCUS General Assembly had urged the lower church courts to consider Girardeau's report on the ecclesiastical relationship between the church and freed persons. Accordingly the synod of Virginia took the matter up at its 1867 meeting. At one point during the meeting "it so happened that Dabney was temporarily absent from the church when the measure was adopted, and when he returned and discovered what had taken place he was furious. After his friends managed to secure a reconsideration of the overture, he attacked it with every forensic weapon at his command."[45] The result of those forensic weapons was the speech later published as "The Ecclesiastical Equality of Negroes." Dabney himself stated that there had "broken out among many a sort of morbid craving to ordain negroes; to get their hands on their heads," which he later claimed stemmed from a "'moral and mental malaria,' a pernicious disease that had infected a large portion of mankind."[46] In his response to Girardeau's report and the synod's action Dabney offered several arguments why the church could not "grant" ecclesiastical equality to African Americans freed persons.

First, Dabney held that the time to extend equality was not the present. He believed that this question could not be decided with the hearts of men so strained by "unusual passions" still lingering from the Civil War. During Reconstruction, the former enslaving population of the South was struggling to retain some sort of power within its society, which had been recently conquered. It was the first time many Whites had seen African Americans living and working around them freely. Further some like Reverend Gibbs were coming from the North and were positioning newly freed African Americans in political offices and ministerial positions. In the midst of these actions Dabney was steadfast in his resolve to maintain southern White dominance: "When I see [the freedmen] almost universally banded to make themselves the eager tools of the remorseless enemies of my country, to assail my vital rights, and to threaten the very existence of civil society and the church at once," Dabney declared, "I must beg leave to think the time rather mal apropos for demanding of me an expression of particular affection."[47]

Second, Dabney believed that the Memphis Assembly's decision was right in principle but wrong in its details concerning principles. Dabney believed that African Americans were equals spiritually but he did not believe that the church should sponsor educational ministries to help them secure ecclesiastical equality. He agreed that ordination should be granted to those who were called by God and qualified for the work, but he noted that Blacks were automatically disqualified to minister to Whites saying: "But in which meaning is it to be taken? Does it imply that we may properly decide that the evidence of God's call and qualification is fatally defective, where an insuperable difference of race, made by God and not by man, and of the character and social condition, makes it plainly impossible for a black man to teach and rule white Christians to edification?"[48] This argument stated that the call and qualifications of ministry could come to Blacks but only in the context of an all-Black church. However this same call and qualification could not be granted were Blacks to shepherd and lead a White congregation.

The third reason that Dabney opposed freed persons' ecclesiastical equality was that he saw it as impractical. He argued based on his assumption that the only "effect that it can have will be to agitate, and so to injure our existing churches."[49] Dabney believed that no African American could ever meet the standard of character, prudence, and morality that the Presbyterian standards required to minister to Whites.[50] Fourth, something that undoubtedly served to frighten his fellow ministers was the claim that ecclesiastical equality would lead to racial amalgamation (or the mixing of the Black and White races), which according to Dabney was nothing less than "the work of the devil."[51] If Dabney could not win the day based on his biblical and practical arguments he would resort to fear tactics to gain the desired result. Dabney even went so far as to claim that the blood of persons like George Washington, Robert E. Lee, and Thomas J. Jackson would be corrupted with such amalgamation. "Yes, sir, these tyrants know that if they can mix the race of Washington and Lee and Jackson with this base herd which they brought from the fens of Africa," then "the adulterous current will never again swell a Virginian's heart with a throb noble enough to make a despot tremble."[52]

Dabney dealt briefly with the scriptural arguments that Girardeau and others put forth as reasons for freed persons to have ecclesiastical equality. In response to Galatians 3:28, "There is neither Jew nor Greek . . . for you are all one in Christ Jesus," Dabney responded that while the blessings of redemption were offered to all races, it does not mean that the responsibilities of church office are available to all believers, irrespective of class or race. Dabney cited the Old Testament qualifications of the priests of the Israelites being limited specifically to the tribe of Levi. What Dabney failed to exegete however was that while

God may have chosen a certain people (the Israelites) to be his own in the Old Testament, he did not single out an "entire race of people to be specifically degraded and dishonorable. According to Paul, all humanity is degraded by the virtue of sin and rebellion against God and all need redemption through Jesus Christ."[53] Dabney revealed in his scriptural justification the ecclesiastical inequality of African Americans, a racial prejudice rather than sound biblical exegesis. Dabney's belief in the inherent inequality of the African American race and his agenda to maintain a White-governed church drove his approach to the biblical text. As Lucas well stated, "Dabney's racial orthodoxy was not biblical orthodoxy. Far from proving his case that nonwhites were biblically banned from holding church office, Dabney revealed his intense racial prejudice."[54]

Fifth and finally, Dabney claimed that the early church refused to ordain enslaved persons even though they were freely admitted into the church.[55] What Dabney failed to understand however was that early church leaders were not necessarily White; neither were enslaved persons in Roman society always Africans. Slavery in the Greco-Roman culture of the early church differed greatly from mid-nineteenth-century southern American enslavement. Mostly it differed because the institution of enslavement in the United States chose a particular race of people (sub-Saharan Africans) as the only race that could be stolen, bought, sold, and brought into plantations in the Western Hemisphere. Roman enslavement as it existed in the New Testament was not race based, and there was not one particular race chosen above others as somehow more desirable to be enslaved. Household enslaved persons such as Onesimus (a slave for whom the Apostle Paul wrote a letter to Philemon) had a different status in Roman society than did a slave who worked in the mines or in the fields. Members of Roman society occasionally sold themselves into enslavement (under a contract agreed upon by both enslaved person and patron) to a wealthier patron in hopes of gaining social advancement through the care and financial support of the patron. Once these household enslaved persons were granted freedom by their patrons after the agreed-upon time economic as well as social advancement in Roman society was available. There was no such comparison that could made in the American South. If you were African American in the U.S. South, enslavement was for life and the life of your offspring.

Likewise Dabney's racial antipathy would not have been shared by the early church. Dabney made a mistake in his logic by comparing his own situation and context of American enslavement to that of the early church under the Roman Empire. There is no biblical or historical evidence of racial distinctions being made as to preventing the appointments of elders or deacons in the first-century church. Rather when the first deacons were chosen Jewish men selected Greek men to care for the needs of Greek widows. Furthermore it was common among the first-century church leaders to appoint Gentiles and Jews alike to various positions of deacon or elder. Gentiles in the church came from a variety of racial backgrounds including peoples from the continents of Africa, Asia Minor, western Asia, and Italy. This is evidenced in Titus when Paul tells him to "appoint elders in every town as I directed you." This is even the case on the island of Crete, upon which Paul is called to labor among and train church leadership in a place full of "degraded and dishonorable peoples."[56]

Dabney had two possible solutions to the "problem" of ecclesiastical equality for African Americans. One was for African Americans to remain in the church with the same status that they had before the war: as second-class enslaved members. The other was that they should separate and form a Black Presbyterian Church, ecclesiastically independent from the White church, while continuing to maintain bonds of friendship. There were the only two ways Dabney was willing to extend ministerial and ecclesiastical equality.[57] Eventually the PCUS would try Dabney's second solution and opt for segregation or what was called "organic separation," forming the Afro-American Presbyterian Church in 1874.

Providing ecclesiastical leadership toward what would later be adopted by the logic of Jim Crow Dabney proposed and the church acceded to segregation and the doctrine of a "separate but equal" church. Those who were there and heard Dabney's speech describe the effects of it as "powerful: 'His audience was held in agony of suppressed emotion.'"[58] One of the audience members noted that "when he finished, we felt as men feel when a tornado has just swept by them. We drew a long breath to relieve the lungs."[59] The synod voted overwhelmingly to request the General Assembly to overturn their previous decision, and the topic of licensing and ordaining men to gospel ministry was placed in the hands of the presbyteries. The 1867 General Assembly rescinded its resolution from the previous year, and Dabney's speech served as the turning point against racial ecclesiastical equality in the Southern Presbyterian Church.[60]

Despite Dabney's victory in the church courts Girardeau continued to serve as pastor of Zion Church and sought the enhanced ecclesiastical status of African American members during and after Reconstruction. One glowing remembrance of this postbellum work described, "It was like a first love with him to serve these children of Africa, and with all the burdens and the attractions and the encouragements of a large and influential white city congregation to minister unto, his heart ever yearned for the salvation of the negro and his development into efficient Christian service."[61] Many African American congregants expressed a recognition of Girardeau's work. His son-in-law recorded a story of two freed persons after the Civil War. "One of his (Girardeau's) negro members asked another negro to go with him to the church. The latter, refusing on the ground that the church had a white preacher, received this prompt reply from Dr. Girardeau's friend, 'Yes, he face is white, but he heart is black.'"[62]

On December 23, 1866, Girardeau recommenced services at Zion Presbyterian. "Once the air began to clear in Charleston, Girardeau intended to resume his ministry with the African Americans of Charleston. Slave or free, they were the object of his affection, and that had not been changed by the war."[63] In April 1866, the presbytery ordered the consolidation of the Glebe Street Church with Zion. The formal installation service took place on December 29, 1867. This consolidation included both African American as well as White members. Zion retained "the offices of both congregations in the united church, including the pastor, and holding the name Zion Church, the regular worship being conducted on the building on Glebe Street. And thus Mr. Girardeau entered upon his memorable pastorate in Charleston after the war."[64]

Zion expanded its membership after the war, and the annual reports show a steady growth of new members. This growth was mostly a result of the continuance of sabbath schools, of which Girardeau was a strong advocate. In a letter to Reverend Thomas H. Law Girardeau discussed this model of sabbath education extensively. He commented, "I have never seen any results equal to those which are secured by this method," which was entitled "A Key to the Shorter Catechism, etc."[65] He went on, "I am delighted with it. And this I say from constant observation, for I attend the Sabbath school regularly and take charge of the main question and the analytical exercise when the school is brought together en masse." Girardeau believed in education for his newly freed congregants, and he claimed that "it is a glorious privilege and a grand opportunity. I regard the exercise as one of the most promising in the circle of pastoral labors. We are trying to train the scholars as Presbyterian Christians." Education was a top priority to Girardeau, and he chose not to separate his classes along racial lines. Both Whites and African Americans attended and the educational experiences at Zion through Girardeau prompted some congregants to go to seminary and into the ministry.[66]

In 1867, more African American members determined they wanted to be a part of Zion with Girardeau as their pastor. As one witness remembered many "were ready to come back to their old church and remained loyal to their former faithful and devoted pastor, and sometimes large congregations attended the services."[67] On March 25, 1867, the (White) session of the church nominated seven (African American) individuals to be superintendents over the new congregation.[68] Many were the same men who had served as class leaders and "watchmen" in the old Zion before the Civil War. Between Old Zion and Zion Glebe Street there were 440 African American members not including 60 new members added in 1868. By March 1869, the total congregation numbered 561.[69]

On Tuesday, July 27, 1869, "the Session of Zion Presbyterian Church formed the Zion Presbyterian Church (Colored), Calhoun Street. Indeed, the black membership constituted more than one-half the total membership of Girardeau's flock in 1869." Later that year Girardeau's work toward ecclesiastical equality of the newly freed persons came to fulfillment. W. F. Robertson recorded that "upon recommendation of the Session, the following African-American men were nominated to serve in the office of Ruling Elder–Paul Trescot, William Price, Jacky Morrison, Samuel Robinson, William Spencer, and John Warren."[70] As a result Girardeau became the first White member of the Southern Presbyterian Church to ordain African Americans to the position of ruling elder, the highest position in the local Presbyterian Church Session.[71]

In 1871, Girardeau, hindered by throat problems, was doubtful whether he should continue to work at Zion. Later that summer he drafted a letter of resignation to both his congregations. He "felt constrained, in the face of the vigorous opposition of the Session and the earnest remonstrance of the people, to tender his resignation, which he pressed so urgently that the pastoral relation was actually dissolved by the Presbytery." However when Girardeau actually came to the congregation to give them his farewell address, "the people, and their earnest desire that he should remain as their pastor had taken such shape that he decided at once not to leave them." "The congregation proceeded to call him again, and the Presbytery, after a season of rest on his part, reinstated him pastor without his having separated from his cherished and devoted flock."[72] This act demonstrated that by the 1870s African American congregants still desired to retain Girardeau as their pastor. After taking an extended leave Girardeau returned to Zion but with increasing problems of racial separatism in the denomination and escalating racial tensions in South Carolina because of Reconstruction his work among the African American community in Charleston was tenuous.

John Boles once wrote, "he kinship between the white and black churches of today is readily apparent, and it points back to a time more than a century ago when the religious culture of the South was fundamentally biracial."[73] Girardeau's postbellum work has had a lasting impact on the Charleston African American community. While many of Girardeau's contemporaries fought integration, African American ecclesiastical leadership, and the rights of the newly freed persons after the Civil War, Girardeau worked for ecclesiastical reform in a resistant and embittered White South. This work is significant in several ways to the modern landscape. For instance in the wake of the Emmanuel AME massacre in Charleston in 2015, there were many relationships between historic White churches and historic Black churches that had been in existence for almost two centuries. If you spoke to both White and African American pastors and church members on the ground in Charleston, South Carolina, during those terrible days in 2015, the biracial relationships bubbled up from previous kinship, biracial fellowship, and stop-and-start racial reconciliation efforts ongoing in Charleston throughout the late twentieth century. One member of Mount Zion AME on Glebe Street has even gone so far as to say that the affection of the AME church on Glebe Street for its White Presbyterian friends in town was still very strong and much had to do with Girardeau's legacy. In 2017, Jemar Tisby and I hosted a racial pilgrimage in Charleston for a large campus ministry organization, and one of the evenings centered around the racial reconciliation efforts happening between Mount Zion AME on Glebe Street and Grace Church Cathedral Episcopalian Church next door. Girardeau's legacy and the memory of biracial efforts on Glebe Street at Zion were the glue around which much of the evening's discussion centered. In 2020, and again in 2025, DeSean Dyson and I would lead similar pilgrimages for the organizations CRU and Telos. Charleston has become a city for racial healing pilgrimages and this research plays a pivotal role in that work.

In 1873, Girardeau penned that "the work of the Presbyterian church among blacks was reported as 'languishing,' and the status of those already within the fold of the Southern Presbyterian church had become increasingly problematic." Further, "the South Carolina Synod of that year hotly debated the issue of effecting an ecclesiastical separation from the blacks and the establishment of an Independent African Presbyterian Church." In 1873, the Synod of South Carolina had overtured the 1869 decision adopted by the General Assembly to have separate congregations for African Americans. In April 1873, the resignation "by the Rev. Peter Gowan" from his "connection with the Calhoun Street Coloured Presbyterian Church" further complicated the situation in Charleston, and it again "devolved upon the Rev. John L. Girardeau to take charge of the Congregation." From 1873 to 1874, Girardeau continued to be the pastor of the church and conducted the session meetings.[74]

In 1874, Benjamin M. Palmer, among other Southern Presbyterian leaders at the Columbus, Mississippi, General Assembly, called for the organic separation of African Americans from White Presbyterian churches. Girardeau was the lone voice in the southern Presbyterian Church arguing for continued integration. Girardeau's effort to retain an integrated church ultimately failed, and "with the establishment of the African Presbyterian Church, Girardeau's cause for an integrated church was lost."[75] Further "when Girardeau convened the black members of Zion and explained that they might withdraw from the church, he found that while the elderly members vigorously opposed the idea of separation," but "Young Africa, which was in the majority, favored it."[76]

Girardeau later wrote about this separation and his stance: "I advised the congregation to adopt it, notwithstanding the fact that my judgment had been opposed to it as a threatening ultimate danger to the spiritual interests of the coloured people. But the drift of events now lies in the direction of organic separation, and it was idle for me to stand alone." Girardeau was considerably troubled by both the General Assembly's as well as the Presbyterian Church's adoption of the plan. He wrote, "There was a want of interest in the work, whether rightly or not, I undertake not to judge. I cannot feel that I am responsible for the severance of my pastoral relation to the colored people." Displaying the sentiments for Girardeau members of the congregation responded, "when I stated to them that the effect of their adoption of the Assembly's recommendation would necessarily be to sunder my pastoral relations to them, a great part of the Congregation broke forth into loud wails and cries. I have never witnessed such a scene." Girardeau described the "greater portion of the congregation suddenly bowed their heads to their knees and sobbed and wailed aloud. The great majority of the women opposed the change, the great majority of the men adopted it."[77]

One can only speculate why women opposed the change, while most of the men adopted it. The notes hint that most of the men adopting it were younger. Perhaps this had something to do with a realization that an autonomous African American–led congregation was preferred, given recent civic freedoms and the postwar climate, which was growing increasingly more hostile toward African Americans. Young men already realized that the society was segregating, and many Whites were simply trying to impose old power structures onto new social and civic climates. It is possible that they saw Girardeau as representative of the old power structure. However youthful ambition and resolve might not have been the predominant position. Women and some older men in the congregation might have had their own ideas of what they were gaining and losing.

Women and older men were certainly aware of antebellum power structures as well as postbellum attempts at reasserting those old power dynamics. While they were more vulnerable than their younger counterparts, older men and women could have provoked action on this issue with regard to considering their own protection. Sobbing and wailing could have been as much about losing an advocate and protector as much as losing a pastor. It is possible that these individuals grew accustomed to using Girardeau's privilege as a shield protecting them from an increasingly violent White society. Girardeau sometimes functioned as an antebellum symbol of protection, provision, and safety. Perhaps this group of African Americans in Charleston was hesitant to sever those ties knowing that Girardeau's advocacy would continue to be important in its community. Perhaps wanting to continue under his leadership was the wiser and more politically pragmatic position. Regardless the congregation split over the decision, which displayed complexity within Zion Church about the relationship between Girardeau and the African American membership in 1874.

The General Assembly decided for something called "organic separation" along racial lines and on July 5, 1874, "after much discussion the members unanimously voted their agreement 'to the severance, in good feeling, of our organic relations to said church, with a view to the formation of a separate Coloured Presbyterian Church with its Presbyteries, Synods, etc.'"[78] Girardeau later wrote, "That was how the breach occurred. The colored people voted for it, and I gave them the road."[79] However Girardeau's task was not yet over. In a heartrending letter written to the Reverend J. B. Mack on July 29, 1874, Girardeau penned, "Dear Brother Joe . . . Last night the mystic tie which has so long bound me to the coloured people in this city was formally severed. The Calhoun St. Congregation adopted the Assembly's recommendation for organic separation. I am to correspond with parties as to securing a coloured minister for them. There is Robert Carter in Savannah—there is the man licensed as an Evangelist by Presb. of Memphis." Girardeau also thought of a man named Gee but later said that "Gee reads his sermons and his health is not strong." The sadness with which Girardeau wrote regarding the separation from Zion Calhoun Street displayed a perspective of the former slave missionary that further complicates our understanding of slave missions as well as post–Civil War race relations and ongoing interracial worship during Reconstruction. Girardeau's fight for a racially harmonious, ecclesiastically equal, and integrated worship service was now lost.[80]

Overwhelming denominational pressures for racial separatism combined with the African American male and "Young Africa's" exodus brought Girardeau's postbellum work with the African American population of Charleston to a close in 1874. Girardeau eventually accepted James H. Thornwell's position teaching Didactic and Polemic Theology at Columbia Seminary in Columbia, South Carolina. His farewell letter dated December 20, 1875, expressed the degree of sadness at his resignation of working and laboring with African Americans of the South Carolina Lowcountry: "Your affectionate and generous conduct towards me has increased my obligations to you, and bound my heart to you more closely than ever. I am profoundly grateful to you for all of your kindness; I love you tenderly and deeply; and only a conviction of duty impels me to take this painful step."[81]

In 1878, over 350 of Girardeau's African American members left Zion. He later remarked, "It was in past days, my privilege to enjoy with those courteous and noble gentlemen. They were my warm friends, and I hope, through grace, to meet them when not long hence it shall be my turn to go."[82] By 1879, Zion Presbyterian Church on Calhoun Street affiliated with the Atlantic Presbytery of the Northern Presbyterian Church along with Hopewell, Aimwell, and Salem Churches.[83] Working for ecclesiastical reform for African Americans within the PCUS was not the only legacy of Girardeau's postbellum work. Girardeau's legacy of working toward the education of African American Presbyterian communities in Charleston lasted well into the twenty-first century.[84]

The legacy of Girardeau's antebellum slave missionary work combined with his postbellum pastorate of newly freed African Americans left an imprint on the history of African Americans in the Lowcountry of South Carolina. During Reconstruction Zion would house the first school for African Americans in Charleston. Zion was also the first site for political discourse among African American political candidates. Finally the African American leadership that Girardeau helped to establish in the 1850s and later ordained in 1869, went on to serve as a crucial foundation for later guidance in the Presbyterian Church's Atlantic Presbytery as well as the larger African American community in Charleston.

In 1878, "Zion became a USA church. The first colored minister—listed in Atlantic Presbytery pastured Zion–Rev. Wm. C. Smith."[85] It was no coincidence that the first ordained African American pastor/reverend in the entire

Atlantic Presbytery came from the same church that Girardeau helped establish. Perhaps another reason for much activity at Zion after the war was the sheer size of the building, which could seat almost three thousand people. The building's size made it a prominent gathering spot, which met logistic as well as communal needs. Both the familiarities with Zion and the building itself were direct results of the work of Adger and Girardeau who helped create the building and the mission. Zion was not only the center for African American activity in Charleston; it was also the location of the first freed persons' school.

Others around the country knew of Girardeau's work as well. In 1865, Daniel Payne visited Charleston as bishop of the African Methodist Episcopal Church in hopes of reestablishing a church there that would later be called Emmanuel. The first place at which he preached was at Zion Presbyterian Church. Erskine Clarke wrote that "it was not by accident that Payne preached on his first Sunday morning in the Zion Presbyterian Church. Zion had become identified in the years immediately before the war as a center of the black community in Charleston. It would remain so during the years immediately after the war."[86] The African American community was certainly familiar with Zion and connected it as a place that was "for" them. It would have been natural for Payne to preach at Zion. Indeed it was the building built for African Americans, where they were at the center of the worship service. It was no coincidence that after the Civil War Zion became a central meeting ground for the African American community religiously, politically, and educationally.

As historian Bernard Powers argued, "Black churches were instrumental in promoting freedmen's education. When one representative of the A.M.A arrived at Plymouth Church, he found a school already organized and operated by a black superintendent and black teachers"[87] Powers was referring to one of the first schools established for freed persons in Charleston. Teachers held school in Zion Church's basement starting in 1865, with 199 boys and 225 girls.[88] The school, founded by Reverend Johnathan C. Gibbs, was originally the Zion School and then the Siloam Church but changed its name to Wallingford Academy "after a Pittsburgh donor."[89] The school was approved by the state of South Carolina, "recognized by the board of education as highly rated," and went from grades one through eight.[90]

Eventually the school moved to Wallingford Presbyterian Church on Meeting Street, but it continued to grow and produced a number of African American scholars throughout Reconstruction. By 1868, the school had about 532 students.[91] The curriculum included courses in reading, writing, arithmetic, English literature, history, natural philosophy, physiology, and algebra. By the

1880s the enrollment had grown to well over 600 students, and "Wallingford would play for more than sixty years an important role in the education of Charleston's black community."[92] In 1968, the Reverend R. R. Woods of Wallingford Church said that "the church was organized from Zion Presbyterian Church on March 3, 1867," and that "the Presbyterian Church (Northern) basically had in mind educating the Negro. The white missionaries came to teach and preach."[93] While there was not a focus on education because there was not a formal school under Girardeau, Woods did not separate the work. It would have been very easy to simply leave out the work of Girardeau and the White missionaries, but it was included. What was happening under the teaching and preaching of the antebellum missionaries and postbellum pastors while it was not formal undergirded and provided a space for the more formal postbellum education of freed persons. Further Wood's comment displayed the interconnectedness of these two periods and how the post–Civil War experience for both African Americans and Whites was directly linked to their antebellum relationships.

A museum exhibition held in Charleston in 1988 entitled "Climbing Jacob's Ladder: The Rise of Black Churches in Eastern American Cities, 1740–1877" also noted Zion's early involvement in the education of African Americans. The exhibition illustrated "the education of black children under church auspices after the Civil War, citing Charleston's Zion Presbyterian Church school as an early example." During Reconstruction African American churches such as Zion "became centers for political activity and black church leaders frequently entered the political arena."[94] This was no coincidence. There is a reason why this space was a center for political activity, education, leadership development, and promoting civic equalities for African Americans. As the antebellum choosing of the name Zion for the mission church was a symbol of deliverance and freedom so too was the postbellum choosing of the site as a space in which symbols could become realities.

It was natural for Zion Church to be associated with a place for education by the African American community during Reconstruction. "These schools, no more than the churches, did not drop suddenly from the sky on a people who previously had no interest in education. The African American Presbyterians and Congregationalists had been nurtured in a tradition that had emphasized the importance of education even while largely denying any formal education to them."[95] The classrooms used were the same rooms in which Girardeau and his class leaders had taught just six years earlier. This school would educate thousands of African American Charlestonians such as Zion's first historian, Lois Simms. Zion contributed to education "culturally as well since the old Zion Church was a venue large enough to house concerts and commencement exercises."[96]

Zion was also the initial place for the establishment of political leadership for African Americans in South Carolina during Reconstruction. "The meeting at Zion Church in Charleston during the late fall of 1865 was by all accounts unprecedented." Experiencing the freedom of political expression for the first time many "black Charlestonians crowded into the Church's galleries to hear the daily debates and to applaud speeches of their newly emergent, largely indigenous leadership at nightly mass meetings." It was at Zion that "Black men–mostly freeborn and relatively affluent–met to demand new liberties and to fashion their first major political manifesto."[97] Zion was a space that enslaved African Americans felt was their own. After the war it was a space in which expanded ecclesiastical equalities occurred. Further Zion became a space in which African American freed persons first exercised their newly won political rights as citizens.

The antebellum Zion Presbyterian Mission Church was a space in which views of enslaved African American humanity, leadership, education, value, and dignity were challenged. By no means was it pushing for the civic rights of enslaved African Americans, but the very experiences of the membership underscored a subtle challenge to the status quo. The church's existence pointed to a tension and a struggle within southern antebellum society. Were the enslaved human or chattel property? This subtle challenge, which was rooted in theological understandings of the *imago dei* and in the recognition that enslaved African Americans were human beings who deserved religious dignity and an independent space, perhaps provided a glimpse of a future, longed-for civic freedom. Freedom was unfulfilled, but the ecclesiastical opportunities experienced at Zion provided hope that other equalities might one day come.

At Zion Church during the postbellum era and the fall of 1865, previously enslaved peoples as the result of the bloodiest war in American history became freed persons and realized those hopes and dreams. The familiarity that existed within Zion among African Americans lent a sense of relaxed enthusiasm to the occasion as "the large church was too small to handle the crowd; the overflow spilled anxiously into the surrounding streets, where the stench of fire damage lingered still in this war-torn city." Further "gnarled but enterprising old men and women with newly found economic liberties hawked peanuts and plied other sundries to black onlookers along Calhoun Street." Such was the enthusiasm for freedom that organizers and ministers from Zion held "a massive parade to celebrate their day of jubilee."[98]

Later in November of 1865, a convention of freed persons met to produce the "first statewide meeting of the Negro leadership for the announced purpose of 'deliberating upon the plans best calculated to advance the interests of our people, to devise means for our mutual protection, and to encourage the industrial interests of the State.'"[99] This convention, attended by forty-one African American delegates, took place at Zion Church. Zion became the space in which not only the first freed African Americans gained their education but where the political leadership of African American Charlestonians during Reconstruction emerged. While Adger's and Girardeau's efforts led to the building of this facility and began the ministry that happened within it, it was the African American community before the war that seized ministry opportunities and after the war continued education, religious leadership, political activity, and leadership development at Zion.

The African American leadership that Girardeau helped to establish in the 1850s and later ordained in 1869, went on to serve as a foundation for later guidance in the larger African American community in Charleston. Clarke pointed out the importance of the antebellum leaders and their continued significance after the Civil War: "Among important bearers of African American traditions were the old leaders or watchmen from the antebellum days." These individuals "along with the lay elders, helped to keep alive (often to the frustration of those who sought the people's 'advancement') the traditions of congregations that reached back many generations."[100]

African Americans also used the Zion Church building as a place to discuss civil rights activities. "For years this church was reputedly the largest building for blacks in Charleston; it would remain a center for community activities long after the Civil War."[101] Reverend Metz later wrote that when the Zion-Olivet United Presbyterian Church merged in 1959 and relocated in 1964, its "long range goal was to prepare and equip the members of both church and the community to confront the institutions in Charleston and action oriented to help make them more responsive to the needs of human beings. In order to accomplish this goal, it has been necessary that the Zion-Olivet Church be progressive and action oriented."[102] In 1968, amid racial tensions across the South, 'the Spacious temple of Zion,' that Girardeau built for the black slaves, was demolished to make way for urban progress, so called."[103]

In the 1970s the church's leadership promoted civic equality. Indeed the mission statement at Zion in 1971 carried a deep sense of the importance of human rights and civil justice: "We at Zion believe that at our given location, the good news of God's reconciling love should have impact in the areas of racisms, poverty, the quality of family life, and housing in the expanding community." The congregation became activists in their new home at 134 Cannon Street believing that "love must take both the form of caring for the needs of individuals through direct services, and by equipping people to change or replace those systems and institutions which oppress or dehumanize human beings."[104] The remnant of what was once "Old Zion," "Big Zion," or "Girardeau's Church" was now fighting for expanded civic freedoms for African Americans into the latter half of the twentieth century. This was part of the legacy of the enslaved African Americans who labored in the antebellum church, the freed persons who labored during Reconstruction but also the legacy of Girardeau, who only a century before had fought for expanded ecclesiastical freedoms within the PCUS. Zion-Olivet became an activist church for human rights and social justice in the 1970s but there is continuity over time with regard to the African American experience in this church going back to the 1840s.

Zion-Olivet also remembered and honored the work of the antebellum missionaries to enslaved persons, Girardeau and Adger, in 1948 on the church's ninetieth anniversary. Reverend Sandy David Thom produced a souvenir booklet noting in the foreword that "we now come to this ninetieth anniversary with grateful hearts and souls overflowing with thanksgiving. This booklet is dedicated to the Honorable Past, the Prosperous Present and the Promising future." He went on to remark, "Here we view the road long and dismal; the white friends that shepherded the slaves in the Second Presbyterian Church and later organized them into a separate Church. We can never know the great multitudes of lives that have been awakened . . . and must never forget or be ashamed to 'Look unto the rock whence ye are hewn and to the hole of the pit whence ye are digged.'"[105] Throughout the booklet produced by this congregation of African Americans in the very midst of a segregated Jim Crow South, a sense of thanksgiving and remembrance appeared for the "white friends" who had "shepherded" the enslaved African Americans of the 1840s and 1850s. Within this booklet there was a large article entitled "Dr. Girardeau Devoted to Negro Work" filled with stories of his kindness and warmth towards African Americans, both slave and free.

The legacy of Girardeau and the Charleston Presbyterian missionaries to enslaved persons has had a far-reaching effect even into the twenty-first century when in 2002 the first African American, the Reverend Donnie Woods, was elected leader and executive presbyter of the Charleston-Atlantic Presbytery.[106] African Americans of the Atlantic Presbytery in the twenty-first century were mindful of the history of Presbyterians in the nineteenth century, of which Girardeau and Adger were such integral parts. Woods remarked, "those traditions are to be respected for their long history and what they have contributed to the well being of each. All of that is a part of culture." Woods has continued the work toward racial harmony by switching pastors with local White churches and choirs of Black and White churches regularly as well as mixing Bible studies, conferences, and camps to "give our young people the opportunity to begin building bridges." Woods went on to say that through the building of bridges members of both races could learn to trust one another and that "it could help to ease some of the tension, some of the mistrust that exists, not only in society in general, but particularly in the church." Woods said, "I think that if we are going to transform society, the church will have to take the lead."

Certainly in the twentieth century, African Americans took the lead in attempting efforts toward racial healing, trust, and easing tension between races. In some ways enslaved African Americans and Girardeau began the process of bridge building between the two races more than a century ago, and Girardeau was the first to take the lead toward integrated worship, racial harmony, ordaining African Americans to be elders, and the building of bridges between the two races within a southern and largely White denomination.[107] However, the overwhelming majority of White southern Presbyterians supported segregation, and this support continue into the twentieth century and into the 1980s and 1990s when it became acceptable for White southerners to engage in conversations on racial reconciliation.

When the Zion-Olivet United Presbyterian Church merged in 1959 and relocated in 1964, its long-range goal was to "prepare and equip the members of both church and the community to confront the institutions in Charleston and to help make them more responsive to the needs of human beings. In order to accomplish this goal, it has been necessary that the Zion-Olivet Church be both progressive and action oriented."[108] When F. P. Metz, pastor at Zion-Olivet in 1971, remarked, "We at Zion believe that at our given location, the good news of God's reconciling love should have impact in the areas of racisms, poverty, the quality of family life, and housing in the expanding community.

Love must take both the form of caring for the needs of individuals through direct services, and by equipping people to change or replace those systems and institutions which oppress or dehumanize human beings," he was speaking of a much longer history than many were aware of.[109]

Girardeau's postwar ministerial career in Charleston, South Carolina, was multifaceted. He was a slave missionary before the Civil War who became an advocate for ecclesiastical reform for freed persons during Reconstruction while simultaneously arguing that White Charlestonians should defend a Lost Cause, which would eventually undo any potential civic or social equality.[110] Charlestonians, Presbyterians, Lost Cause advocates, educators, and scholars have all used his life and memory to display different aspects of religion's role in the South. Presbyterians remember Girardeau as the great missionary to the enslaved persons who devoted his life to their spiritual growth, theological education, and leadership development. The administration of the College of Charleston erected a marble plaque in Randolph Hall in 1937 commemorating the college's "first honor graduate" and "distinguished theologian" who was a "pioneer" in interracial work in the city. Scholars of the Lost Cause have viewed Girardeau as a staunch advocate of the Confederacy and representative of an unreconstructed mentality in the South. African Americans at Zion-Olivet Church, the remnant church of Girardeau's Zion Mission, who were forced to leave the PCUS and join with the northern and later national Presbyterians (PCUSA), remember Girardeau as a benevolent missionary.

The memory and legacy of Girardeau is mixed based on who is speaking, which is indicative of the complex nature of southern interracial worship as it flowered and wilted during denominational conflicts and the rise of a Lost Cause civil religion. John Lafayette Girardeau's legacy as an interracialist on matters of race and the church runs parallel to his career as an orator of the Lost Cause. Girardeau therefore complicates our understanding of southern White clergy and competing notions of masculinity, identity, and morality in the postwar South, while displaying how some White missionaries elected to promote racial ecclesiastical integration while also buttressing the Lost Cause.

Despite Girardeau's efforts toward ecclesiastical reform, it was the Lost Cause that ultimately left a legacy on the post-Reconstruction South's religious landscape. The southern population had the language and even authorization from Girardeau as a Confederate chaplain to maintain an antebellum order at all costs. The leading lights of Southern Presbyterianism not only helped defend an antebellum southern way of life in the postbellum South but also helped mobilize an embittered and resentful population toward reclaiming political, economic, and social control through violence. The church, an organization that was to be a place for all people, would become a steadfast bastion in the effort to fight for issues of racial inclusion.

While the legacy of Girardeau's and Adger's work in Charleston might be small within the larger framework of southern Presbyterianism, it does highlight the importance of sustained bridge building between races which, while intermittent over time, does continue in a variety of ways in Charleston. Certainly racial violence, tension, and resistance to African American equality have been the status quo in Charleston over three centuries. But there is also something to be said for the unique ways in which the Charleston community dealt with situations like the Mother Emmanual AME massacre, the murder of Walter Scott, and the ways in which White and African American communities came together in a show of biracial support after these 2015 events.

One can also continue to find examples like the Charleston City Council's attempts to revive the Human Affairs and Racial Conciliation Commission, racial reconciliation book clubs, prayer meetings, and organizations like 1Charleston, a multiethnic group focused on racial reconciliation led by pastor Philip Pinckney of Radiant Church. Since 2015, White and Black churches in Charleston have become leaders in racial unity and healing and have hosted numerous events and programs on the topic. One historically White congregation, which is now Anglican (Anglican Church in North America), called the Cathedral Church of St. Luke and St. Paul, pastored by the Reverends Peet Dickinson and Patrick Schlabs, has actively studied its own racist past, its former leader's commitment to enslavement, and begun racial healing efforts in Charleston while also providing resources to local African American congregations and communities in its neighborhood in hopes of beginning to repair prior economic damage caused by enslavement and segregation.

I would be remiss if I did not include the work of my own pastor when I was growing up, Apostle Herman Robinson, longtime pastor of Trinity Worldwide Outreach Ministries at 997 King Street in Charleston with my mother and my friend Heidi Ravenel. Herman was known his entire life for his work across racial lines in Charleston. He personally pastored me, a young White boy in Charleston, and my mother, Martha Westbrook Pickett, and her friend Heidi. We attended Herman's weekly services, attended prayer meetings and Bible studies, most of which focused on racial healing and how to come together in love for one another. Herman served as the chaplain for the College of Charleston basketball team, and he was known across racial and denominational lines in Charleston for his passion to meet with, pray for, and help White folks understand the importance of racial unity. At his funeral in January 2019, there were almost as many White folks present as there were African Americans. Each person who gave a eulogy talked about Herman driving hundreds of miles a week across Charleston County to attend racial healing Bible studies and prayer meetings. There is a long legacy of racial violence, racism, White supremacy, and oppression in Charleston. But there are also stories of racial healing which have largely gone untold and that give this historian hope that we can one day achieve something resembling a beloved community here in South Carolina.

Chapter 6

"The Evils Which Now Oppress Us"

Southern Civil Religion and the Lost Cause

The name John Lafayette Girardeau carries conflicting meanings depending on the context. Among southern Presbyterians he is known as a great orator, preacher, seminary professor, missionary to enslaved African Americans, and the first southern Presbyterian (PCUS) to ordain African Americans to the office of ruling elder. Among African Americans in Charleston, South Carolina, Girardeau is known as a minister to the antebellum enslaved community, as well as an advocate for education and racial reform through ecclesiastical equality in the years after the Civil War. In stark contrast historians and Lost Cause advocates are mostly familiar with the name Girardeau for his role in perpetuating a civil religion that served to undergird the tenets of the Lost Cause during Reconstruction.[1]

However Girardeau's life and world displayed a much more complex picture than his missionary activity, representative Calvinism, efforts toward ecclesiastical reform, or Lost Cause ideology often reveal. In *Race and Reunion: The Civil War in American Memory*, David Blight gave three disparate visions of the Civil War's legacy in American memory. Girardeau can be found in all three (reconciliationist, White supremacist, and emancipationist) each during the same epoch.[2] Girardeau complicates our understanding of Christian clergy's roles in the Civil War era and displays that they could often possess different personas and competing ideologies among different groups. Girardeau's career encompassed an antebellum missionary to enslaved African Americans, his work in the biracial missions church, as well as his ecclesiastical reform from 1866–74 combined with his legacy of embodying defeat as a former Confederate chaplain through Lost Cause ideology. The competing visions of Girardeau during Reconstruction further cloud the already murky waters through which historians have examined the role of clergy in the Civil War era South.

Applying Blight's visions to three separate phases of Girardeau's career perhaps paints a more representative picture of a conflicted Southern clergy whose theology and ecclesiology often challenged their views on race and enslavement while fully embracing and supporting the social, economic, political, and racial status quo. Girardeau's postbellum ecclesiastical reform in ordaining African Americans and pushing for their ecclesiastical equality placed him among those with the emancipationist vision. His work on the battlefield as a Confederate chaplain, his helping the public to cope with death and destruction after the Civil War, and his serving as pastor of an integrated church places him in the reconciliationist camp. His work as a defender of the Lost Cause, which helped justify the racial violence perpetuated by its adherents, undoubtedly also places him among the White supremacist vision.

While attempting to deal with Christianity, enslavement, and a changing landscape during the Civil War and Reconstruction era, Girardeau found himself captive to a society whose central tenet was preserving the institution of enslavement. Later a strict adherence to the racial status quo brought about by a violent political redemption, driven by the Lost Cause during Reconstruction. By the end of Reconstruction, Girardeau and Southern Presbyterians would find themselves also pushing the culture in promoting Lost Cause ideology and modeling racial segregation twenty-two years before *Plessy v. Ferguson*.[3]

In Charles Reagan Wilson's *Baptized in Blood: The Religion of the Lost Cause, 1865–1920*, Wilson uses Girardeau to display the "traditional Calvinist explanation" for an interpretation of the Civil War and also as an example of the "hope of future vindication."[4] As Girardeau penned in 1866, Confederate ideals would one day "in some golden age, sung by poets, sages and prophets, come forth in the resurrection of buried principles and live to bless mankind, when the bones of its confessors and martyrs shall have moldered into dust."[5] In W. Scott Poole's *Never Surrender: Confederate Memory and Conservatism in the South Carolina Upcountry* the religion of the Lost Cause was rooted in a deep pessimism about "the possibilities of society that issued in both sad praise for a conquered past and a critique of the materialistic and utilitarian present."[6] We see this on display in Girardeau's Lost Cause apologetics during Reconstruction. However at the same time Girardeau was speaking at Confederate Memorial Day ceremonies and disseminating a Lost Cause ideology, he was also challenging the racial status quo in one of the most racially conservative denominations in the country: the Presbyterian Church United States (the southern branch of the Presbyterian Church).

Girardeau seemed to be a man torn between two worlds. Yet these worlds collided during Reconstruction in familiar ways, reflecting similar tensions in southern culture in the antebellum context. In one context Girardeau was a Civil War veteran who fought with and served the Confederacy as a chaplain in the Twenty-Third Regiment of South Carolina Volunteers. In another he was a missionary to Charleston's enslaved African American population, many of whom saw him as a spiritual father, as a racial moderate, and as a man who advocated for their ecclesiastical rights.[7]

After the war a strange marriage occurred between these two competing visions. Girardeau was called upon by leading lights of the Lost Cause in Charleston to speak on the justness and holiness of the Confederate cause, a cause that defended the perpetual enslavement of African Americans as one of its main tenets.[8] Girardeau engaged in this activity partly because he was attempting to cope with and help his listeners grasp the changing nature of their surroundings. He was also providing the men and women in the audience a vision to cope with defeat by displaying a postbellum southern honor built on both gentility and violence through continued sectionalism and White superiority.[9] There is a staunchly unreconstructed tone throughout this speech, and even in defeat Girardeau remained defiant arguing that there "are two senses in which it must be admitted that they [Confederate soldiers] lost their cause, -they failed to establish a Confederacy as an independent country, and they failed to preserve the relation of slavery," which led southerners to forms of government considered the "evils which now oppress us."[10]

Serving as a minister of civil religion in the Lost Cause provided Girardeau with a powerful postwar public platform. He found himself in the process of redefining what it meant to be a southern Presbyterian minister in the latter half of the nineteenth century, helping the landscape heal after a crippling military defeat while also helping shape, define, and put into practice what would later become Jim Crow segregation buttressed by racial violence. Girardeau had never had such broad audiences, and he found himself not only preaching to his biracial church but also preaching to the broader citizenry about the justness, rightness, and holiness of the Confederate War effort and how these characteristics should be maintained. He went from being a local missionary to enslaved African Americans to a Confederate chaplain to becoming a statewide and regional defender of the memory of the Confederate dead and advocate for the Lost Cause. As advocate for the Lost Cause, he helped forge a postwar identity of White South Carolinians bent on redemption and wresting political, economic, and social control away from African Americans and Republicans.

While serving as a minister of the Lost Cause, Girardeau also became the leading southern Presbyterian advocate for ecclesiastical integration. It seemed as if Girardeau was either comfortable with this contradictory clash between African American ecclesiastical equality and civic inequality, was completely unaware of the distinctions between the two, or was adapting and redefining his Christian identity by publicly serving as a minister-patriot of the Lost Cause while also in a local church context helping to expand ecclesiastical rights for African Americans.

His unquestioned loyalty to the Lost Cause and his embodiment of it as a living testament to Confederate memory in Charleston would make it difficult for detractors to question the old chaplain when it came to his moderate stance on race in the church. Girardeau seemed to use those powers of influence in complex ways in ecclesiastical circles, which oftentimes ran counter to accepted broader cultural standards of racial hierarchy and sometimes even contradicted basic tenets of Lost Cause dogma. The complexity of Girardeau's life complicates our understanding of southern White clergy who often moved in competing circles, were sometimes conflicted, and even contradicted themselves based on the context in which they found themselves at a given moment.

Increasing hostility throughout the South toward freed persons from 1871 to 1873 led to complete racial segregation in southern Presbyterian churches in 1874. In 1871, Girardeau began speaking at Confederate Memorial Day ceremonies openly advocating a racially charged Lost Cause ideology by prompting his audience to never forget the cause for which Confederate veterans died. The beginning of Girardeau's public life as a Lost Cause apologist in 1871 paralleled the period of his fight for ecclesiastical reform among southern Presbyterians.

In the late nineteenth century, Confederate Memorial Day ceremonies often included ex-Confederate chaplains who not only reaffirmed the holiness of Confederate troops, but who also helped embed the sanctity of the Confederate cause in the southern landscape. These clergy were central to the development of a collective Confederate identity and memory. The combination of their education, oratorical skill, and first-hand account of the events of the Civil War gave Confederate chaplains powerful positions in postbellum southern society. Furthermore their education, spirituality, and ability to comfort and inspire their audiences made them effective speakers for Memorial Day events, such as the one that the Ladies' Memorial Association of Charleston hosted at Magnolia Cemetery on May 10, 1871.

That day four ministers participated in the event: Reverend John Bachman, Reverend Ellison Capers, Reverend Edward R. Miles, and Reverend John Lafayette Girardeau. Of these four ministers, Capers and Girardeau served as Confederate chaplains. Girardeau delivered the main address.[11] The purpose of the event was the reinternment of South Carolinian Confederate troops who died at Gettysburg. As Girardeau wrote, "The circumstances which assemble us in the streets of this City of the Dead are" that "the bones of our brethren have for nearly eight years been sleeping in the bloody battlefield of Gettysburg" and are now returned to "the State that they had loved so well." In some strange combination of afterlife mysticism (not common among Calvinist Presbyterians of the nineteenth century) and sectionalism he awkwardly proposed the theory that the soldiers, "as dying children to a mother, yielded up their gallant spirits" and "breathed the fervent entreaty: 'Send our bodies to South Carolina to be buried there!'"[12] This is a strange statement from a southern Presbyterian who, according to theological principles laid out in the Westminster Confession of Faith (to which Girardeau ascribed), the "bodies of men, after death, return to dust, and see corruption: but their souls, which neither die nor sleep, having an immortal subsistence, immediately return to God . . . where they behold the face of God."[13] Girardeau's comments seemed to be in stark contrast with the views of the writers of the confession.

Girardeau was insulted at the thought of South Carolina's sons lying in a grave for "rebels and traitors." If Girardeau believed these men to be "beholding the face of God" and had immediately "returned to God" along the lines of an orthodox view of the Westminster Confession, then why would the souls in question be worried about whether their bodies of dust were in Pennsylvania? Worse Girardeau presumed that the corpses were deeply offended. He asked his audience, "Was it in their latest moments of consciousness" that "they recoiled from the thought that they would be interred in an enemy's soil?"[14] This important question from an authority about religion, death, and the Civil War implanted in the listeners' subconscious a memory of their dying fathers, brothers, and sons. This statement implied that to honor these men properly the listeners to and preservers of their fallen men's memory could not see the soil of Pennsylvania as in any way common, shared, unified or in union with soil of South Carolina. To Girardeau and his audience Pennsylvania in 1871, six years after the surrender at Appomattox, was still the enemy's soil.

To honor the dead Girardeau's listeners had to remember that their sons gave their lives in defense of a state, a cause, and a way of life. "There are living issues which emerge from these graves," Girardeau claimed, "gigantic problems affecting our future, which starting up in the midst of these solemnities demand our earnest attention. The question which thrills every heart is, 'Did these men die in vain?'"[15] Girardeau's assertions in addressing this question, which point to an ideology of preserving the memory, sacrifice, and cause of Confederate soldiers seemed to have undermined his work in ecclesiastical racial reform.

Girardeau first declared that these soldiers "had, as a peculiar people, occupied graces by themselves—in death as in life adhering to a noble and sacred, though despised and execrated, Cause." The cause to which Girardeau was referring was a right to preserve the southern cultural, social, political, and economic way of life. The most important aspect of this way of life was the preservation of the institution of enslavement and perpetuating an antebellum racial hierarchy in the late nineteenth and twentieth centuries. In admitting failure on behalf of the Confederate dead Girardeau noted, "They failed to preserve the relation of slavery," which along with other issues "underlay and pervaded that complex whole which we denominated our Cause."[16]

Girardeau asserted that it was the duty of those left living to remember this cause in noble and sacred ways rather than to accept current political, social, or economic conditions as a possibility for an acceptable future. Rather than admit that the soldiers died in vain, in the sense that the cause was ultimately lost and that neither enslavement nor the Confederacy was preserved, Girardeau implored his listeners for a type of southern civic duty. "Shoulder to shoulder they stood; now let them lie side by side. Confederates in life, confederates let them be in death." This duty was to honor and possess an "unspeakable love," a "boundless admiration," and an "undying gratitude" for the "heroes of a defeated but glorious Cause."[17]

In clear terms Girardeau asserted what this cause was about: "There are two ways in which it must be admitted that [the soldiers] lost their cause,—they failed to establish a Confederacy as an independent country, and they failed to preserve the relation of slavery."[18] Underneath these two main tenets Girardeau placed other fundamental principles, such as preserving an antebellum social order as well as civil and religious liberty. According to Girardeau's statements, it may be properly assumed that the intent of the Confederate cause was to establish a government under which enslavement might continue to grow, flourish, and perpetuate. The question posed to the audience members forced them to consider how antebellum social relationships could be perpetuated in a country that had outlawed enslavement and the Confederacy had been defeated and ceased to exist.

Girardeau then connected the listener to his or her role in this cause: "And the question whether those who fell in its support died in vain . . . must depend for its answer upon the course which will be pursued by the people of the South." In a not-so-subtle shift Girardeau transferred the burden of supporting the principles of the "cause" from the fallen Confederate soldiers to the remaining civilian population of the South. He claimed that "our brethren will not have died in vain, if we cherish in our hearts . . . the principles for which they gave their lives."[19]

Therefore for Girardeau and his audience it became the duty of every southern man and woman to remember the cause, to continue to preserve state sovereignty in practical ways, and to keep freed persons in a separate and unequal social order. Girardeau was carving into the hearts and minds of his listeners a sense of transferred guilt and duty thus perpetuating the cause of the Confederacy onto the next generation. Not honoring and remembering the dead—and the cause for which they died—was akin to desecration of their graves. Girardeau therefore helped contribute to the development of an explicit southern White memory of the Civil War using overtly religious language. This memory was not just philosophical and ethereal. It had real, tangible, and palpable application for his listeners and for the African Americans now living in Charleston, who would become the focal point of yet another century of racial violence. It would mean buttressing racial divides, perpetuating an antebellum structure of racial hierarchy, and committing violence if necessary to preserve this way of life. To the men in the audience who did not fight in the Civil War Girardeau was communicating that they could still prove their masculinity by upholding these tenets in the memory of their slain forefathers. They could even act violently to preserve this way of life because it adequately honored the memory of the veterans.

In Girardeau's view how were the audience members to respond to Reconstruction government and African American political participation? Girardeau did not mince words: "Let us cling to our identity as a people! The danger is upon us of losing it—of its being absorbed and swallowed up in that of a people which having despoiled us of the rights of freemen assumes to do our thinking, our legislating and our ruling for us," which would remove and "wipe out every distinctive characteristic which has hitherto marked us."[20] This firmly unreconstructed statement displayed continued defiance of federal authority and disdain for South Carolina's largely integrated state government during Reconstruction. The identity not so subtly referred to was that of White superiority solidified in a "states' rights" ideology promoting African inferiority and thus forcing African Americans to exist in a state of subservience.

For Girardeau the characteristic that marked southern people was their commitment to White control, virtue, and resistance to racial amalgamation. He mentioned that "there is a race, which, coming down through the centuries enveloped with antagonistic influences and hostile nationalities, has stood out in perpetual protest against amalgamation with other peoples."[21] With this statement Girardeau connected the listeners' identity with a European ancestry, which had supposedly remained unmixed and even "today preserves its characteristics, as the current of the great Wester River flows into, without blending with, the multitudinous waters of the Gulf."[22] To continue the Lost Cause the listeners would need to maintain White solidarity and supremacy and would be responsible for teaching the next generation of the virtues of social order. It would be this kind of oratory that would help set the stage for decades of Jim Crow segregation in southern schools, public facilities, private businesses, intermarriage laws, and even church membership.

Connecting this philosophy to practical implementation Girardeau insisted that "appointing anniversaries" for the commemoration of "the deeds of men who died for our fundamental liberties and constitutional rights" would be necessary to maintain the cause. Further a dogmatic adherence to perpetuating "the phraseology of the past—making it a vehicle for transmitting our posterity ideas which once true are true forever, all opposition to them by brute force to the contrary notwithstanding."[23] It was clear that education of new generations of southerners would be necessary to maintain antebellum political, economic, and social relations. It would be necessary to make "nurseries, schools and colleges channels for conveying from generation to generation our type of thought, sentiment and opinion; by stamping on the minds of our children principles hallowed by the blood of patriots."[24]

In a seemingly eerie glimpse toward a post-1954 era, Girardeau predicted the prevalence of segregated southern public and private universities replete with Confederate markers and flags, the development of segregationist academies after *Brown v. Board of Education*, and pervasiveness of history textbooks, all of which perpetuated myths of Reconstruction and in some cases used Lost Cause rhetoric into the late twentieth century. As Wilson noted the southern jeremiads, mysticism, evangelism, and education all rooted in southern civil religion perpetuating a Lost Cause was "the story of the use of the past as the basis for a Southern religious moral identity, an identity as a chosen people."[25] Religion played an absolutely central role in perpetuating a Lost

Cause ideology, which helped cement a solid Jim Crow South, in some cases into the late twentieth century.

Girardeau closed with the image of a dying Thomas J. "Stonewall" Jackson, who "faint from the loss of blood, and suffering from excruciating pain, . . . partly raised himself from his prostrate posture and in a tone of authority said: 'Hold your ground, Sir!'" One can only speculate as to the heightened volume and theatrics Girardeau offered in this moment. Given his use of pronounced language and facial expressions to drive home a point in the pulpit it was likely that Girardeau expanded his presence at this juncture in an attempted recreation of the scene for his audience. He was turning the hearts and minds of the listeners to the revered Confederate general and who by this time had taken on the kind mystical power reserved only for mythical legends. Girardeau was calling on the crowd to hold its own cultural, economic, political, and social ground. He said, "We must, by God's help, hold our ground, or consent to be traitors to our ancestry, our dead, our trusts for posterity, to our fire-sides, our social order, and our civil and religious liberties."[26]

With this statement Girardeau was essentially offering what can only be called a military-style order to a civilian population to continue to fight. Invoking the memory of Jackson and recreating his call for them to "hold their ground" was a clear clarion call to maintaining the antebellum order at all costs. This kind of rhetoric proved incredibly successful as South Carolina would help lead the nation over the next century in preventing integration, perpetuating racial violence, and holding its ground on issues of state versus federal authority, refusing to implement antilynching laws, and regaining White control of state politics as well as limiting educational and economic opportunities for African Americans into the twentieth century.

However just a year and a half before this speech Girardeau became the first White Presbyterian to ordain African American freed persons to leadership positions in an interracial church. While giving this speech Girardeau was simultaneously pastor of a church with African American members, many of whom he helped gain expanded ecclesiastical rights. How was Girardeau able to reconcile these two ideologies? Perhaps he was suggesting that White men and women of the South ought to choose a public and political course supporting a social order that reflected a belief in the Lost Cause for which their fallen soldiers died, all while blatantly rejecting the same order in their own local church and more private ecclesiastical contexts. Or perhaps Girardeau even saw the church as a vehicle for helping to promote the kind of education and instruction that he called for to maintain the Lost Cause. Maybe Girardeau saw the church as an institution that could over time help bring African Americans beyond ecclesiastical equality to full civic equality, and he needed to play a contrasting public role to give him space to maneuver in the ecclesiastical sphere. Whatever his designs might have been, broader denominational forces were at work to prevent the latter from happening.

Girardeau's postwar career and legacy of memory in Charleston were multifaceted. He was a slave missionary before the Civil War who became an advocate for the ecclesiastical equality of freed persons during Reconstruction while simultaneously arguing that White Charlestonians should defend a cause undoing any potential civic or social equality.

The memory and legacy of Girardeau is mixed based on who is speaking, which is indicative of the complex nature of southern interracial worship, memory, and Lost Cause mentality. While the postwar career of John Lafayette Girardeau was somewhat ambiguous because of the conflicting nature of his perspectives, his legacy as a southern moderate on race and the church ran parallel to his career as an orator of the Lost Cause. Girardeau complicates our understanding of southern White clergy and competing notions of masculinity, identity, and morality in the postwar South. His work also helps us understand further the positions that White southern moderates on issues of racial ecclesiastical integration played in a burgeoning Lost Cause movement.

Despite this southern pastor's efforts toward ecclesiastical reform it was the Lost Cause that ultimately left a tremendous legacy in the post-Reconstruction South. Indeed the southern population would now have the authorization and even orders from a Confederate chaplain to maintain an antebellum order at all costs. The leading lights of southern Presbyterianism not only helped defend an antebellum southern way of life in the postbellum South but also helped mobilize an embittered and resentful southern population toward reclaiming political, economic, and social control through violence. The church, an organization that was to be a place for all people, would become a steadfast bastion in the effort to "hold your ground" on issues of racial inclusion. At different points in his career Girardeau embodied all three of Blight's visions. Ultimately however Girardeau could not detach himself from the White supremacist vision so common among Lost Cause advocates in the postwar South.

Girardeau continued to honor, make sacred, and memorialize a Lost Cause movement into the end of Reconstruction. Simultaneously his work in the church undermined several of the tenets of the Lost Cause. However capitulation to culture on issues of race became inevitable. Like his predecessors

Girardeau would more and more reflect the broader cultural mores of fellow southerners bent on maintaining segregation, White control, and the political and economic exploitation of African Americans. Rather than being captive to culture, southern Presbyterians like Girardeau helped model to the rest of the South what practical White control might look like after Reconstruction. The Presbyterian Church United States became segregated in 1874 and helped set the tone for the rest of the South on how to go about a process like "organic separation." Unlike the cultural captivity of the early nineteenth century southern Presbyterian Christians in the latter half of the nineteenth century lead the way and pushed the culture on issues of segregation.

Through reading the letters of many Presbyterian missionaries, such as those of Thomas Donnelly, T. C. Stuart, Charles Colcock Jones, John Adger, and John Girardeau, to enslaved African Americans and Native Americans it seemed as if some of these men privately despised the dehumanizing aspects of the institution of enslavement. Perhaps these Presbyterian missionaries with very distinct philosophies regarding missions to enslaved African Americans and Native Americans were consciously even attempting to subvert the peculiar institution or at least the accepted racial attitudes of their surroundings. Eugene Genovese avowed in *Slaveholders Dilemma* that most Christian pastors believed in the Gospel as a liberating force. John Boles argued that many missionaries and Southern Presbyterian pastors operated with a "limited emancipationist impulse" and some like Girardeau would end up pushing for ecclesiastical reform during Reconstruction.

However what we see more fully is that while there may have been private misgivings most Southern Presbyterian shepherds succumbed to the prevailing notions of race and the institution of enslavement. They used theology, biblical exegesis, and ecclesiology to force the church to conform to the aforementioned prevailing notions on race throughout the South. In short southern shepherds let the savage wolves in to ravage the flock. Further creating second-class worship spaces for African Americans led the southern Presbyterians not only to become supporters of pro-enslavement theology but created the very structures needed to accommodate, support, and practice pro-enslavement ecclesiology. Southern Presbyterians would become early adopters of segregation as yet another acceptable biblical, theological, and ecclesiological framework.

Twenty years before *Plessy v. Ferguson* the PCUS would adopt "organic separation" and segregated worship spaces for Whites and African Americans with one dissenting voice in the 1874 General Assembly: John L. Girardeau.

Southern Presbyterians played a major role in sanctioning American enslavement by creating a space for it in the life of the church, nurturing the system, and even creating separate worship spaces to accommodate it. Southern Presbyterians led the charge in responding to abolitionism with theological arguments, biblical references, and even ecclesiological structures that attempted to show northern Christians that southerners were more adept at theology, biblical understanding, and how the church "really worked." Southern Presbyterians could more appropriately model and display to northern Christians how to "properly and in good order" accommodate enslavement, make room for slave holders/enslavers, salve their consciences, and simultaneously provide spaces in which enslaved African Americans could worship in a second-class manner and not be granted full ecclesiastical rights.

Therefore the savage wolf of racism and practitioners of the institution of enslavement drove the work of slave missions as much or in some cases more than as an interest in gospel ministry. Ultimately White southern Presbyterians did not believe that African Americans were equal to Whites either civically or within the kingdom of God. African Americans were to have churches without full rights as members until they "matured" to the point at which they could function within the church as equals. Southern Presbyterians desired to missionize enslaved African Americans and convert them to Christianity, but once there was conversion the same Presbyterians were not willing to grant full rights to African American members of the church. While adult African Americans were conducting ministries as watchmen, class leaders, exhorters, and all manner of leaders, White Southern Presbyterians considered these grown adult leaders as little more than children. For most Southern Presbyterians even as African Americans were ordained to the office of ruling elder in 1869, it would be many years in their minds before any freed persons were ready to discharge the offices of a teaching elder.

Other savage wolves were let in to ravage the flock. One main wolf was fear. The entire system of enslavement in the South was built on the perceived inferiority of the African American race. It was made clear through the South Carolina ordinance of secession that White southerners believed Africans and African Americans were inferior people who were only created to labor physically. A great deal of fear undergirded the White response to missions and later an integrated church. Robert Dabney displayed this fear perfectly in his belief that racial amalgamation or "the mixing of races" would happen if the churches remained integrated. Southern Whites feared their children would marry Blacks. This fear would continue into laws against intermarriage in the

South until the 1960s. This issue is still a major problem in multiethnic Presbyterian churches and youth activities in Reformed circles into the twenty-first century. It is fine for little children to play together, but once the children reach adolescence many White families remove their children from integrated schools, integrated youth groups, and multiethnic churches across the South. This fear, rooted in racism, gripped the church in the antebellum context and during Reconstruction and continues to grip southern Presbyterianism (and perhaps even national Presbyterianism) into the twenty-first century.

While there are many wolves that these southern shepherds let in to ravage the flock, another major wolf was greed. Again and again Southern Presbyterians chose the pursuit of mammon, wealth, and economic growth over the love and care of their fellow persons. This pursuit is typical in the American church as enslavement touched every aspect of American society from the seventeenth century up to the late nineteenth century and beyond. The unique contribution of southern Presbyterians was the complete way southern pastors prostrated themselves before their members' profits. The leaders (ruling elders and deacons) of the antebellum southern Presbyterian Church tended to be wealthier, landholders, and somewhat educated. Most of these persons were either enslavers or benefited financially from their connections to enslavement.

This greed is especially poignant when considering that many of these elders and deacons were holding stolen persons in perpetual enslavement (violating Old Testament law), that many of these men and women were fellow Christians, and many of these elders and deacons were having children outside of wedlock with enslaved African American women. There seems to be no discussion, rebuke, or accountability on these issues from southern Presbyterian pulpits from 1830–65. What this should tell us is that wealth and the pursuit of wealth in America was and is the true god. It had a massive impact on the church in America that has unquestioningly connected wealth with God's blessing and the pursuit of wealth as the ultimate product and form of a good "Protestant work ethic." For antebellum southern shepherds owning enslaved persons was acceptable labor and a very acceptable way to earn a living. Further enslavers were growing their wealth by having children with enslaved women largely through rape and sexual abuse. This practice went unquestioned. The wolves ravaged the flock, and the shepherds stood by silently.

This book has examined how some missionaries created functional spaces in which some equalities were a part of the ecclesiastical life of a multiracial community, and these rights expanded under Reconstruction. What we ultimately see is that southern Presbyterian Christians sanctioned enslavement and went a step further to formalize a space inside the church to make room for pro-enslavement theology, that theology's application to an ecclesiological setting, and its function in church practices. Rather than admit equal status to enslaved African American members and Native American members, Southern Presbyterians created a second-class church in which there existed some but not all membership rights. This separate and nonequal space set an example and precedent for other southern spaces such as schools, parks, drinking fountains, and other public spaces throughout the twentieth century.

Slave missions were more than just about conversion of the enslaved. They were about justifying the southern way of life, supporting pro-enslavement ideology, and providing a functional space in which pro-enslavement theology could be put into practice in the life of the church or what I have referred to as a functional racist ecclesiology. The goal was to prove to northern abolitionists that Southern Presbyterians were more correctly reading their Bibles and creating a more "biblically acceptable" church for enslaved people, which became the slave mission church. Southern Presbyterians attempted to respond to abolitionism with their own version of what was acceptable biblically, theologically, and functionally. What was created was the enslaved persons' mission church. However, for all their reworking of the scriptures, for all their theological gymnastics, for all their ecclesiological innovations to accommodate race, southern Presbyterians ultimately failed and fell short of understanding that there is no room in God's church for second-class members, and second-class children of God.

These wolves—the pursuit of mammon, greed, fear, obsession with profit over care for one's neighbor, and racism—ran rampant. The wolves not only destroyed the sheep but rendered the shepherds defenseless, impotent, and voiceless. As the shepherds accommodated these wolves the sheep suffered tremendously. As we will see in the latter sections of this final chapter, it would not be the last time that these southern shepherds would let savage wolves in to ravage the flock. Southern Presbyterian shepherds would let other wolves that fit within a southern evangelical worldview like segregation, White supremacy, resistance to civic equality, resistance to justice movements, fear, and politics into the church while excluding other political positions. Southern Presbyterians hid behind a "spirituality of the church" doctrine and used it to remove themselves from issues surrounding integration, civil rights, justice, and even the intermarriage of different races. All these wolves would feast on the flock into the twentieth century. That feasting continues in different ways into the twenty-first century.

It is the historian's job to examine continuity and change over time. While there have been important changes in southern Presbyterianism, there has ultimately been great continuity with regard to race, greed, fear, and politics. The twenty-first century has seen southern Presbyterians shrink from justice movements, work to connect their religion with alt-right conservative movements, and marginalize, isolate, or remove African American members or congregants who speak out. For a denomination with such strong theological acumen, biblical literacy, borderline obsession with catechisms, standards, rules of governance and order southern Presbyterian churches still tend to stand with the regional cultural forces that drive economics, racial hierarchies, politics, consumerism, and lack of care for a just society for all. For a denomination that believes in God's predestined plan, his will, his authority over all things, and his rule there seems to be a great deal of fear that resides in southern Presbyterianism: fear of a shrinking church, losing political power. demographic change, providing justice for all, people who do not look like them, the outside world, culture. What does the Bible say about this? "Do not fear, for I am with you; do not be dismayed, for I am your God." It says, "For God has not given us a spirit of fear, but of power and of love and of a sound mind." It says, "There is no fear in love. But perfect love drives out fear, because fear has to do with punishment. The one who fears is not made perfect in love."[27]

If all the above is true one must reconcile biblical accounts that point to a trajectory of freedom with the overt Christian support of the institution of enslavement in the antebellum South and submission to segregation during Reconstruction. It is difficult to reconcile the two since an overwhelming number of southern pastors supported the institution of enslavement and segregation so vehemently. However history is complex, and Presbyterian mission churches might also serve as spaces in which a biblical tenor of humanity's trajectory toward freedom existed in some lived context in the antebellum South. The fact that there were many ecclesiastical reforms at Zion, Girardeau argued for ecclesiastical equality after the Civil War, Zion became a place for African American community after emancipation, Thomas Donnelly preached manumission of the enslaved, and T. C. Stuart expanded roles of enslaved members at the Monroe Mission shows it is possible that a liberating ideal concerned about ecclesiastical equality, racial justice, and love of one's fellow persons existed among some Presbyterian missionaries to enslaved persons and can exist again. Where this mind-set existed ecclesiastical, social, and educational opportunities were more prevalent for enslaved African Americans and Native Americans. As opposed to other interracial spaces in the South, these Presbyterian mission churches both failed African Americans and Native Americans while also creating opportunities for enhanced ecclesiastical reforms for African Americans and Native American members, which would become important for both communities.

As Stuart continued to work with the Chickasaw and enslaved African Americans in Monroe his views on enslavement softened. As Girardeau continued to work with enslaved African Americans, he grew to realize that they were human beings made in the *imago dei* and hence worthy of ecclesiastical rights with White congregants during Reconstruction. Many of the preceding facts in this book, some of the most poignant being Stuart's willingness to ask Dinah to translate preaching, Donnelly's willingness to preach emancipation, Girardeau's work for postbellum ecclesiastical equality and ordaining ex-enslaved persons to the office of elder in 1869, evidence these beliefs.

Enslaved African Americans at Monroe and Zion experienced more expanded ecclesiastical opportunities than at many other historically White churches throughout the South. Preaching to the congregation, learning in the mission schools, experiencing new ecclesiastical freedoms, securing the place of honor in seating, availing themselves of leadership opportunities as class leaders and later as ruling elders, teaching and reading in Sunday school classes, and choosing their surnames as well as the name of the church were all part of the development of southern Presbyterian missionaries to enslaved persons. All of these facts combined with a continued and long-lasting relationship after Native American removal and the Civil War suggest that there was something distinct and unique about the way Presbyterians conducted Native American missions, missions to enslaved African Americans, and post–Civil War race relations.

Presbyterians were not as historians have declared an afterthought in the work of missions to enslaved persons. In contrast they might provide nineteenth-century models of promoting integrated worship, pushing for ecclesiastical reforms, engaging in interracial worship, and might even push modern conversations about racial reconciliation, ecclesiastical integration, and racial healing and solidarity movements. In contrast Southern Presbyterian missionaries to enslaved persons might also be innovators in creating second-class church memberships for African Americans, segregating worship on Sunday morning, and ongoing racism within White churches. While the overall numbers of congregants may have been fewer than those of the Baptists or Methodists, the Presbyterians also provided examples of missions and missionaries to the enslaved in the antebellum South that were unique. Presbyterianism lent itself to a depth of theological inquiry, ecclesiology, and biblical study that pushed Girardeau's position on ecclesiastical reform. Other denominations without the benefit of in-depth theological training before circuit riding or church planting were perhaps more vulnerable to cultural captivity.

Evaluation of southern Presbyterian ecclesiology and the theology undergirding principles of missionary work with Native Americans and enslaved African Americans is largely missing from historiography. Despite Donnelly's work to manumit enslaved African Americans in Rocky Creek, T. C. Stuart starting the first multiethnic churches on behalf of South Carolina in north Mississippi, Charles Colcock Jones's legacy as the father of missionaries to enslaved persons, as well as Adger and Girardeau's creation of one of the largest churches for enslaved African Americans in the US South, the Presbyterians of South Carolina have not received enough attention in their roles as missionaries to enslaved persons. They have also not received enough attention for their ecclesiological segregationism, which left a tremendous impact on the southern landscape through creating second-class churches for enslaved African Americans and laid the blueprints and moral justification for the region into continuing racial segregation on a larger scale. Missions to enslaved persons in South Carolina are distinct and their missionaries have been overlooked as innovative individuals who were simultaneously pushing for expanded ecclesiastical reform and ecclesiastical segregation. This history also needs to be placed into the larger contexts of American, southern, and African American history as well as American religious history so that a fuller understanding of the broad range of southern race relations in the church is better understood. To grasp the complex roles of religion and race in the history of the South a fuller understanding of Presbyterian missionaries to Native Americans and enslaved African Americans brings forth a more complex and complete picture.

Finally both autonomous congregations of Native Americans after removal and of enslaved African Americans after emancipation played pivotal roles in the provision of leadership for each community. The remnant ecclesiastical spaces of former missions continued to serve as respites from an often-hostile White environment in the last half of the nineteenth century and into the first half of the twentieth century. There is little doubt that the Presbyterian missionaries to Native Americans and enslaved African Americans of South Carolina assisted in establishing an ecclesiastical leadership base from among Native American and African American communities and helped create a legacy of engagement, education, civil activity, and service. These leaders, as early as Dinah and the Colbert family in the 1820s, to Zion's "leaders" in the 1850s, who later served as elders in 1869, guided both Native American and African American communities in South Carolina through removal, Reconstruction, a violent Jim Crow era, and a revolutionary civil rights period.

The leadership abilities, education, and experience in race relations proved to be vital tools in combating a hostile southern White community that sought to deny rights to Native Americans and African Americans into the mid- and even late twentieth century. The roles that Rocky Creek, Monroe, Jones's mission work, and Zion played in helping to establish this base of ecclesiastical leadership that promoted political activity and provided an important ecclesiastical space for community amid a difficult time period cannot be underestimated. Education and leadership development also played a substantial role in the lives of the various Native American nations as well as African American communities throughout the latter half of the nineteenth century and into the twentieth century.

As Don Mathews has reminded us, "This is not to deny that forms of Protestant Christianity were used to create a means of social integration, leadership selection, and ideological expression. There is much evidence that they did. But black religion was as much a creation of the slaves themselves as it was a gift of the white man. Jones could not create his biracial community because it expected too much of the white man and too little of the black."[28] Indeed this leadership base was just as much the result of Native American and African American creation as it was of the missionary's work. Developing a leadership base among Native American and African American Presbyterians in South Carolina was partly due to White missionaries creating those spaces but mostly due to the enslaved and Native peoples who chose to use what was provided to improve their situations.

Before Chickasaw removal and before the Civil War, throughout occupation of reservations in Oklahoma, and throughout Reconstruction, Christian missionary men and women worked alongside and cultivated relationships with populations of Indigenous people as well as enslaved African Americans. While slave missions in South Carolina were fundamentally biracial, Native American missions were multiracial. Enslaved African Americans belonging to the Chickasaw were also vital members of these multiracial, ecclesiastical communities. These multiracial communities and complex relationships within these communities reveal human beings from various racial, cultural, and religious backgrounds struggling to communicate, to know one another, and to make some sense of their changing worlds. In many ways it was not unlike our twenty-first-century efforts to overcome divisions of race, religion, and culture. Studying the experiences of these mission communities can help navigate the multiracial dimensions of our own national identity.

Some have interpreted missionaries as only imperialistic entities. Missionaries only living among Native Americans and African Americans attempted to proselytize them to Christianity to dominate, acculturate, and indoctrinate with a westernized, highly individualistic view of education and religion. From this perspective both enslaved African Americans and Native American peoples were robbed of their own religious traditions, their children stolen and sent to boarding schools away from the bosom of community and kinship—all to dominate them or make them culturally speaking more "civilized."

This interpretation robs both the White missionaries and Native American and African American members of these churches of agency. All three communities made decisions that at times ran counter to the prevailing notions and openly challenged or violated the racial status quo. Native Americans and African Americans seized opportunities presented to them to improve their lives and the lives of their children. White missionaries sometimes wrestled with and challenged the expectations of the racial ecclesiastical hierarchy and perhaps even whether the institution of enslavement was the best system for labor. Sometimes these missionaries made decisions that supported the status quo, and other times openly challenged them. These actions present a much broader and more complex understanding of interracial religious communities in the nineteenth century and complicate our understanding of history through the complexity of human relationships.

It is easy to write off missionaries as little more than well-meaning imperialists, but a closer inspection reveals relationships of immense complexity. This position may only serve to weaken our understanding of antebellum US history, African American history, Native American agency, interracial relationships, church history, and the missionaries themselves. More important this view robs us of hope for future racial reconciliation, solidarity, and unity within ecclesiastical structures. That there were glimmers of reform provides hope. In the long arc of history, and while the work is slow, perhaps we can push those glimmers into bright shining beacons. A hope that can trace its roots in surprisingly harmonious interracial missionary communities two hundred years ago provides modern churches with a precedent, a history, and an identity that work that has started can be picked up once again. To know that Southern religious history once fostered not only fellowship but also ecclesiastical reform among races means that perhaps the twenty-first century southern Presbyterian church can once again pick up the baton, learn from the mistakes of the past, and help to create a beloved community that reflects God's love.

Missionaries to enslaved African Americans and Native Americans sacrificed much. They suffered limited career opportunities, familial isolation, and cultural ostracism, acting in some cases as the only White advocates for enslaved African Americans and as mediators of Native American rights with government agents. Missionaries occupied a difficult and tenuous middle ground. They were often torn between loyalty to their own region and the state as well as a concern for the people they served. Historian Ernest Trice Thompson described their commitment, noting that they

> renounced titles and estates to engage in the work; most of them were of finished scholarship and refined habits . . . They faced all manner of privation merely for the sake of making some portion of the world a better place in which to live, or to improve the condition of a fellow mortal, no matter how unworthy the latter may have been considered in the esteem of mankind.[29]

Perhaps we can begin by walking through and dealing with a horrific past. We should not gloss over our history or neglect to repair its offenses. But we should also look to the past for examples of somewhat peaceful and positive interactions that give us hope and cause us to pause to begin the work toward a genuine and lasting reconciliation and solidarity. We need to look at history and expose its problems but also claim and celebrate moments of meaningful coexistence as touchstones that can lead us forward. Perhaps the lives of T. C. Stuart, Thomas Donnelly, Charles C. Jones, John Adger, and John Girardeau as well as the lives of the Colbert family, Dinah, Paul Trescot, William Price, Jacky Morrison, Samuel Robinson, William Spencer, John Warren, and Jonathan Gibbs can provide examples of Christian men and women who while deeply flawed also made decisions that complicate our understanding of religion in the US South. The members of these mission churches provide examples of communities who sought opportunities for humanity and dignity in an institution filled with degradation. These members and later ruling elders, persevered, served, taught, preached, ministered, and cared for their own families while laboring under the dominance of enslavers. They would see freedom in 1865 and use these spaces to assert their rights to education, a political voice, and economic uplift. The missionaries, while no doubt paternalistic and deeply flawed, could in some way provide a historical model for what it looks like to challenge entrenched, unjust institutions as well as examples of what can happen when we remain silent and sit by as the wolves come in to ravage the flock. May we all strive to be good shepherds.

ACKNOWLEDGMENTS

There are many people who and institutions that I wish to thank for the completion of this manuscript who have supported my research, thinking, and writing over the years. A scholar incurs many debts along the way and is supported by many. I would first like to thank my mother Martha Westbrook Pickett and my father Otis Moncure Pickett III for instilling in me a love of history. Both parents studied, loved, taught me about, and talked about history often so the study of it came very naturally. I was not pressured to study in a "more employable" major, and my parents allowed me to pursue my passion. This is a gift that a lot of folks do not have. Thank you and I love you both, Mom and Dad, for this gift. They nurtured my interest at the dinner table and in political discussions and made sure historical site visits were common in our travels. Most of all both taught me to love my fellow humans and to care about my community, state, and nation. They also taught me to respect others and to empathize and as much as possible advocate for them and treat them with respect and dignity in the process. Thank you for your investment in me and all that you sacrificed so that I could be a professional historian. I am a product of you both. Thank you for always telling me you love me, that I am smart, and that you were proud of me. I have learned that not a lot of children are told this, and I am privileged to call you Mom and Dad.

I also was the product of some wonderful teachers. I had some truly great social studies teachers in elementary, middle, and high school. Mrs. Fetner taught me to love reading and writing; she "published" my first book, which was a helicopter version of *Top Gun*, in fourth grade. The Reverend Callie Walpole at Bishop England High School in Charleston, South Carolina, taught me Spanish and how to be a good human being who cares for his or her community. Mrs. Renee McCrae at Trinity Collegiate School in Florence, South Carolina, was an amazing US history teacher and presented me with the 1995 History Award. As an aside . . . awards matter. When I was contemplating whether I had what it took to get a PhD in history I came across that award one day and thought "you know what, I can do this. I have been doing it my whole life." William and Mary Durst were a constant source of encouragement at Bishop England High School and pushed me to read the works of C. S. Lewis, J. R. R.

Tolkien, and Christian history. The Reverend Herman Robinson at Trinity International Ministries in Charleston, South Carolina, taught me about African American history and the importance of an oral tradition. Mrs. Herron taught me English and allowed me to write about *Les Miserables* and religion, Donna Logan introduced me to dystopian novels and stirred my imagination, Bill Runey is the only person on this earth who has ever made me love math (geometry), and he extended his instruction onto the coaching field. For the first ten years of my career I trained social studies teachers, and I will say that this group plays one of the biggest roles in our society for the next generation learning to engage history.

History was in the very water I drank in Charleston, South Carolina. My summers were spent on Sullivan's Island long before Hurricane Hugo and before it became a posh haven for America's wealthiest citizens to have second or third homes. Back then very few homes had air conditioning, most people lived on the island year-round, and I spent many of my days at the Fort Moultrie Museum watching the documentary and reading the exhibit notes all because it was one of the few air-conditioned spaces on the island. My friend Vernon Burton always says, "two things changed the US south: the voting rights act and air conditioning." Both are true.

My aunt Lark was an intellectual force. She was the first in our family to earn a PhD, and she and my uncle Dan took me on trips to Italy, Spain, and France during their summer vacations. They were teachers and used their summers to travel, often taking young cousins in our family along. Their son, my cousin Ian, worked in South Africa just after apartheid and wrote me letters about the work he was doing to teach people to vote and help bring that country together. He is one of my heroes and has always helped me see the connection between historical study and its important link to work we must do in the present to be active agents in history. I am indeed the beneficiary of many special people acting intentionally in my life. My aunts and uncles on both sides of my family were always supportive, kind, engaging, and nurturing of my interests. Both sets of grandparents are heroic for different reasons. One served in WWII and Korea, was a medical doctor (Otis M. Pickett, Jr.) and another (Robert Alexander Westbrook) served in Korea and was an agricultural education teacher, educator, farmer, and business owner. Mostly, I thought they hung the moon because of how they loved others and how others were drawn to them. My grandmothers, Ruth and Martha, saw and lived through most of the twentieth century and both were sources of love, support, and teaching me how things were. One of the great honors of my life was coming home to work at Clemson and saying the prayer at my grandmother's ninetieth birthday in Monticello, South Carolina. Home, land, history, culture, food, language, and laughter in the South have always been important to me and my family has played a central role in shaping me and this book.

Clemson University played a very important role in my scholarly development, and that continues to this day. Drs. Paul Anderson, Rod Andrew, Bruce Ransom, William Steirer, Laura Olson, Keith Morris, Edwin Moise, James Burns, Alan Grubb, Don McKale, Richard Saunders, Steven Grosby, and Nancy Hardesty at Clemson were amazing professors who challenged my thinking and writing at the undergraduate level. They are incredible and innovative professors and scholars. These individuals supported me, instilled in me a passion and desire for the study of history and religion, and played tremendous roles in becoming the kind of historian, teacher and writer that I am today. Further, Dr. Jerry Reel modeled a love of institutional history and Clemson history, and I would not be where I am today without his commitment to Clemson's history and to teaching it so passionately and eloquently to Clemson students over the years.

At Clemson, I met my amazing partner, spouse, and wife, Julie Thome. Julie was in the honors college, had served as the student founder of the ring ceremony at Clemson, and was serving as the cochief of staff to the first female student body president in Clemson's history, Rita Bolt. The book is dedicated to her as I have always called her "Jules." Through Julie I met Peggy and Tom Thome (my in-laws). They have cared for us in ways too many to mention and they have supported Julie and me in times of financial hardship and in times of plenty. They have always encouraged me to pursue my dream of being a professional historian and have supported us every step along the way. They both love history. Peggy offers the best history tour one can get of Aiken, South Carolina, and Tom has become very involved and passionate about history and racial justice in Aiken. They are wonderful examples of service, of a loving fifty-plus year marriage, and are the best in-laws a son-in-law could ask for. I love you both and thank you for your support of almost twenty-five years. I am also deeply thankful as an only child to have a brother and a sister in Eric and Eloise Thome. I love you both and thank you for how you have always supported me, coming to my presentations and encouraging me every step of the way. The Thome family members are some of the finest people I know.

I thank Covenant Theological Seminary for supporting me in pursuing an MA in theological studies and letting me take church history independent studies with Drs. Sean Lucas and David Calhoun. I am indebted to Sean and

David for introducing me to nineteenth-century Presbyterian history and to helping guide me throughout seminary and into graduate school in history. Sean, this book started because of you and research papers I wrote for you at Covenant Seminary in 2004–2005. Thank you for nurturing and guiding me down this road. I am also thankful to Wayne Sparkman, director of the PCA Historical Center and Archives, who allowed me to work as a graduate assistant in the archives. I gained much valuable knowledge and experience from Wayne and am thankful for him and the important work he is doing to preserve the history of Presbyterianism. Drs. Greg Perry, Jack Collins, Anthony Bradley, Michael Williams, Jerram Barrs, and David Chapman also played a tremendous role in my education at Covenant. They taught classes that challenged me deeply while encouraging and nurturing my love of history, theology, Greek, civil religion, and apologetics. I would not be the kind of scholar of religious history I am today without my educational experiences in seminary. These experiences helped me better understand the people I write about because they too had a seminary experience. To go through that experience myself helps me as I reflect upon what shaped their own worldviews and experiences.

The College of Charleston and The Citadel, my hometown institutions at which I attended basketball camp and summer camps as a child, were the places I continued my graduate studies in history through their joint MA in history program. I would like to thank Dr. Bernard Powers and the College of Charleston for offering me a graduate assistantship at the Avery Center for African American History and Culture. Bernie, this would not be a publication if you had not brought me to CofC and given me a great opportunity. Thank you for your feedback on my thesis and for being a friend and mentor throughout my entire career. I am thankful for Dr. W. Scott Poole, who served as my thesis adviser and was a terrific mentor and friend. As an adviser Scott Poole was incredible. He helped prepare a section of my thesis for a journal publication and was always available to discuss ideas and help with revisions. His careful attention as an MA adviser was second to none. Drs. David Gleeson, Jeffrey Diamond, Christophe Boucher, Blain Roberts, and Marvin Dulaney worked with me and supported me throughout this time as professors, mentors, and friends. I would like to thank my colleagues Mary Jo Fairchild, Kolo Rathburn, Miles Smith, Timothy Fritz, David Dangerfield, Kate Jenkins, Ramon Jackson, Charles Wexler, and Jason Farr for their encouragement, support, and important work over the years. I am so proud that many of us have gone on to earn PhDs, MLIS degrees, and other terminal degrees and succeeded in our respective fields. Many of us have earned tenure-track positions at great institutions or wonderful jobs in museums and archives across the state and country. We all continue to write and research, and I am so proud to know you all. It was a special group. I would also like to thank the Colonial Dames Powder Magazine Scholarship, the Charleston Scientific Cultural and Educational Fund, Mr. Charlton DeSaussure, Joe Riley, and the Avery Center for their financial support in helping me obtain my MA in History.

I thank the University of Mississippi Department of History for offering me assistantships, graduate instructorships, and travel support to pursue a PhD in history. I would also like to thank the UM Graduate School for a dissertation-writing fellowship. Drs. Charles Reagan Wilson, Ted Ownby, Robbie Ethridge, and Nancy Bercaw were wonderful to work with as a dissertation committee, and I appreciate all their work in guiding me through the process and offering edits and feedback on the dissertation. Thanks to Ted for connecting me with the St. George Tucker Society and for all you did to support my work over the years. Dr. Ethridge played a huge role in some of this research being published in the journal *Native South*. She is one of the most amazing people I have worked with, and her feedback on Native American experiences makes this book more robust and interdisciplinary in bringing an ethnohistoric and anthropological lens to the work. I am also indebted to the work of Dr. Susan Glisson and the William Winter Institute for Racial Reconciliation. Susan is one of my heroes, and she supported me to present this research at the John Hope Franklin Conference on Racial Reconciliation as well as the Duke Divinity Summer Institute on Racial Reconciliation. I am so honored to have an article in *The Southern Quarterly* about her work alongside Governor William Winter in Mississippi, and her expertise in applying history to racial healing is second to none. Thank you to Dr. Darren Grem and Jimmy Thomas for their friendship and work on my chapter on Girardeau and the Lost Cause in *Southern Religion, Southern Culture: Essays Honoring Charles Regan Wilson*. Thank you to Drs. Sheila Skemp, John Neff, Douglas Sullivan-Gonzalez, Deirdre Cooper Owens, Marc Lerner, Jarod Roll, Charles Ross, Charles Eagles, Elizabeth Payne, and Chiarella Esposito for their support, wonderful classes, and encouragement. Thank you to Dr. Patrick Alexander for encouraging me and being my friend. I love teaching in prison with you, my brother. Helping cofound the Mississippi Prison to College Pipeline with you was one of the greatest programs of which I have ever been a part in my career.

I would like to thank Dr. Charles Reagan Wilson who was my adviser, friend, and scholarly model. I was one of Charles' final PhD students at UM before he retired. He is everything a person could want in an adviser. Someone once told me not to just look for the best scholar in an adviser but the best scholar you can find who is also a kind person. I got the best of both worlds. Charles's friendship, support, guidance on my dissertation, and subsequent manuscript was a source of constant encouragement. I am not sure there is a better history PhD adviser in the country, a better historian, a better mentor, or a finer gentleman. Thanks for leading the way, Charles! I am a big fan and always will be.

I thank my graduate student colleagues at UM: Evan Nooe, Miller Bill Boyd III, Amy Fluker, Tony Klein, Greg Richard, Rob Krause, Ryan Fletcher, Amanda Nagel, and Ben Guest. Many thanks also go to Drs. Kim Hartman, Susan McClelland, Rosemary Oliphant-Ingham, Ann Monroe, Amy Wells Dolan, and the Department of Teacher Education in the School of Education at the University of Mississippi who supported me financially and allowed me to teach courses in their department all throughout graduate school as a graduate instructor. Dr. Ellen Foster, a true friend and mentor, was incredibly supportive along the way in helping me navigate a different academic terrain while nurturing my interest in history, geography, and social studies. I will never forget her kindness and support. It was amazing to be a faculty member in the department and to work with wonderful colleagues like David Rock, Joel Amidon, Lane Gauthier, Mark Ortwein, Andy Mullins, Jim Payne, and William Sumrall. You all made me feel so welcome and were wonderful colleagues.

I also thank many scholars who had a tremendous impact and input on this manuscript. Thank you to Luke Harlow and his colleagues at the University of Tennessee for reading sections of the manuscript and pushing me to think in new ways. Thank you to Charles Irons for his kind feedback and thoughts. Many thanks to Don Mathews for always helping me process and think about C. C. Jones. At the St. George Tucker Society meeting in 2010, Bertram Wyatt-Brown was sitting in the audience and breathing through an oxygen mask. He was taking copious notes as I was presenting, and afterward he walked up and handed me a paper that said "Otis: I think your work will make its mark in Southern scholarship. Grand research, eloquent prose, excellent structure. What more could one ask? I would be honored if asked to write a comment for the dust jacket when it appears in print. Best wishes, Bert." I thought I would melt right then and there. I am saddened by Don's and Bert's passing and wish they were still here to help me. Perhaps we will meet again one day on some blissful shore. Thank you to Regina Sullivan for reading and offering thoughts. Thank you to my Tucker friends Trae Welborn, Pete

Slade, David Dangerfield, David Moltke-Hansen, Charles Joyner, Beth Barton Schweiger, Doug Thompson, Jay Richardson, Tammy and Matthew Byron, Jim Farmer, Jay Langdale, Robert Greene, Sarah Gardner, Ken Startup, Carolyn Renee Dupont, Trudier Harris, Ted Delaney, Larry MacDonnell, and Matthew C. Hulbert for always being there to support, work on drafts, discuss the book, and help me think through everything related to this history.

Thank you to the archives and teams of archivists for helping me conduct research over the years. I am especially thankful to the PCA Archives and Historical Center in St. Louis, Missouri; the Avery Center for African American History and Culture in Charleston, South Carolina; the South Caroliniana Library at USC; the South Carolina Historical Society; and the good folks in Archives and Special Collections at Addlestone Library at the College of Charleston. Thank you to Archives and Special Collections at the University of Mississippi in Oxford, Mississippi, and the Mississippi Department of Archives and History in Jackson, Mississippi. Thank you to the University of Oklahoma Western History Archives in Norman, Oklahoma, and the Oklahoma Department of Archives and History in Oklahoma City. Many thanks to Columbia Theological Seminary in Decatur, Georgia, and to the wonderful folks at RTS Jackson for giving me access to their special collections reading room and the Blackburn papers for the years I lived in Clinton, Mississippi. I am most indebted to Wayne Sparkman at the PCA Archives for introducing me to Alexander McCleod. Special thanks to Graham Duncan at the South Caroliniana for his patient support for many years and Georgette Mayo at the Avery Center for her insights. Mary Jo Fairchild at CofC is second to none, and Jennifer Ford was amazing to work with at UM. Thank you all for your help in researching what would become this book.

Thank you to my fellow scholars in the Conference on Faith and History and at CCCU schools across the country. Thank you to Beth Allison Barr (and the Anxious Bench for letting me write for you), Kristin Kobes Du Mez, John Fea, Mark Noll, George Marsden, John D. Wilsey, Darin Tuck, Paul Thompson, Chris Gehrz, Blake Ball, Jay Green, Trisha Posey, and Karen Johnson. Your work as faithful scholars and truth tellers is inspiring to me daily. Thank you for sharing your work over the years, for coming to hear me present at the CFH, and for being "flying buttresses and pillars" (thank you, Lisa Clark Diller) all these years.

Thank you to friends at Mississippi College who encouraged me to keep at it, especially Steven Patterson, Martha Hutson, Jonathan Randle, Patrick Connelly, Glenn Antizzo, Harry Porter, Evan Lenow, Chris Weeks, Kirk Ford, and Ivan Parke. Thank you to Dr. Blake Thompson for your friendship, encouragement, and support. I would also like to thank Dr. Stuart Rockoff at the Mississippi Humanities Council for its financial support of teaching in prisons and to Randy Akers at the South Carolina Humanities Council. It is so great to advocate for the humanities with you over the years as partners and board members.

Thank you to my editor Ehren Foley and the University of South Carolina Press for their long interest in this work and their ongoing support and commitment despite many years of heavy teaching loads, losses, moves, and sparse times to write. Thank you for believing in this book and for helping "shepherd" it to completion.

Thank you to my Presbyterian History Posse: Jemar Tisby, Bobby Griffith, Ansley Quiros, Brian Franklin, Malcolm Foley, Alicia Jackson, Bo Morgan, David Irving, Nick Pruitt, and Bob Elder. Y'all were always there for me to help process this history and pushed me to continue. It has been an honor to present with you and alongside you at the CFH and the PCA General Assembly. Thank you for your friendship and willingness to speak truth even when it was difficult.

Thank you to Vernon Burton for being a wonderful friend, colleague, and encourager to get this published. Vernon was in the audience at the South Carolina Historical Association the first time I presented a paper on this topic back in 2008 and has pushed and encouraged me ever since. I am honored to call him a friend, mentor, and now colleague at Clemson University who has been my constant advocate and chief encourager. The SCHA ended up publishing a section of this work, and I most thankful to the editorial committee and peer reviewers with *The Proceedings* who named that chapter the "South Carolina Historical Association's Best Article from a Graduate Student in *The Proceedings*, 2010–2012" Award.

To all my friends and supporters at Clemson University: Thank you. Thank you to Provost Bob Jones and Dean Chris Cox for giving me the freedom to research and write. Thank you to Allen Wood, Paul Lewis, and Thomas Austin for holding me accountable to write every week and for praying for me. Thanks to the Department of History for binging me on board as an affiliated scholar. Thanks to George Petersen, Dave Fleming, Brooke Whitworth, and the Department of Teaching and Learning at Clemson for bringing me on the faculty and giving me a teaching home. Thank you to my fellow colleagues in the libraries at Clemson University for making room for a university historian and for offering me a tenure-track role as an assistant professor of libraries. Thanks especially to Renna Redd and my colleagues the associate deans (Shamella Cromartie, Ariel Turner, and Elias Tzoc). Thank you to my awesome team in the Department of Historic Properties including Naomi Gerakios Mucci, James Bostic, Mairead Downes, Kristen Fink, Dominick Bucca, Charleigh Sprawls, Helena Harte, Eli Kernaghan; y'all rock. It is so awesome to be on your team. Thank you to Dr. Rhondda Thomas for your amazing work. To everyone on the Archives and Special Collections team at Clemson University, especially Drs. Nick Richbell, Tara Wood, Sean Baker, Carl Redd, Jim Cross, Olivia Brittain, Emily Shelton, and Laurie Varenhorst for putting up with me while I was writing this and enduring the "southern word of the day." Y'all are an amazing group of folks to come in every day and with whom to work. You are more than that. You are like family.

James Bostic, this book couldn't have gotten done without you. You carved out the time, created space, encouraged, and supported me through it. Thank you. You changed my life by coming to Clemson. I will never forget your advocacy, accountability, and pushing me every day. You are one of the best things that has ever happened to me in my career and the best operations manager, chief of staff, and colleague a person could ask for. I am forever grateful to you and appreciate you so much. I am excited to see where your journey as a historian will take you.

DeSean Dyson, thank you for always believing in me and encouraging me to write and get this out there. You and I have spoken together and put this book into practice in Charleston, South Carolina; Charlottesville, Virginia; Jackson, Mississippi; and all over the South. Thanks for doing this work with me. I love you, brother. I love that we have been able to be and do this work together as brothers. Thank you for being my family. Excited to see what we will do together in the future.

Thank you to all my students at the University of Mississippi, Mississippi College, Gordon Conwell, and Clemson University over the years who have listened to me talk about religion and the discussions we have shared because of this research in and out of class. I would like to thank Mark Rushing, Cade Barlow, Jerry Ainsworth, Bryan Hendricks, Camryn Bruce, Mason Fahy, Solomon E. Zinn, Anthony P. Causley-Jackson, Austin King, Sarah Grantham, Emilee Robbins, Tiki Broome, Stephen Griffin, Sophie Abuzeid, Kaleb Jefcoat, Cami Phillips, Nathan Morris, Zach Ashcraft, Shay Gregorie, Patrick Schlabs, James Ritchey, Austin LaBrot, Aaron Boersma, Jonathan Kettler, and Drake Terry. There are so many others. There are thousands. Please forgive me if I left you out.

To my faith communities and church families at Fort Hill Presbyterian Church, Clemson Presbyterian in Clemson, South Carolina; Two Rivers in Charleston, South Carolina; Christ Presbyterian Church in Oxford, Mississippi; and Redeemer Church in Jackson, Mississippi; the Alliance for Mission and Renewal, The Old Stone Presbyterian Church Board; and the Girardeau Society. Thank you for being the hands and feet of Jesus to me and my family. Thank you especially to Reverends Jimmy Agan, Phil Stogner, Curt Presley, Les Newsom, Mike Campbell, Elbert McGowan, Rob Porter, Bryan Counts, and Laura Conrad. You shepherded me and my family well as I was thinking through this history and writing it. Redeemer Church, thank you for working so hard to model a multiethnic community. I will never forget my time among you from 2013–22. You cared for us so well in the loss of our sweet daughter Sadie Margaret, you were an honor to be a member of, and it was a great honor you called me as an undershepherd and ruling elder. Thank you for your willingness to hear me talk about issues of race in the church and difficult history in the denomination. Thank you to many of these churches and others in the PCA for hosting me for conferences on race and history, Sunday schools, and lectures on these topics. Thanks to the PCA for letting me present on these topics at Pre-GA history conferences and seminars and for inviting me to serve on the Race and Ethnic Reconciliation Ad-Interim Committee for the denomination. It is my hope that this research makes us all better and allows us to see the past more clearly so we can make a better future.

I want to thank Rick Hove, Barry Bouchillion, and my Faculty Commons friends in CRU for supporting our first and second Charleston Pilgrimage during which we got to walk through this history and use it to help bring unity, peace, and understanding on issues of race and the church to bear in a difficult time in American history (2016–20). I cannot thank you enough for doing that, Rick. CRU was investing in this work when it was not popular to do so. For that CRU should be commended as should Rick Hove.

Thank you also to Mitch Landrieu, Scott Hutcheson, and the team at *E Pluribus Unum* for supporting me with the first Eminent Scholar Award from EPU in 2022–23 and for supporting my podcast *Purpose that Prevails*, which examines many of the questions contained in this book. All the guests on that podcast have left a tremendous impact on me, my life, and my career. Thank you to Jenniger "Bingo" Gunter, Sam Perry, Howard and Kellie Brown, Dr. Robert P. Jones, Dr. Russell Moore, and all the incredible folks who helped produce like J. T. Tittle and his incredible team at Next Chapter Podcasts. I am thankful for my good friend and cohost Thomas Austin for your long support and encouragement. Excited to see where this podcast takes us.

To my scholarly communities at the St. George Tucker Society, the Conference on Faith and History, the Southern American Studies Association, the Southern History of Education Society, the South Carolina Historical Association, the Mississippi Council on the Social Studies, the Southern Historical Association, and my friends at the OAH and AHA: Thank you for giving me spaces to present my work over the years; share it with other scholars; and for offering me encouragement, thoughts, edits, criticism, and feedback to continue honing my work. The field of history is truly blessed with some wonderful people, and I have known many of them in my short career through attending and presenting at these conferences.

To my amazing dog Marcel Ledbetter Pickett who always loved me and put her head in my lap when she could tell I had a bad day. Dogs are the best, and every historian/author/writer needs one.

I want to thank my family. Thank you to my incredible children Martha Jane Caroline Pickett, Otis Westbrook Pickett Jr., and Thomas William Pickett. One of the great joys of my life has been being your father. Being a father has meant sometimes focusing less on my academic research and writing, but this was necessary and important to be with you, love you, shepherd you, and be your dad. That is the great honor of my life. The book is also better for having waited and not rushed to publication. The maturing process and time to think and work through the argument has made the manuscript better. Thank you for putting up with all my talks, teaching, travel, and for enduring all the informal "history lectures" you received over the years. I hope one day you will understand how your own history has shaped you and how broader forces in history have shaped who we are as a people. Also your local history and your family shape you. Don't be ashamed of who you are. Learn about who you are and try to make the world a better place. I know that you will. You are each special, unique, and wonderful people, and I see pieces of me and your mother in each of you. At different times in your life I was working on what would become this book. Martha Jane, the first months of your life I was putting the finishing touches on my thesis; Otis, when you were born, I was just starting my dissertation; and Thomas, you came right after I finished my dissertation. I was honored to help raise y'all in Oxford, Mississippi; later in Clinton, Mississippi; and now here in Clemson, South Carolina. Your smiling faces, laughs, warmth, and voices bring me great joy. I know you will do incredible things, and I cannot wait to sit back and watch. I love you. May God bless you and always be with you wherever you go. May you also find work that is as satisfying to you as being a historian has been for me.

Julie, my everything, this book is dedicated to you and the ways you shepherd my heart, soul, and mind and is written in your honor. I would not have become a history major if it were not for you. I would not have made it through two master's degrees and a PhD if it were not for you. I would not have made it through being a graduate instructor, clinical assistant professor, assistant professor, tenured associate professor, university historian, clinical assistant professor again, affiliated scholar, tenure-track assistant professor again, and living this life if it were not for you. We have been through a lot: broken backs, sickness, the death of a child, broken teeth, every medical issue one can imagine, and not only have you gotten more beautiful, I fall in love with you more every day. You have walked so faithfully with me through it all. You daily make me a better person, and you are the absolute love of my life. There is no one else, only Jules. I love you my sweet, wonderful, amazing, beautiful wife.

NOTES

Introduction: Southern Religion and Domestic Missions to Enslaved Persons

1. Joshua 4:1–7 (English Standard Version Bible).

2. Luke 15:6 (English Standard Version Bible).

3. Presbyterian Church in American, *Book of Church Order.* Lawrenceville, GA: Presbyterian Church of America: ch. 8-1.

4. Revelation 7:9 (English Standard Version Bible).

5. Sean Michael Lucas, *For A Continuing Church: The Roots of the Presbyterian Church in America* (Phillipsburg, NJ: P&R Publishing, 2015).

6. Racial Reconcilation (2002). https://pcahistory.org/pca/studies/race.html; Personal Resolution on Civil Rights Remembrance (2015), https://www.pcahistory.org/topical/race/2015_Personal%20Resolution%20on%20Civil%20Rights%20Remembrance.pdf.

7. The PCA called for a committee to write a report on racial and ethnic reconciliation to the forty-sixth General Assembly. The report contains a survey from over five thousand pastors and ruling elders in the denomination on their views on race. The report was accepted in omnibus at the forty-sixth General Assembly in Atlanta, but members of the committee were called "critical race theorists, communists, radicals and progressives," which are all considered pejorative terms in the PCA. https://resources.pcamna.org/resource/report-on-racial-and-ethnic-reconciliation/.

8. Acts 20:29–30 (English Standard Version Bible).

9. Luke 4:18–20 (English Standard Version Bible).

10. Baird transcript (2015). https://www.pcahistory.org/topical/race/2015_Baird_transcript.pdf.

11. Report on Racial and Ethnic Reconciliation (2018). https://resources.pcamna.org/resource/report-on-racial-and-ethnic-reconciliation/

12. The Christian believes that before regeneration or rebirth a person is a slave to sin, is not free, and is a child of wrath. Christians, especially Presbyterians in the nineteenth century, believed that one could only truly be free in Christ. This is one of the reasons why Presbyterians took up the missionizing of slaves in the early to mid-nineteenth century. They truly believed that they were liberating the souls of enslaved Africans and thus doing something socially aware and just. However they either did not recognize, were culturally captive to, or simply ignorant of the fact that they were simultaneously desiring to free people from sin yet keeping them enslaved in body. This is not consistent with Christianity. This is instructive for Christians and all human institutions today that we can say we believe one thing and yet live in a way that completely contradicts those principles and be completely blind to it.

13. Anne C. Loveland, *Southern Evangelicals and the Southern Order* (Baton Rouge: Louisiana State University Press, 1981), 245–46. Loveland forged a three-pronged conceptualization of enslaved persons missions. Before this work it was widely believed that enslaved Africans worshipped either in white-led mixed churches or in "chapels" set up on larger, more rural plantations. Loveland also pointed out that some congregations created actual separate congregations for the enslaved Africans themselves. These types of churches were rare throughout the 1830s and 1840s according to Loveland, and many early missionaries such as James O. Andrews and Charles Colcock Jones opposed this idea of separation in worship. However into the 1850s the model of the church built separately for enslaved Africans was a collective "decided improvement" over the models that tended to be more laborious for the missionary to enslaved persons. Finally Loveland did an excellent job of pointing out the various ways in which an individual could work as a enslaved persons missionary. According to Loveland they were not all puppets of the planter class, nor were they all anti-enslavement progressives. However some did seem to be more passionate about working with enslaved African Americans. An enslaved persons missionary who perhaps was trying to mitigate the effects of enslavement believed that Christianity was liberating of the soul. This type of missionary moved in two separate spheres of influence to placate southern whites while also working to alleviate the condition of enslaved African Americans.

14. There are so many historiographical threads running throughout this study that it is too difficult to limit the scope of the work to only one historiographical discussion. Therefore, to better engage in an ongoing historical dialogue, this work fits best under the broad historiographical category of southern religion. However, the historiographical framework for this research fits within a period of the nineteenth century, from 1802 to 1874, specifically focusing on antebellum southern religion, race, and mission spaces. Focusing the historiographical scope to the antebellum South from 1802 to Reconstruction is necessary because it places the study in a particular framework under a two very broad lenses: antebellum southern religion and religion in the South during Reconstruction. It is necessary to have some understanding of the religious context of the South during Reconstruction since the research carries the relationships forged in multiracial antebellum mission churches beyond the Civil War and into the Reconstruction. Further the institution of enslavement is so dominant in the antebellum southern landscape and plays such a vital role in southern religion during this period that the religion of enslaved African Americans and the historiography of slave missions are central to understanding the context of domestic Presbyterian missionaries in South Carolina. Certainly there are multiple other historical discussions that touch on this topic, but antebellum southern religion with a particular focus on the southern religious frameworks of enslaved African Americans and Native Americans is a lens that best fits for the purposes of this work.

15. John Boles, ed. *A Companion to the American South* (Malden, MA: Blackwell Publishing, 2004), ch. 10. See also Randy Spark's "Historiography of Southern Religion," in

Interpreting Southern History: Historiographical Essays in Honor of Sanford W. Higginbotham, eds. John Boles and Evelyn Thomas Nolen (Baton Rouge: Louisiana State University Press, 1987), 156–57. In this historiographical essay focusing on antebellum southern religion, Randy Sparks noted that the entire notion of southern religion was built on an idea of "southern exceptionalism: that there is a unique region called the South with a distinctive history worthy of examination on its own terms." As the field of southern history developed over time, so has its importance in a national Atlantic world and global perspectives. For Sparks southern religion has been an integral part of the developing global South. Indeed as Sparks mentioned, "the importance of religious institutions and refugees within it, offers exciting possibilities for the integration of southern religious history into a larger, more comprehensive theoretical framework." Sparks saw the colonial era placing the South as an important sphere in European religious history, the Atlantic world as well as linking it to Spanish South America and the British West Indies. Therefore a multireligious Atlantic world was the context that linked Europe, South America, and Africa to the United States South. This world informs and helps create the context for Charleston, South Carolina as a home for Barbadian planters, Anglicans, and large numbers of enslaved Africans. Sparks corroborated for southern religious history what historian Jon Butler argued about American religious history in *Awash in a Sea of Faith:* that a transatlantic focus was absolutely *sine qua non* for understanding the history of religion. Part of this focus was the close cultural connections between the Americas and Europe, the conscious attempt on the part of the Americans to follow European models, as well as the "overwhelmingly derivative" nature of American society. However the role of western Africa, the experiences of enslaved people in the British West Indies, and the influence of the Spanish in early South Carolina with Native Americans also played a tremendous role on the religious landscape of South Carolina. Both Sparks and John Boles place the beginning of historical attention to southern religion in the 1960s. Kenneth K. Bailey, Samuel Hill, and John Boles all began publishing works on southern white Protestantism and southern churches in crisis and revival in the mid- to late 1960s. The field of southern religion has grown tremendously over the last several decades as scholars continue to place the American religious experience into larger and more comprehensive frameworks. Virtually no limits will exist to understanding, tracing, and conceptualizing the impact of southern religion throughout the last four hundred years in an Atlantic and even global context.

16. Charles R. Wilson, ed. *Religion in the US South* (Jackson: University Press of Mississippi, 1985), 41–44. This work was adapted in part from C. Eric Lincoln's larger work *Race, Religion, and the Continuing American Dilemma* (New York: Hill and Wang, 1984.). Charles Reagan Wilson edited a collection of essays with chapters from John Boles, Samuel Hill, Edwin Gaustad, and J. Wayne Flint entitled *Religion in the South*, which is a collection of essays that came out of the Porter L. Fortune Chancellor's Symposium on Southern History Series at the University of Mississippi and published

through the University Press of Mississippi. This book positions religion in the South as a powerful force adding to the region's distinctive culture. The focus was on different time periods, the history of evangelicalism, religious diversity of the South, the social gospel in the South, politics and religion, and even geographical distributions of religious groups. The article most pertinent to this book is C. Erin Lincoln's article on missionary efforts among enslaved African Americans in the US South. Lincoln makes the argument that "by the 1840s the missionary movement among the slaves had the support of most of the denominational churches. The Methodists were most zealous, closely seconded by the Baptists, with the Presbyterians and Episcopalians active but less prominent in the plantation ministry." Lincoln's argument is largely connected to the Charles C. Jones model of preaching to the enslaved African Americans on plantations, and he mentions it being "considered by most white clergyman to be a contemptible ministry, if not an actual abuse of the calling." He does not focus at all on the Presbyterian style but largely examines Methodist and Baptist missions due to the large numbers of attendees. While this is true the Southern Presbyterians tended to "out punch their weight" with theological ability, education, and influence in terms of thought and ideas. Because they were a smaller denomination their impact was theological, writing systematic theology and offering commentaries on the Bible. Southern Presbyterians created unique mission churches with their own theology, ecclesiology, and implantation of that academic work into church life. This makes southern Presbyterians worthy of their own examination on this topic. However Lincoln's discussion of the invisible church, autonomous African American congregations, and African American ecclesiastical community are very important to the corpus on works on slave missions.

17. Beth Barton Schweiger and Donald Mathews *Religion in the American South: Protestants and Others in History and Culture* (Chapel Hill. University of North Carolina Press, 2004). Beth Barton Schweiger and Don Mathews also contributed an edited collection of articles on the topic and nature of southern religious history titled *Religion in the American South: Protestants and Others in History and Culture.* In this book several authors who focus on southern religion such as Paul Harvey, Jon Sensbach, Jerma Jackson, and Emily Bingham examine the development of religion across the US South through three centuries from the early eighteenth century up to the civil rights era.

18. Charles Irons, *The Origins of Proslavery Christianity: White and Black Evangelicals in Colonial and Antebellum Virginia* (Chapel Hill: University of North Carolina Press, 2008). This book plays a tremendous role in shaping the field of southern religious history particularly on the ways in which whites and enslaved African Americans shared religious worship spaces in the colonia era. While whites and African Americans prayed together, sang together, worshipped and heard many of the same sermons as well as attended similar church functions, Irons argued that the white Protestant owners of enslaved persons became the chief and most virulent defenders of

race-based chattel enslavement. Irons also argued that it was enslaved African American evangelicals and their actions that helped shape the nature of pro-enslavement doctrine. When enslaved people participated in different churches, rejected colonization, and promoted autonomous congregations, their actions displayed to white enslavers that the need to control the actions of enslaved people was necessary and defended biblically.

19. Other important works pertaining to religion in the South and the important role of African Americans include Albert Raboteau, *Slave Religion: The "Invisible Institution" in the Antebellum South* (New York: Oxford University Press, 1978); Albert Barnes, *The Church and Slavery* (New York: Negro University Press, 1857); William G. McLoughlin, ed. *The American Evangelicals 1800–1900* (New York: Harper and Row, 1968); John B. Boles, *Black Southerners, 1619–1869.* (Lexington: University Press of Kentucky, 1983); Robert M. Calhoon, *Evangelicals and Conservatives in the Early South, 1740–1861* (Columbia: University of South Carolina Press, 1988); David B. Cheesebrough, *Clergy Dissent in the Old South, 1830–1865* (Carbondale, Southern Illinois University Press, 1996); Kenneth Moore Startup, *The Root of All Evil: The Protestant Clergy and the Economic Mind of the Old South* (Athens: University of Georgia Press, 1997); Edward R. Crowther, *Southern Evangelicals and the Coming of the Civil War* (Lewiston, NY: E. Mellen Press, 2000); Samuel S. Hill, *Southern Churches in Crisis Revisited* (Tuscaloosa: University of Alabama Press, 1999); *One Name but Several Faces: Variety in Popular Christian Denominations in Southern History* (Athens: University of Georgia Press, 1996); Samuel S. Hill, ed., *Varieties of Southern Religious Experience* (Baton Rouge: Louisiana State University Press, 1988); Donald G. Mathews, *Religion in the Old South* (Chicago: University of Chicago Press, 1977); E. Brooks Holifield, *The Gentlemen Theologians: American Theology in Southern Culture 1795–1860* (Durham, NC: Duke University Press, 1978); James D. Essig, *The Bonds of Wickedness: American Evangelicals against Slavery, 1770–1808* (Philadelphia: Temple University Press, 1982); Charles Reagan Wilson, ed., *Religion in the South* (Jackson: University Press of Mississippi, 1985); Victor B. Howard, *Conscience and Slavery: The Evangelistic Calvinist Domestic Missions, 1837–1861* (Kent, OH: Kent State University Press, 1990); Mitchell Snay, *Gospel of Disunion: Religion and Separatism in the Antebellum South* (New York: Cambridge University Press, 1993); John R. Mckivigan and Mitchell Snay, *Religion and the Antebellum Debate over Slavery* (Athens: University of Georgia Press, 1998); Paul Harvey, *Freedom's Coming: Religious Culture and the Shaping of the South from the Civil War through the Civil Rights Era* (Chapel Hill: University of North Carolina Press, 2005).

20. John Boles mentioned in *Masters and Slaves in the House of the Lord* that some ministers in biracial churches "placed too much emphasis on the 'slaves-obey-your-master' homily and thereby neglected to preach the gospel in its fullness often sought an alternative worship experience." Other important monographs of slave missions include Milton Sernett, *Black Religion and American Evangelicalism: White Protestants, Plantation Missions, and the Flowering of Negro Christianity 1787–1865* (Metuchen, NJ:

Scarecrow Press, 1975) and J. Morgan Kousser and James M. McPherson, eds., *Region, Race, and Reconstruction: Essays in Honor of C. Vann Woodward* (New York and Oxford: Oxford University Press, 1982). Some important articles on slave missions include, Carlton Hayden, "Conversion and Control: Dilemma of Episcopalians in Providing for the Religious Instruction of Slaves, Charleston, South Carolina, 1845–1860," *Historical Magazine of the Protestant Episcopal Church* 36 (March 1967: 35–61), Timothy Reilly, "Slavery and the Southwestern Evangelist in New Orleans (1800–1861)," *Journal of Mississippi History* 41 (November 1979): 301–18, George C. Whately, "The Alabama Presbyterian and His Slave, 1830–1864," *Alabama Review* 13 (January 1960): 40–51. Helpful dissertations include Donald B. Touchstone, "Planters and Slave Religion in the Deep South," PhD diss., Tulane University, 1973, Marjorie Jordan, "Mississippi Methodists and the Division of the Church over Slavery," PhD diss., University of Southern Mississippi, 1972 and Thomas Erskine Clarke "Thomas Smyth: Moderate of the Old South," ThD diss., Union Theological Seminary, Richmond, 1970.

21. Rhys Isaac, *The Transformation of Virginia, 1740–1790* (Chapel Hill: University of North Carolina Press, 1999) and Robert M. Calhoon, *Evangelicals and Conservatives in the Early South, 1740–1861* (Columbia: University of South Carolina Press, 1988). Two particularly important works on these topics include Rhys Isaac's *Transformation of Virginia, 1740–1790*, and Robert M. Calhoon's *Evangelicals and Conservatives in the Early South*. Isaac's *Transformation of Virginia, 1740–1790* is a fascinating look at the religious, political, and social revolutions in eighteenth-century Virginia that led to a transformation of class, religious affiliation, and social order. To understand southern religion from the late eighteenth century to the mid-nineteenth century, Robert M. Calhoon's *Evangelicals and Conservatives in the Early South* shifts the focus beyond the colonial experience and into the nineteenth century. Calhoon's *book* is an investigation of southern evangelicalism as a belief system that could sustain itself within the conservative political environment of the Old South. Like Isaac's work, Calhoon's argument about the impact of religion on the South and of the South on religion informs the discussion of nineteenth century missions to enslaved Africans and Native Americans. Indeed, in many ways, the mission churches were countercultural spaces, but the churches also served as places in which southern values shaped the culture.

22. Sylvia Frey and Betty Wood, *Come Shouting to Zion: African American Protestantism in the American South and British Caribbean to 1830* (Chapel Hill: University of North Carolina Press, 1998). This reciprocal process was an overarching theme of this book. Making acculturation reciprocal was a key point for Frey and Wood because they believed that if it was not reciprocity then the African Americans were not active agents in participating in Christianization. Additionally Frey and Wood presented a responsible contribution of the roles of women in the African American church. They stated that the role played by African American women was critical in "the formations of revival culture, in the creation of affective ritual worship, in the

establishment of institutional foundations of the early black church, and in the dissemination of religious values within and between generations."

23. Donald G. Mathews, *Slavery and Methodism: A Chapter in American Morality, 1780–1845* (Princeton, NJ: Princeton University Press, 1965); *Religion in the Old South* (Chicago: University of Chicago Press, 1977); H. Shelton Smith, *In His Image but . . . Racism in Southern Religion, 1780–1910* (Durham, NC: Duke University Press, 1972); Albert Raboteau, *Slave Religion: The "Invisible Institution" in the Antebellum South* (New York: Oxford University Press, 1978); Eugene Genovese, *Roll, Jordan, Roll* (New York: Vintage Books, 1972); Kenneth K. Bailey, "The Post-Civil War Separations in Southern Protestantism: Another Look," *Church History*, XLVII (December 1977); Timothy John Nelson, "Every Time I Feel the Spirit: Religious Experience and Religious Ritual in an African American Congregation," PhD diss., University of Chicago (1997); Edward J. Blum and W. Scott Poole, *Vale of Tears: New Essays in Religion and Reconstruction* (Macon, GA: Mercer University Press, 2005); Mark Kelly Tyler, "Bishop Daniel Alexander Payne of the African Methodist Episcopal Church: The Life of a 19th Century Educational Leader, 1811–1865," PhD diss., University of Dayton, (2006).

24. Important works in Presbyterian history as well as Presbyterianism's role in African American history as well as in South Carolina include John B. Adger, *My Life and Times, 1810–1899* (Richmond, VA: Presbyterian Committee of Publication, 1899); Henry Alexander White, *Southern Presbyterian Leaders* (New York: Neale Publishing, 1911); Ernest Trice Thompson, *Presbyterians in the South,* 3 vols (Richmond, VA: John Knox Press, 1963); F.D. Jones and W.H. Mills, eds., *History of the Presbyterian Church in South Carolina Since 1850* (Columbia, SC: R. L. Bryan, 1926); Randall Balmer and John R. Fitzmier, *The Presbyterians* (Westport, CT: Greenwood Press, 1993); William J. Weston, *Presbyterian Pluralism: Competition in a Protestant House* (Knoxville: University of Tennessee Press, 1997); James O. Farmer, *The Metaphysical Confederacy: James Henry Thornwell and the Synthesis of Southern Values* (Macon, GA: Mercer University Press, 1986); and Joseph S. Moore, *Founding Sins: How a Group of Antislavery Radicals Fought to Put Christ into the Constitution* (New York: Oxford University Press, 2015).

25. John Boles's important collection of essays on slave missions entitled *Masters and Slaves in the House of the Lord* has been important to the development of the historiography as well. Indeed, it called for historians to pay more attention to the role of religion in examining the institution of enslavement. The book also dealt specifically with biracial churches and the "white mission to the slaves." Boles showed that early owners of enslaved persons in the seventeenth and eighteenth centuries were hesitant to attempt the conversion of enslaved Africans. Like Raboteau and Genovese, he found "there was no viable religious institution to incorporate the two races into one worshipping community." It was not until the early to mid-nineteenth century, with many southerners feeling compelled to justify the institution to northern abolitionists, that there was a movement towards the religious instruction of enslaved Africans. However

Boles's exposition of slave missions painted a much different picture of slave missionaries. For instance, Boles noted the "limited emancipationist impulse" of many missionaries to enslaved persons who "tended to criticize slavery in the abstract, delineate its evils both to the slaves and even more to the whites, emphasize that slaves were persons with souls precious in the sight of God, and suggest that slavery be ended 'insofar as practicable.'" This pointed to a position that missionaries to enslaved persons were not clear-cut representatives or supporters of the institution and that there were those whose economic position even "enabled them to see blacks as potential fellow believers." Indeed Boles pointed to the expanded freedoms evident within these biracial churches arguing that, "it is still fair to say that nowhere else in southern society were they [enslaved Africans] treated so nearly as equals." Boles went on to argue that the biracial churches "offered a spark of joy in the midst of pain, a promise of life-affirming forgiveness to soften the hopelessness of unremitting bondage, an ultimate reward in heaven for unrewarded service in this world." For Boles, these biracial slave missions constituted the only avenues in which enslaved Africans experienced any sort of equality.

26. Jane Duitsman Cornelius, *Slave Missions and the Black Church in the Antebellum South* (Columbia: University of South Carolina Press, 1999); Erskine Clarke, *Our Southern Zion: A History of Calvinism in the South Carolina Low Country, 1690–1990* (Tuscaloosa: University of Alabama Press, 1996), 131; Victor B. Howard, *Conscience and Slavery: The Evangelistic Calvinist Domestic Missions, 1837–1861* (Kent, OH: Kent State University Press, 1990). Clarke, Howard, and Cornelius furthered the historiography of slave missions. Cornelius's monograph *Slave Missions and the Black Church in the Antebellum South* has been an important reexamination of the role of missionaries to enslaved persons and their interactions with enslaved Africans toward the process of Christianization. Cornelius built on Frey's and Wood's contention that Christianity was a religion in which Whites and Blacks shared reciprocity. Indeed through the interaction of Whites and Blacks, of enslaved Africans, pietistic planters, and pastors, of European interpretations of Christianity and African customs, a unique African American church came into being. "European American Christianity in the South" was "transformed by its interaction with the black church. The slave missions, with all their contradictions, were the vehicles through which this interaction took place when the black church became a reality in the years immediately before freedom." Cornelius also examined the postbellum period by looking at colonization, mass emigration, relations between the newly freed persons and their old "pastors" and the freedom that was found in the African American Church during Reconstruction. The overarching theme of Cornelius's work was that a very complex relationship existed between missionaries to slaved persons, their enslaved congregants, and the planter elite who allowed or did not allow the missionaries onto their plantations. Cornelius's missionaries were introducing slaves to print culture, advocating reading in violation of state law, and hiring Princeton-trained graduates to teach on their plantations.

Further Cornelius found that missionaries were sometimes beaten, ridiculed, and denounced as enemies of enslavement. She specifically focused on the work of Charles C. Jones, William Capers, Richard Fuller, Stephen Elliott, Basil Manly, Thomas Clay, and John Hartwell Cocke. Their work, Cornelius claimed, was "'enigmatic' because studying their contradictions is fascinating, but perplexing." Indeed "conclusions about the white missionaries' motives and accomplishments are difficult to state in simple terms; the goals of the slave missions were primarily spiritual but also secular, with implications for freedom, power, and control." Cornelius built on the assertion that enslaved African Americans were active participants in "slave missions." Both African Americans and Whites served as pastors and teachers in this movement. To be sure, blacks also quickly perceived that the slave mission offered them an opportunity to create a small space in the oppressive conditions of slavery: to conduct their own meeting, to take advantage of the privileges of leadership, to seize chances for literacy, and to build the black community." Experience gained in missions to the enslaved went on to serve the leadership of the emergent African American church after the Civil War. Often the leaders of African American churches became the political, educational, and spiritual leadership of African American communities even into the civil rights movement. Missions to the enslaved, the churches that grew out of them, and early education provided by them were places that yielded racially integrated worship as well as an independent African American leadership base into the twentieth century. Also some missionaries wanted to see an end to the institution and thought like New Orleans Methodist clergyman Holland McTyeire that the "church was the only possible theatre for the slave's ambition." Cornelius spent much time in *Slave Missions* discussing the importance of Charles Colcock Jones, the "father of slave missions" and "the apostle to the Negro slaves." Jones had a tremendous influence on John Girardeau as his mentor and cousin. Indeed Jones who became "Georgia's most devoted missionary to the slaves" conducted the most groundbreaking work in missions to the enslaved throughout the South in the nineteenth century. As has been shown previously religion and enslavement have long been important historiographical themes. However while scholarship has addressed the role of missionaries to the enslaved it has not dealt exhaustively with the variance of conflicting philosophies within the body of missionaries, pastors, and lay ministers working with enslaved Africans.

27. Early historiography of southern religion includes the following publications: Kenneth K. Bailey, *Southern White Protestantism in the Twentieth Century* (New York: Harper and Row, 1964); Samuel S. Hill, Jr., *Southern Churches in Crisis* (New York: Holt, Rinehart, and Winston, 1966); Lester B. Scherer, *Slavery and the Churches in Early America* (Grand Rapids, MI: William B. Eerdmans, 1975); Samuel S. Hill, ed., *On Jordan's Stormy Banks Religion in the South: A Southern Exposure Profile* (Macon, GA: Mercer University Press, 1983); E. Brooks Hollifield, *Gentlemen Theologians: American Theology in Southern Culture, 1795–1860* (Durham, NC: Duke University Press, 1978); Charles R. Wilson, *Baptized in Blood: The Religion of the Lost Cause, 1865–1920*

(Athens: University of Georgia Press, 1980); James O. Farmer, *The Metaphysical Confederacy: James Henry Thornwell and the Synthesis of Southern Values* (Macon, GA: Mercer University Press, 1986); Christine Heyrman, *Southern Cross: The Beginnings of the Bible Belt* (New York: Knopf, 1997); Eugene Genovese, *A Consuming Fire: The Fall of the Confederacy in the Mind of the White Christian South* (Athens: University of Georgia Press, 1998); Janet Duitsman Cornelius, *Slave Missions and the Black Church in the Antebellum South* (Columbia: University of South Carolina Press, 1999); Erksine Clarke, *Wrestlin' Jacob: A Portrait of Religion in Antebellum Georgia and the Carolina Low Country* (Tuscaloosa: University of Alabama Press, 2000); Stephen R. Haynes, *Noah's Curse: The Biblical Justification of American Slavery* (New York: Oxford University Press, 2002); C. N. Willborn, "John L. Girardeau: Pastor to Slaves and Theologian of Causes," PhD diss., Westminster Theological Seminary, 2003.

28. Charles R. Wilson "Southern Religion(s)," in Richard Gray and Owen Robinson, *A Companion to the Literature and Culture of the American South* (Malden, MA: Blackwell Publishing, 2004); Steve Longenecker, *Pulpits of the Lost Cause: The Faith and Politics of Former Confederate Chaplains during Reconstruction* (Tuscaloosa: University of Alabama Press, 2023). As Charles R. Wilson argued there is a trifocal vision of religion in the postwar South. The Confederate vision grasps a divine purpose in the result of the Civil War: the purification of White southerners for a future righteous cause. The northern missionaries had a particular vision: reconciliation of North and South and conversion of White and Black southerners to a "truer" religion than they had known before the Civil War. Finally the evangelical freed people's vision created separate religious denominations from those of Whites, institutionalizing their dreams of ecclesiastical independence. The Confederate vision became the triumphant southern position in which religion was used in buttressing the Lost Cause. Confederate Veterans and the United Daughters of the Confederacy used religious rhetoric to sacralize and memorialize the Confederacy as well as the cause for which it stood. Sanctification of the Confederate experience after the Civil War became one of the orthodoxies at the heart of the southern way of life. African American religion established new denominations and orthodoxies. Freed persons withdrew from biracial churches and sought to control their own religious destinies. The folk spirituality of quarters for enslaved persons merged with organized and orthodox denominational churches. Some leaders championed a social separatism, and others expediently embraced accommodation, but "uplift" was the key orthodoxy of the Black church. Steve Longenecker, in his *Pulpits of the Lost Cause: The Faith and Politics of Former Confederate Chaplains during Reconstruction*, has made the argument that former Confederate chaplains are important figures in understanding the Lost Cause. He argues that some chaplains defended the Lost Cause and that others were more progressive and advocated theological liberalism leading into the twenty-first century. His chapter on John L. Girardeau, Moses Drury Hoge, and George Gilman Smith, "Nearer My God to Thee," puts Girardeau in the predictably conservative camp, accepting orthodoxy and

resisting religious modernization such as multiethnic worship. Longenecker argued that Girardeau was firmly consistent with the Lost Cause ideology and helped turn the tide in South Carolina toward Wade Hampton and a Democratic victory in the late 1870s. Indeed, "In small ways, then, John Girardeau was atypical . . . but in large ways he was typical."

29. Paul Harvey, *Redeeming the South: Religious Cultures and Racial Identities among Southern Baptists, 1865–1925* (Chapel Hill: University of North Carolina Press, 1997). Paul Harvey's *Redeeming the South* examined Black and White Baptists from the end of the Civil War into the 1920s. Harvey found that both denominations in these years became well-organized bureaucracies, with ministers pushing for and achieving professional status. Harvey identified tensions and contradictions such as rural church members continuing to worship in nonmodern ways, and he organized the book as corresponding studies of two Baptist groups (one White, one Black), rather than as an incorporated narrative. Harvey's model as religion providing a space for interracial interaction in the late nineteenth and twentieth century is useful when considering similar religious spaces in the early nineteenth century. Indeed the church not only provided opportunities for racial uplift in postbellum South but also in the antebellum South. The mission churches were spaces in which African Americans could take advantage of education and leadership opportunities as well as forge relationships with influential Whites, some of whom would later help them to freedom and even legitimize their ecclesiastical status by ordaining them to leadership positions in the church. At this point transitioning into an understanding of the historiography of Native Americans and religion, interracial interaction, and missions' history might help provide a framework for considering the history of Presbyterian mission stations among the Choctaw and Chickasaw.

30. Jemar Tisby, *The Color of Compromise: The Truth about the American Church's Complicity in Racism* (Zondervan, 2019) and Anthea Butler, *White Evangelical Racism: The Politics of Morality in America* (Chapel Hill, NC: University of North Carolina Press, 2021). Jemar Tisby's *The Color of Compromise: The Truth about the American Church's Complicity in Racism* suggests that white evangelicalism in the South, as well as the nation at large, connects white evangelical Christians and Protestants with a tendency to compromise on issues of human dignity and equality. Tisby displayed skillfully that a pattern of white supremacy and continuing an oppression of marginalized people of color in America was a kind of *modus operandi* within White evangelical spaces. Tisby's chapter on the southern defense of enslavement and the lead up to the Civil War confirms much of what Presbyterian missionaries in the South believed and acted upon. Anthea Butler's *White Evangelical Racism: The Politics of Morality in America* displays how central White supremacy was in southern evangelical thought. Southern pastors and theologians used the Bible to defend enslavement and during Reconstruction used the Bible to justify violence toward African American freedmen as well as removing the franchise from African American citizens. Butler makes the

argument that the long history of southern white Protestantism is one firmly rooted in racial division, racial oppression, and the rule of white supremacy and southern Whites participating in these churches adhered to the status quo.

31. Donald G. Mathews. "Charles Colcock Jones and the Southern Evangelical Crusade to Form a Biracial Community," *Journal of Southern History* 41, no. 3 (August 1975): 299.

32. There were several other anti-enslavement Presbyterian ministers in South Carolina. James Gilleland, member of the South Carolina Presbytery, was summoned and disciplined by the presbytery for preaching anti-enslavement. He appealed the case to the Synod of the Carolinas, but the synod upheld the presbytery's ruling. The synod stated that Gilleland was free to use his "utmost endeavors in private" if he desired to help enslaved persons. Another included Robert Wilson, a young Presbyterian minister who thought about leaving the state "or the ministry rather than submitting to enforced silence on slavery." In 1798, Johnathan Edwards encouraged Wilson to "remain in his office, for in private he could still assist like-minded brethren and perhaps lead younger ministers to his way of thinking." However both ministers ended up leaving South Carolina: Gilleland in 1804 and Wilson in 1805. This is in Essig's *The Bonds of Wickedness*, 119–20.

33. Otis W. Pickett, *Encyclopedia of Mississippi History*, "Stuart, Thomas C." (Jackson: University Press of Mississippi).

Chapter 1: "A Black Swan in the Flock"

1. Ernest Trice Thompson, *Presbyterian Missions in the Southern United States* (Richmond, VA: Presbyterian Committee of Publication, 1934), 137.

2. D. Faris, "Reminiscences of the R.P. Church in South Carolina," 2.9, *Our Banner* (September 15, 1875): 348.

3. Hugh Thomas. *The Slave Trade: The Story of the Atlantic Slave Trade: 1440–1870* (New York: Simon and Schuster, 1997), 203.

4. Faris, "Reminiscences," 346.

5. Eugene Genovese, *The Slaveholders Dilemma: Freedom and Progress in Southern Conservative Thought, 1820–1860* (Columbia: University of South Carolina Press, 1992), 2.

6. David Brion Davis. *The Problem of Slavery in the Age of Revolution 1770–1823* (Ithaca, NY: Cornell University Press, 1975), 523.

7. Davis, *The Problem of Slavery*, 523.

8. Lester B Scherer. *Slavery and the Churches in Early America.* (Grand Rapids, MI: William B. Eerdmans, 1975), 104.

9. Scherer, *Slavery and the Churches*, 106.

10. Davis, *Problem of Slavery*, 25.

11. Davis, *Problem of Slavery*, 25.

12. Scherer, *Slavery and the Churches*, 115.

13. David Brion Davis. *In the Image of God: Religion, Moral Values, and Our Heritage of Slavery* (New Haven, CT: Yale University Press, 2001), 189.

14. Davis, *Problem of Slavery*, 27.

15. Davis, *Problem of Slavery*, 29.

16. Davis, *Problem of Slavery*, 29.

17. Scherer, *Slavery and the Churches*, 114.

18. Davis, *Problem of Slavery*, 30–31.

19. Samuel Brown Wylie, *Memoir of Alexander McLeod, D.D.* (New York: Charles Scribner, 1855), 13.

20. Wylie, *McLeod Memoir*, 16.

21. Wylie, *McLeod Memoir*, 17.

22. Wylie, *McLeod Memoir*, 17.

23. See https://rpcna.org/trunk/page/convictions.

24. Wylie, *McLeod Memoir*, 21–22.

25. Wylie, *McLeod Memoir*, 33.

26. Wylie, *McLeod Memoir*, 26.

27. Wylie, *McLeod Memoir*, 51.

28. Wylie, *McLeod Memoir*, 52.

29. Faris, *"Reminiscences,"* 346.

30. Faris, *"Reminiscences,"* 346.

31. Faris, *"Reminiscences,"* 346.

32. Wylie, *McLeod Memoir*, 51.

33. Wylie, *McLeod Memoir*, 62.

34. Dwight Lowell Dumond. *Antislavery: The Crusade for Freedom in America* (Ann Arbor: University of Michigan Press, 1961), 80.

35. Dumond, *Antislavery*, 80.

36. Alexander McLeod, *Negro Slavery Unjustifiable: A Discourse* (New York: T&J Swords, 1802.), 4.

37. C. Vann Woodward, *The Abolitionists: Means, Ends and Motivations* (Lexington, MA: D. C. Heath, 1972.), 191–92.

38. McLeod, *Slavery Unjustifiable*, 8.

39. McLeod, *Slavery Unjustifiable*, 9.

40. McLeod, *Slavery Unjustifiable*, 9.

41. McLeod, *Slavery Unjustifiable*, 9.

42. I am taking the term "White supremacy" to mean any system that recognizes Whites as superior and in any way marginalizes people of color as inferior. Many have made the mistake that a White supremacist structure must be akin to a neo-Nazi system or a system that systematically murders any non-White person. While this is White supremacy a White supremacist system may be any system that privileges one race over another and sees one race as superior while another is inferior. It is this description that the author has in view.

43. Willard Swartley, *Slavery, Sabbath, War, and Women* (Scottdale, PA: Herald Press, 1983), 46.

44. McLeod, *Slavery Unjustifiable*, 15.

45. McLeod, *Slavery Unjustifiable*, 15.

46. McLeod, *Slavery Unjustifiable*, 15–16.

47. Some have made the argument that modern historians use race as a modern tool applied to structures and institutions, and those men of the eighteenth and nineteenth century "didn't see race" and were not "influenced by race." Nothing could be further from the truth. These men and women were absolutely shaped by racial categories and used race as a construct to force people into bondage. Modern historians are not putting race into the writings of nineteenth-century ministers or politicians. Race existed, and historians are simply pointing out how our world, our society, our structures and institutions are founded on the worldview that some were superior and others were inferior based on their race and culture. This view was widely accepted in McLeod's context, and he is clearly pointing it out in *Negro Slavery Unjustifiable*. Therefore discussing race is not a modern invention by biblically unorthodox "liberals." It was a discussion many nineteenth-century clergy were comfortable discussing.

48. McLeod, *Slavery Unjustifiable*, 16.

49. McLeod, *Slavery Unjustifiable*, 16.

50. McLeod, *Slavery Unjustifiable*, 22.

51. McLeod, *Slavery Unjustifiable*, 22.

52. McLeod, *Slavery Unjustifiable*, 22.

53. McLeod, *Slavery Unjustifiable*, 24.

jus. McLeod, *Slavery Unjustifiable*, 40.

55. McLeod, *Slavery Unjustifiable*, 38.

56. McLeod, *Slavery Unjustifiable*, 38.

57. McLeod, *Slavery Unjustifiable*, 41.

58. George Howe, *History of the Presbyterian Church in South Carolina*. (Columbia, SC: Duffie & Chapman, 1870.), 700.

59. Howe, *Presbyterians in SC*, 700.

60. Howe, *Presbyterians in SC*, 700.

61. Faris, *"Reminiscences,"* 343.

62. Faris, *"Reminiscences,"* 344.

63. Faris, *"Reminiscences,"* 345.

64. Faris, *"Reminiscences,"* 347.

65. Faris, *"Reminiscences,"* 347.

66. Faris, *"Reminiscences,"* 347.

67. Wylie, *McLeod Memoir*, 53.

68. Wylie, *McLeod Memoir*, 53.

69. Wylie, *McLeod Memoir*, 53–54.

70. Faris, *"Reminiscences,"* 348.

71. Wylie, *McLeod Memoir*, 54.

72. Howe, *Presbyterians in SC*, 707. Other family names mentioned in Faris's history include the Loughridges, the Edgars, the Wyatts, the Mortons, the Mcquistons, the Stormonts, the Rocks, the Hemphills, the Coulters, the Harbisons, the Martins, the Cunninghams, the Smiths, the Montgomerys, and the Blacks. Many of the same names are in Howe's history.

73. Faris, *"Reminiscences,"* 348.

74. Faris, *"Reminiscences,"* 348.

75. Howe, *Presbyterians in SC*, 703.

76. Faris, *"Reminiscences,"* 348.

77. Faris, *"Reminiscences,"* 348.

78. Faris, *"Reminiscences,"* 349.

79. Howe, *Presbyterians in South Carolina*, 704.

80. John Christie and Dwight Dumond, *George Bourne and the Book and Slavery Irreconcilable*. (Wilmington: Historical Society of Delaware, 1969), 66.

81. Lawrence Lesick, *The Lane Rebels: Evangelicalism and Antislavery in Antebellum America*. (Metuchen, NJ: Scarecrow Press, 1980), 3.

82. Lesick, *Lane Rebels*, 4.

Chapter 2: "The Father of Native American Missions in Western South Carolina"

1. Donald G. Mathews, "Charles Colcock Jones and the Southern Evangelical Crusade to Form a Biracial Community," *Journal of Southern History* vol. 41, no. 3 (August 1975): 299.

2. Along with Southern Presbyterians like James Henley Thornwell and Robert Lewis Dabney, who defended the institution of enslavement with an in-depth biblical defense, there were several other Presbyterian missionaries interested in race, anti-enslavement and creating opportunities for multiethnic worship in the nineteenth century. James Gilleland, member of the South Carolina Presbytery, was summoned and disciplined by the Presbytery for preaching anti-enslavement. He appealed the case to the Synod of the Carolinas, but the synod upheld the Presbytery's ruling. The synod stated that Gilleland was free to use his "utmost endeavors in private" if he desired to help enslaved persons. Another included Robert Wilson, a young Presbyterian minister, who thought about leaving the State "or the ministry rather than submitting to enforced silence on slavery." Further in 1798, Jonathan Edwards encouraged Wilson to "remain in his office, for in private he could still assist like-minded brethren and perhaps lead younger ministers to his way of thinking." However both ministers ended up leaving South Carolina: Gilleland in 1804 and Wilson in 1805. This is in Essig, *The Bonds of Wickedness*, 119–20. Presbyterian missionaries to enslaved Africans in South Carolina and Georgia such as Charles Colcock Jones, John Lafayette Girardeau, and John B. Adger created multiethnic ecclesiastical spaces, which further complicates the

role of race in nineteenth-century southern Presbyterianism and Presbyterianism in South Carolina.

3. Clara Sue Kidwell's *The Choctaw in Oklahoma: From Tribe to Nation, 1855–1970* leans on her earlier work regarding Presbyterian missionaries and sees this time period as helpful in understanding later Choctaw notions of private property. Further, Kidwell points to the tensions "between full-blood and mixed blood elements." These tensions help explain pre-removal multiracial tensions within the Choctaw nation and the complexity of a space combined with race, religion and gender. Later Valerie Lambert produced *Choctaw Nation: A Story of American Indian Resurgence*. While this work mostly focused on postremoval history and nation building, Lambert did posit the important role that preremoval Choctaw history played in developing a postremoval political order. Indeed "from the creation of the Choctaw tribe out of the crumbling Mississippian chiefdoms of the Southeast, through forced removal and allotment, the Choctaws have a long historical legacy of upheaval and resurgence that influences Choctaw culture and politics today." Most important Lambert argued that Choctaw identity was something that shifted over time, "from a more inclusive identity based on self-identification to a more tribally sanctioned identity based on legal documentation." Clara Sue Kidwell argued that the missionaries came with a spiritual intent, but the interests of the federal government tainted their teachings. As Kidwell explained, "Government policy fed white land hunger and finally to a policy of separating Indians entirely from white society, and from their lands." Kidwell's contention that while the role of the missionaries "moved full circle in shaping the lives of the Choctaw people" they were essentially turned out to be "major agents of . . . assimilation." While this is no doubt true it is also fair to say that the relationships between missionaries and Native Americans were not solely based on attitudes of assimilation. In many ways the relationships between missionaries and Native Americans existed on a sort of "middle ground" in which Choctaw and Chickasaw leaders exerted influence over the missionaries and forced them to make concessions in their policies. In 2003, Bonnie Sue Lewis built on Kidwell's work with her important *Creating Christian Indians: Native Clergy in the Presbyterian Church*. In the debate on whether a Native American could be both "Christian and Indian" Lewis decidedly assents; Christianizing largely took place through Native American Presbyterian ministers to the Dakota and Nez Perce. Lewis is a careful scholar of congregational life and does well to tease out the notion of "band organization" and its impact on the Indigenous church. Lewis points to several instances through which "many converts explicitly conceived of their new lives in terms of a separation from their non-Christian tribal members." Forming separate communities along religious lines became commonplace.

4. William G. McLoughlin's *After the Trail of Tears: The Cherokees Struggle for Sovereignty, 1839–1880* perhaps provided the most thorough social, cultural and political history of the Cherokee as they struggled to fight for autonomy throughout the antebellum era and into Reconstruction. Due to the time period and focus on the nation

before and after the Civil War McLoughlin's framework fits nicely with the Chickasaw. He also does well to trace the history of the Cherokees by synthesizing a number of historical texts on the nation while uncovering previously unused primary resources. McLaughlin's work pushes this research about the importance of trying to objectively understand the historical context of all parties involved rather than turning a very complex historical situation into a false dichotomy of "good" and "evil." His work provides a space to examine this ongoing tension. McLaughlin's treatment of missionaries among the Cherokee was more nuanced. More at home in the sphere of religion McLaughlin did an excellent job in *Cherokees and Missionaries* of displaying the complexity and distinctions of the historical cast of characters. Indeed he argued that the Cherokees were focused on "ideological and social reorientations" as a result of Christian influence as well as maintaining Cherokee religious traditions. McLaughlin also saw white missionaries' interactions with Cherokee and how these forced the missionaries to "make critical reevaluations of their own culture." This framework provided a lens through which to think about how missionaries to the Choctaw and Chickasaw were able to reflect on their own culture and what was acceptable eschewing what was not useful. To fully understand missionaries and religion among the Choctaw and Chickasaw an overview of Cherokee history is needed. In *Cherokees and Missionaries* McLoughlin for perhaps the first time in the historiography of Native American missionaries went beyond an examination of the preacher in the pulpit and into the Native Americans occupying the pews. McLoughlin reminded us that Native American indifference and outright opposition to the teachings of missionaries was common. However, those who did attend the congregations of the Moravians, Methodists, Congregationalists, and Baptists often picked and chose what they wanted to hear and believe. McLoughlin argued that few missionaries intermarried with the nation or attempted to learn Cherokee or adopt cultural patterns. Indeed the missionaries gravitated toward interacting with mixed-race Cherokees of European descent. This interaction helped tremendously in thinking about the missionaries to the Choctaw and Chickasaw. According to McLoughlin missionaries were often comfortable with cultural patterns, married into the nation, and began to soften on entrenched Eurocentric philosophies. Further McLoughlin's expansive denominational overview included the Methodist James J. Trott and the Baptist Evan Jones, both of whom fought for the rights of the Cherokee even with their own denominations renouncing their efforts. It is from McLoughlin that we understand syncretism with regard to a blending of Native American religion with Christianity.

5. In terms of early missions to Native Americans some important colonial and eighteenth-century texts have been Robert F. Berkhofer's *Salvation and the Savage: An Analysis of Protestant Missions and American Indian Response, 1787–1862;* Francis Jennings's *The Invasion of America: Indians, Colonialism, and the Cant of Conquest*; James P. Ronda's "The Sillery Experiment: A Jesuit-Indian Village in New France, 1637–1663"; and "We are Well as We Are: An Indian Critique of Seventeenth-Century

Christian Missions." Each of these texts pointed to early Christian activity among Native Americans using both Catholic and Protestant examples. Similar to Jennings's title the thrust of this historiographical argument was that missionaries were similar to other imperialistic endeavors and sought to invade, destroy, and acculturate with little regard for the theological positions of the missionaries, the interracial nature of the mission churches, and with regard for accepted interracial ecclesiastical interaction of the time period. There is some truth to this with regard to Presbyterians and early nineteenth-century missionaries, but further analysis of the aforementioned issues points toward enhanced clarity of a very complex interracial situation. Further Neal Salisbury's works "Red Puritans: The 'Praying Indians' of Massachusetts Bay and John Elliot" and *Manitou and Providence: Indians, Europeans, and the Making of New England, 1500–1643* have moved the field forward. Further important works considering the first missionaries to Native Americans in the colonial era were George E. Tinker's *Missionary Conquest: The Gospel and Native American Cultural Genocide* and James Treat's *Native and Christian: Indigenous Voices in Religious Identity in the United States and Canada*. Both texts carry similar theoretical frameworks in which the missionary was little more than a religious conquistador attempting to claim the souls of Native Americans as European explorers did with territory. Conquest, acculturation, and the indoctrination of European religion on an already existent religious community were the overwhelming themes. However Salisbury's *Manitou and Providence* provided important distinctions on how Native Americans in New England used Christianity to continue perpetuating their own communities in the face of European incursion into their society. Indeed using a hybrid Christianity with their own religious practices was one of the ways Native Americans convinced Europeans of their "civilization." The Choctaw and Chickasaw used the Presbyterian missionaries in similar ways from 1817 throughout the Civil War.

6. Theda Perdue's *Slavery and the Evolution of Cherokee Society, 1540–1866* traces the history of the Cherokee from colonialism to the mid-nineteenth century while examining how the institution of enslavement played a role in each period. Perdue found that the Cherokee adopted the culture of the Europeans to survive. Duane King's collection of essays entitled *The Cherokee Indian Nation: A Troubled Nation* shed more light on this issue of cultural survival. Theda Purdue's essay on enslavement and its transformation over time examined the slaves' role in mission churches.

7. Randy Sparks's *Religion in Mississippi* and his more general study of evangelicalism in Mississippi, *On Jordan's Stormy Bank* are both helpful. The fields of anthropology and ethnohistory, particularly the work of Robbie Ethridge, have certainly enhanced the understanding of Native American culture in Mississippi. Ethridge's works include *From Chicaze to Chickasaw: The European Invasion and the Transformation of the Mississippi World, 1540–1715* and her coedited volume *The Transformation of the Southeastern Indians, 1540–1760* have enhanced historians' understanding of how European incursions and invasions into Chickasaw country in the Southeast created

much transition across the cultural landscape and left a tremendous impact on Native American society moving into the nineteenth century.

8. Minges's *Slavery in the Cherokee Nation: The Keetowah Society and the Defining of a People, 1855–1867* pushed understanding of the impact of Christianity and mission churches on the Cherokee view of enslavement. According to Minges the Keetowah society had its own trifocal ecclesiastical relationships in which white missionaries, enslaved Africans, and Native Americans functioned within a church structure with relative equality. Daniel Littlefield's *Africans and Creeks: From the Colonial Period to the Civil War* examined the relationships among whites, the mixed-race elite, enslaved Africans, and the Creek. His findings illuminate similar relationships especially in the context of the church among the Chickasaw. Littlefield sees the federal government as well as the southern slavocracy playing a tremendous role in proliferating enslavement among the Creek and Chickasaw. Littlefield also found that racial mixing between the Whites and Creeks created a "mixed offspring" that "dominated Creek affairs, carried Anglo-Saxon values into the Creek nation, and readily accepted government efforts to 'civilize' the Creeks." Littlefield also saw racial prejudice among the Creek's "divide and conquer strategy" to keep enslaved Africans from aligning with the Creeks against them. However Littlefield found that the small number of enslavers among the Creek was minor compared to that of the Choctaw. Soon after his work on the Creek Littlefield examined the freed Africans among the Chickasaw in his *The Chickasaw Freedmen: A People without a Country*. Gary Zellar's *African Creeks: Estelvste and the Creek Nation* argued that African Creeks played important roles in the formation of cultural identity. As workers, interpreters, and even political figures these individuals left their imprint on the nation. Similar to the Chickasaws, African Creek embraced Christianity early, adopted it, and grew its teachings from their own communities to the rest of the Creek nation. Zellar examined how groups divided themselves along racial lines. Celia E. Naylor's *African Cherokees in Indian Territory: From Chattel to Citizens* builds on Daniel E. Littlefield's *The Cherokee Freedman: From Emancipation to American Citizenship*, but she did so by paying close attention to the WPA narratives and how African Cherokee actually saw themselves. Naylor argued that African Cherokee never really gained full equality within the Cherokee nation, somewhat mirroring the Jim Crow South through the exclusion of African Americans. This work explores preremoval interracial interaction and is applicable to understanding multiethnicity in mission churches.

9. James F. Brooks's *Confounding the Color Line: The Indian-Black Experience in North America* was incredibly insightful in helping historians of race understand the significance of "blood" and racial identity. Brooks's collection of essays brought fuller understanding of how the lives of enslaved African peoples became so interwoven with those of Native Americans, especially in the colonial and antebellum contexts. Both Susan Sleeper-Smith and Circe Sturm point to this racial self-awareness and identity with regard to native women marrying French traders as well as the "construction of

blood status" among the Cherokee in Oklahoma. To be sure mission schools as well as churches, are helpful spaces for examining these identities. Theda Purdue tackled issues of interracialism and biculturalism in *"Mixed Blood" Indians: Racial Construction in the Early South*. In it Perdue argues that terms such as "mixed-bloods," "full-bloods," and "mestizos" don't fully explain or help us understand southeastern Native American culture, behavior, or community. Instead of telling these single stories Perdue reminds us to think through the complexity of human relationships. She started with an examination of marriages between Indian women and European men. She found that initially they were largely on Native American terms with Native American traditions of kinship networks controlling absorption into the nation. European men largely adhered to Native American tradition and raised their children within this context. Perdue also examined why so many mixed-race children ascended to leadership within the Native American political power structure into the late eighteenth and early nineteenth centuries. She found that one's race did not necessarily create leadership opportunities. Instead there were individuals of mixed-race heritage in a variety of political circles as the position of Native Americans became more tenuous. Later Perdue found that mixed-race Native Americans came to prominence due to white European racism. Indeed those who advocated removal argued that it was only the mixed-race Indians who could be "civilized." Perdue is very helpful in thinking through the impact of racism even in the missionaries' thoughts concerning mixed-race and full-blooded Chickasaw. Circe Sturm built upon Perdue's work regarding the impact that race, culture, identity, and the "language of blood" played in postremoval Cherokee society in her book *Blood Politics*. Sturm affirmed that "blood" is a social construct of Cherokee society that Cherokees have altered over their history to fit their own needs. Sturm discussed connection of these notions with the Dawes Commission and the current application for citizenship requiring a certain degree of Indian blood and argued that "citizenship by the virtue of 'blood' is a political construction but that more traditional ways Cherokees define 'blood' in ways that are not necessarily synonymous with ancestry." This work is helpful in the role that race and racial ideology played in the mission churches and its allowance for multiple ethnicities functioning alongside one another.

10. Tiya Miles explored enslavement and mixed-race Afro-Cherokee identity in her *Ties that Bind: The Story of an Afro-Cherokee Family in Slavery and Freedom*. Miles brought to the forefront a topic that had long been neglected by the historiography: owners of enslaved persons by Native Americans. Her narrative of a Cherokee-African family helps provide some insight into this controversial dynamic. Miles "examines the changes over time in Cherokee gender roles, the matrilineal kinship system, and the Cherokee system of African slavery." The Cherokee used enslaved Africans to advance economically but also "and more importantly, as evidence of Cherokee civilization and acculturation. Cherokees wanted to demonstrate their right to exist as a sovereign nation independent of the United States." Therefore while there was an

"Americanization" of Cherokee culture, "the Cherokee Nation borrowed political systems and racial ideologies from the United States to avoid being colonized by the United States." Miles ultimately concludes that initially the Cherokee system of enslavement was more in flux than previously thought and largely reflected attitudes of equity in the Cherokee's historical relationship to human beings. Miles's work is helpful in understanding how a largely White enslavement of persons had a tremendous impact on the cultural landscape. But this perspective also robs Native Americans of their own agency and ability to maintain a cultural autonomy in the face of an Anglocentric hegemony. Indeed the Chickasaw were able to achieve syncretism in enslavement and their religious attitudes and pragmatically borrow what was helpful to them from the institution of enslavement while also negating aspects that seemed outside their own cultural value system. This framework certainly applies to how the Chickasaw used the missionaries to achieve their own, as we will examine later. Miles, along with Fay Yarbrough, continued to examine issues of race, enslavement, and the Cherokee in important recent works: *Race and the Cherokee Nation* and *The House on Diamond Hill.* Nancy Shoemaker produced a monograph addressing this issue entitled *A Strange Likeness: Becoming Red and White in Eighteenth-Century North America.* Shoemaker is particularly helpful to this work in examining religious commonality. This work contributed to an understanding of the multiracial nature of the Chickasaw mission churches and the peaceful as well as hospitable nature of the relationship between the variety of races worshipping, teaching, and learning in these spaces.

11. Clara Sue Kidwell, *Choctaws and Missionaries in Mississippi, 1818–1918* (Norman: University of Oklahoma Press, 1995), xiv.

12. Kidwell, *Choctaws and Missionaries, xiv.*

13. Kidwell, *Choctaws and Missionaries, xiv.*

14. Robert Milton Winter, *Outposts of Zion: A History of Mississippi Presbyterians in the Nineteenth Century* (Holly Springs, MS: self-pub., 2014), iii.

15. Winter, *Outposts of Zion*, iii.

16. EE. T. Winston, ed., *"Father" Stuart and the Monroe Mission* (Meridian, MS: Press of Tell Farmer, 1927). This work will be used heavily throughout the paper as the edited volume by E. T. Winston included church session records from Monroe Church, interviews with members and individuals of the church, Stuart's own letters and memoirs from 1861, as well as secondary historical narrative regarding the Chickasaw, the Monroe Mission, and the town of Pontotoc. For the sake of brevity the papers will be referred to as Winston, *Stuart* for the remainder of the paper. Most of the papers are housed at the Reformed Theological Seminary Library Rare Book Room in Jackson, Mississippi.

17. Thompson, *Missions*, 137.

18. Thompson, *Missions*, 138.

19. Winter, *Outposts of Zion*, 1.

20. Winter, *Outposts of Zion*, 1.

21. Winter, *Outposts of Zion*, 5.
22. Winter, *Outposts of Zion*, 1.
23. Winter, *Outposts of Zion*, 8.
24. Thompson, *Missions,* 141.
25. Thompson, *Missions,* 141.
26. Winter, *Outposts of Zion*, 9.
27. Winter, *Outposts of Zion*, 10.
28. Winter, *Outposts of Zion*, 10.
29. Winter, *Outposts of Zion*, 11; William C. Davis, *A Way through the Wilderness: The Natchez Trace and the Civilization of the Southern Frontier* (New York: HarperCollins, 1995).
30. Winter, *Outposts of Zion*, 26.
31. Winter, *Outposts of Zion*, 27
32. Thompson, *Missions,* 145.
33. William A. Love, "The Mayhew Mission to the Choctaws," *Publications of the Mississippi Historical Society*, vol. 11 (1910): 386–87.
34. Howe's *History of the Presbyterian Church in South Carolina.* In Winston's *Stuart*, 66. These letters were originally written for and published in the *Southern Presbyterian*, a journal of the southern Presbyterian Church throughout the late nineteenth century and up until the early twentieth century.
35. Howe's *History of the Presbyterian Church in South Carolina.* In Winston's, *Stuart*, 66.
36. E. T. Winston, *"Father" Stuart and the Monroe Mission.* (Meridian: MS: Press of Tell Farmer, 1927), 19.
37. Winston, *"Father" Stuart*, 19.
38. Winston, *"Father" Stuart*, 19–20.
39. George E. Tinker, *Missionary Conquest: The Gospel and Native American Cultural Genocide* (Minneapolis: Fortress Press, 1993).
40. Winston, *"Father" Stuart*, 20–21.
41. Thompson, *Southern Missions*, 145–46.
42. C. W. Grafton, *History of Presbyterianism in Mississippi* (Jackson, MS: papers photocopied from microfilm and bound, 1927).
43. C.W. Grafton, *History of Presbyterianism in Mississippi.*
44. Winter, *Outposts of Zion*, 46.
45. Winston, *Stuart*, 20.
46. Winston, *Stuart*, 20.
47. Winston, *Stuart*, 44.
48. Winston, *Stuart*, 44.
49. Winston, *Stuart*, 44.
50. Winston, *Stuart*, 44–45.
51. Winston, *Stuart*, 44–45.

52. Winston, *Stuart*, 45. An elder is a term in Presbyterian polity and church governance indicating church authority and leadership. The session, or group of elders, govern church business and there are normally teaching as well as ruling elders. Stuart would have been a teaching elder, and he would have shared governance of the church with the ruling elders.

53. Winter, *Outposts of Zion*, 45.

54. Winter, *Outposts of Zion*, 45.

55. William L. Hiemstra. "Presbyterian Missions among the Choctaw and Chickasaw Indians, 1845–1862" (master's thesis, University of Mississippi, 1947), 6.

56. Thompson, *Presbyterian Missions*, 146.

57. Winston, *Stuart*, 20.

58. Thompson, *Presbyterian Missions*, 146.

59. Winter, *Outposts of Zion*, 48.

60. Thompson, *Presbyterian Missions*, 146.

61. Winter, *Outposts of Zion*, 48.

62. Thompson, *Presbyterian Missions*, 147.

63. Ursula Smith, *Pioneer Women: The Lives of Women on the Frontier* (Norman: University of Oklahoma Press, 1996), 119.

64. Presbyterians use language of a mission church and a "particularized church" to display the church's autonomy. A particularized church typically has its own leadership, budget, membership, building, and recognition from a presbytery that it has gone through a process to transition from a mission church to a particularized congregation. This means the church is not dependent upon another church for its survival and can raise its own money to function as well as elect its own leaders rather than borrowing leaders from nearby churches.

65. Numerous historians like John Boles, Charles Irons, Paul Harvey, Erskine Clarke, and others have discussed the role of interracial worship in an antebellum context. But there has not been as much investigation into western frontier mission spaces as religious communities in which a white hierarchy was not as clearly established as it was in spaces like Charleston, Savannah, and Norfolk. Indeed the frontier mission space in the 1830s and 1840s saw Chickasaw and African American leadership within an ecclesiastical context while providing for and supporting white families struggling for survival.

66. Ben Robertson, *Red Hills and Cotton* (Columbia: University of South Carolina Press, 1991), 197–98.

67. This is true particularly of Presbyterian missionaries as evidenced by the work of Cyrus Kingsbury, Cyrus Byington, and T. C. Stuart among Native Americans and by John Adger, John Lafayette Girardeau, and John Leighton Wilson among Africans and enslaved African populations of Georgia, South Carolina, and in western Africa.

68. Thompson, *Presbyterian Missions*, 147. Given the fact that the Presbyterian Church commissioned Thompson to write this history one must take this comment

with a grain of salt. Thompson although an able historian would naturally want to paint Stuart in this light. However much of what we know of Stuart seems to bear out a narrative of at least a peaceable existence among the Chickasaw. We must be careful with such self-congratulation as "in the four centuries of American history there is no more inspiring chapter of heroism, self-sacrifice and devotion to high ideals than that afforded by the Indian Missions."

69. Thompson, *Presbyterian Missions*, 147.

70. Hiemstra, "Presbyterian Missions among Chickasaw," 64.

71. Winter, *Outposts of Zion*, 48.

72. Winter, *Outposts of Zion*, 48.

73. Winston, *Stuart*, 17.

74. Thompson, *Presbyterian Missions*, 146.

75. Winston, *Stuart*, 23.

76. Winter, *Outposts of Zion*, 48.

77. Winston, *Stuart*, 23–24.

78. George Howe, *History of the Presbyterian Church in South Carolina* (Columbia, SC: Duffie and Chapman, 1870), 72. These letters were originally written for and published in the *Southern Presbyterian*.

79. Winston, *Stuart*, 23–25

80. Winston, *Stuart*, 53.

81. Winter, *Outposts of Zion*, 48.

82. A session is a court of the Presbyterian Church that is typically nominated and elected by members of the congregation. A session consists of teaching elders/pastors and ruling elders who meet regularly to conduct the business of the church in a court-like "session."

83. Winter, *Outposts of Zion*, 48.

84. Winter, *Outposts of Zion*, 25

85. Winter, *Outposts of Zion*, 53.

86. Howe, *History of the Presbyterian Church in South Carolina*, 72.

87. Otis W. Pickett, "We Are Marching to Zion: Zion Church and the Distinctive Work of Presbyterian Slave Missionaries in Charleston, South Carolina, 1849–1874." *Proceedings: Journal of the South Carolina Historical Association* (Spring 2010): 91–104.

88. Winston, *Stuart*, 26.

89. Winston, *Stuart*, 25.

90. Winston, *Stuart*, 25–26.

91. Winston, *Stuart*, 34.

92. Church session records showed many enslaved Africans and individuals of African descent added as members to the Monroe Church. December 24, 1823, showed that "three black persons, John, Daniel and Rebecca, were added to the communion on examination. March 4 "Affy, a black woman. May 6 Three black persons, Agnes, Mary

and Bob were admitted. Sept 30 Two black women, Sarah and Indah, were admitted on examination. December 24, 1825 Three black persons, John, Daniel, and Rebecca were added to the communion of the church on examination." Several others joined in the mid- to late 1820s according to the session records.

93. This is not the only instance in church records of an enslaved African "owned by an Indian" being accepted for membership. July 2 showed that "Chloe, a black woman belonging to an Indian, applied for privileges to the church."

94. Winter, *Outposts of Zion*, 54–55.

95. Winston, *Stuart*, 26.

96. Although it took a bit longer for Native Chickasaw to begin to join the church, records from May 7 showed that "Molly Colbert, a native, came forward and offered herself as a candidate for admission."

97. Howe, *History of the Presbyterian Church in South Carolina*, 72.

98. Hiemstra, "Presbyterian Missions among Chickasaw," 63.

99. Winston, *Stuart*, 27–30.

100. Howe, *History of the Presbyterian Church in South Carolina*, 72.

101. Pickett, *Zion Presbyterian Church*, 96.

102. Hiemstra, "Presbyterian Missions among Chickasaw," 63

103. Winter, *Outposts of Zion*, 49.

104. Hiemstra, "Presbyterian Missions among Chickasaw," 9

105. Howe, *History of the Presbyterian Church in South Carolina*, 72.

106. Winter, *Outposts of Zion*, 49.

107. Howe, *History of the Presbyterian Church in South Carolina*, 72.

108. Winston, *Stuart*, 53.

109. Winston, *Stuart*, 39.

110. Winston, *Stuart*, 30–32.

111. Winston, *Stuart*, 34.

112. Winston, *Stuart*, 40.

113. Winston, *Stuart*, 41.

114. Albert Raboteau, *Slave Religion: The "Invisible Institution" in the Antebellum South* (New York: Oxford University Press, 1978), 15–36.

115. John R. Swanton, *Chickasaw Society and Religion* (Lincoln: University of Nebraska Press, 2006), 87.

116. Howe, *History of the Presbyterian Church in South Carolina*, 67

117. Howe, *History of the Presbyterian Church in South Carolina*, 68.

118. Thompson, *Presbyterian Missions*, 147.

119. Winston, *Stuart*, 48.

120. Winston, *Stuart*, 48.

121. Howe, *History of the Presbyterian Church in South Carolina*, 69.

122. Winston, *Stuart*, 60–62.

123. Hiemstra, "Presbyterian Missions among Chickasaw," 10.

124. Hiemstra, "Presbyterian Missions among Chickasaw," 12. In 1832, General John Coffee arranged for a land cession treaty with the Chickasaws. In 1834, there was another treaty with those who remained, and in that year the mission to the Chickasaw, as an official entity, ceased to exist. William Colbert along with William Spencer, James Hodges, Henry Love, Ishtohotopah, and James Perry, an interpreter, signed the treaty, which sent the Chickasaw west to Oklahoma. Later, Presbyterians and other denominations attempted to set up mission stations among the Chickasaw in Oklahoma, but it took years before the memory of 1832 and 1834 disappeared. That memory of betrayal despite Washington's promise to Colbert was palpable.

125. Hiemstra, "Presbyterian Missions among Chickasaw," 12.

126. Winston, *Stuart*, 56–57.

127. Winston, *Stuart*, 56–57.

128. Fred R. Graves, ed., *The Presbyterian Work in Mississippi* (Sumner, MS: Sentinel Press, 1927).

129. Howe, *History of the Presbyterian Church in South Carolina;* Winston, *Stuart*, 66. These letters were originally written for and published in the *Southern Presbyterian*, which was a journal of the southern Presbyterian Church.

130. Winston, *Stuart*, 76.

131. Winston, *Stuart*, 76.

132. Otis W. Pickett, "T. C. Stuart and the Monroe Mission among the Chickasaws in Mississippi, 1819–1834," *Native South* 8 (Lincoln: University of Nebraska Press, 2015), 63–88.

133. Winston, *Stuart*, 76–77.

134. Winston, *Stuart*, 78.

135. Winston, *Stuart*, 78.

136. Winston, *Stuart*, 78–80.

137. Winston, *Stuart*, 57.

138. Winston, *Stuart*, 57.

139. Otis W. Pickett, "Hope for Racial Healing: Rethinking Christian Missions among the Chickasaw," *Oklahoma Humanities Magazine, no.* 23 (Summer 2012).

Chapter 3: "To and Fro Like a Forest in a Storm"

1. Donald G. Mathews, "Charles Colcock Jones and the Southern Evangelical Crusade to Form a Biracial Community," *Journal of Southern History* 41, no. 3 (August 1975): 299.

2. Mathews, "Jones Crusade," 299.

3. Mathews, "Jones Crusade," 300.

4. Erskine Clarke, *Wrestlin' Jacob: A Portrait of Religion in Antebellum Georgia and the Carolina Low Country* (Tuscaloosa: University of Alabama Press, 2000), 7.

5. Mathews, "Jones Crusade," 300.

6. Janet Duitsman Cornelius. *Slave Missions and the Black Church in the Antebellum South* (Columbia: University of South Carolina Press, 1999), 78.

7. Robert Manson Myers, ed. *The Children of Pride: A True Story of Georgia and the Civil War* (New Haven, CT: Yale University Press, 1972), 12.

8. Clarke, *Wrestlin' Jacob*, 10.

9. "Docetism, (from Greek *dokein,* "to seem"), Christian heresy, and one of the earliest Christian sectarian doctrines, affirmed that Christ did not have a real or natural body during his life on earth but only an apparent or phantom one. Though its incipient forms are alluded to in the New Testament, such as in the letters of John (*such as* 1 John 4:1–3; 2 John 7), docetism became more fully developed as an important doctrinal position of gnosticism, a religious dualist system of belief arising in the second century AD that held that matter was evil and the spirit good and claimed that salvation was attained only through esoteric knowledge or gnosis." https://www.britannica.com/topic/Docetism.

10. Andover Seminary in Massachusetts and later Princeton Seminary in New Jersey.

11. Mathews, "Jones Crusade," 301.

12. Charles C. Jones to Elizabeth J. Maxwell, October 4, 1825, Charles Colcock Jones Collection, Tulane University (JCTU); Clarke, *Wrestlin' Jacob*, 11.

13. Victor B. Howard, *Conscience and Slavery: The Evangelistic Calvinist Domestic Missions, 1837–1861* (Kent, OH: Kent State University Press, 1990), 18.

14. Clarke, *Wrestlin' Jacob*, 12.

15. Charles C. Jones to Mary Jones, July 22, 1829, JCTU.

16. Mathews, "Jones Crusade," 301.

17. Jones to Mary Jones, October 5, 1829; see also Jones to Mary Jones, October 24, 1829, JCTU.

18. Charles C. Jones to Mary Jones, September 8, 1829, JCTU. Clarke, *Wrestlin' Jacob*, 13.

19. Charles Colcock Jones to Mary Jones, May 30, 1829, Sept. 8, 1829; Cornelius, *Slave Missions and the Black Church*, 79.

20. Mathews, "Jones Crusade," 303.

21. Cornelius, *Slave Missions and the Black Church*, 81.

22. Cornelius, *Slaver Missions and the Black Church*, 83.

23. Boles, *Masters and Slaves in the House of the Lord*, 6, 122.

24. Cornelius, *Slave Missions and the Black Church*, 82.

25. Matthew 7:15 (English Standard Version Bible).

26. Cornelius, *Slave Missions and the Black Church*, 83.

27. Mathews, "Jones Crusade," 303.

28. Eugene Genovese, *The Slaveholders' Dilemma: Freedom and Progress in Southern Conservative Thought, 1820–1860* (Columbia: University of South Carolina Press, 1992), 27.

29. Clarke, *Wrestlin' Jacob*, 19.

30. Cornelius. *Slave Missions and the Black Church*, 72.

31. Mathews, "Jones Crusade," 303.

32. Mathews, "Jones Crusade," 303–4. Others like Jones include William Capers, Stephen Elliott, John B. Adger, John L. Girardeau, and Thomas Smythe. Smythe battled those who sought to deny the humanity of enslaved Africans, and he would later refute the dual origin theory, which held that Africans were not of the same origin as Whites. James Henry Thornwell also recognized a need for slave missions against those that would say that Africans were "heathens." Conflict was present in the lives of these shepherds. It was a conflict that they did not know how to act upon without being cast aside socially or even fearing death. However it is this conflict and subversive behavior toward the institution that separate them from other slave missionaries. The importance of Jones was that he created a sphere that dealt with this conflict.

33. Cornelius, *Slave Missions and the Black Church*, 79–81.

34. Cornelius, *Slave Missions and the Black Church*, 8.

35. Eugene Genovese. *Roll, Jordan, Roll: The World the Slaves Made*. (New York: Vintage Books, 1974), 188.

36. Mathews, "Jones Crusade," 305.

37. Clarke, *Wrestlin' Jacob*, 36–37.

38. White, *Southern Presbyterian Leaders*, 294.

39. Genovese, *Roll, Jordan, Roll*, 260–61.

40. White, *Southern Presbyterian Leaders*, 294.

41. Eugene Genovese. *A Consuming Fire: The Fall of the Confederacy in the Mind of the White Christian South* (Athens: University of Georgia Press, 1998), 19.

42. Mathews, "Jones Crusade," 310.

43. Cornelius, *Slave Missions and the Black Church*, 138.

44. Genovese, *Roll, Jordan, Roll*, 206–7.

45. White, *Southern Presbyterian Leaders*, 295.

46. Biblical texts referring to enslaved persons obeying their masters can be found in the Ephesians and Philemon. Many pro-enslavement theologians used these texts as well as Old Testament verses in which God considered Abraham's slaves to be part of his household whom he would bless and therefore according to southern theologians approved of the institution.

47. Clarke, *Wrestlin' Jacob*, 41–43.

48. Don Mathews, ed. *Religion in the American South: Protestants and Others in History and Culture* (Chapel Hill: University of North Carolina Press, 2004), 49.

49. Clarke, *Wrestlin' Jacob*, 41.

50. Cornelius, *Slave Missions and the Black Church*, 83.

51. John Boles, *Masters and Slaves*, 9.

52. Mathews, "Jones Crusade," 306.

53. Mathews, "Jones Crusade," 313.

54. Mathews, "Jones Crusade," 306.

55. Boles, *Masters and Slaves*, 1–8

56. Boles, *Maters and Slaves*, 1–8.

57. Zion Presbyterian was perhaps the largest congregation of enslaved Africans in the entire South seating almost three thousand people in sabbath worship. Girardeau also continued to work toward ecclesiastical equality and education for free African Americans after the Civil War. More will be said on this in chapters 3 and 4.

58. Mathews, "Jones Crusade," 317.

59. Mathews, "Jones Crusade," 315.

60. There are several sources here on the idea of cultural captivity and how the church was simply held captive by the prevailing culture of racism, enslavement, and the influences of these frameworks. This perspective is not in the works of Samuel S. Hill: *Southern Churches in Crisis Revisited* (Tuscaloosa: University of Alabama Press, 1999); *Religion in the Southern States: A Historical Study* (Macon, Georgia: Mercer University Press, 1983); *One Name but Several Faces: Variety in Popular Christian Denominations in Southern History* (Athens: University of Georgia Press, 1996).

61. Mathews, "Jones Crusade," 316.

62. Mathews, "Jones Crusade," 319.

63. Most prominently was in May of 1845 in an address to the public on the religious instruction of the Blacks. This is discussed at length in Erskine Clarke, *Wrestlin' Jacob*, 100–107.

64. Smyth, *Autobiographical Notes, Letters, and Reflections* (Charleston, SC: Walker, Evans, & Cogswell, 1914), 218; C. N. Willborn, "John Lafayette Girardeau: Pastor to Slaves and Theologian of Causes," 93.

65. Adger was a long-time member, pastor, and associate minister of Second Presbyterian throughout the nineteenth century.

66. Willborn, "Girardeau," 95.

67. Clarke, *Wrestlin' Jacob*, 145.

68. By "full" I mean that while enslaved Africans were offered a membership status they still could not be nominated for the ordained offices of deacon or elder. They could not vote alongside White congregants to call a pastor or on matters related to the building, hold their session accountable in any church court, or attend or ask that a session member give them an account of the presbytery or General Assembly. These are all rights that full members in Presbyterian Churches possess.

69. Clarke, *Wrestlin' Jacob*.

70. Clarke, *Wrestlin' Jacob*, 144–45.

71. *Second Presbyterian Minutes of Session*, South Caroliniana Library, 1–2.

72. Erskine Clarke stated that the author of "Many Citizens" was no other than A. G. Magrath, who became "judge of the United States District Court and would serve as governor of South Carolina during the last days of the war. As a fire-eating judge, he would declare that the foreign slave trade was not piracy when the slave ship *Wanderer* was captured illegally selling African slaves in Georgia."

73. Willborn, "*Girardeau*," 100.

74. Clarke, *Wrestlin' Jacob*, 146.

75. Clarke, *Wrestlin' Jacob*, 147. In 1817, Denmark Vesey had been a member of Second Presbyterian Church. Vesey had maintained his membership at Second Church and there had been little to distinguish him from other black members. That was what made his memory so dangerous for the religious instruction of slaves. White ministers had all been saying that if Vesey and other conspirators had been under the influence of a white minister, there never would have been a plot. It had not prevented him from being at the center of the most dangerous insurrection planned by urban slaves.

76. Clarke, *Wrestlin' Jacob*, 147.

77. Willborn, "*Girardeau*," 127.

78. Second Presbyterian Minutes of Session, South Caroliniana Library, 9.

79. Second Presbyterian Minutes of Session, South Caroliniana Library, 10.

80. Starobin, Robert, ed. *Denmark Vesey: The Slave Conspiracy of 1822* (Englewood Cliffs, NJ: Prentice Hall, 1970), 131.

81. Willborn, "*Girardeau*," 127–30.

82. There were other slave churches in Charleston, such as Paul Trapier's Calvary Episcopal and several Methodist churches (such as Trinity or Bethel), which held over 150 classes for enslaved Africans across the city. Zion, however, was the only church to have such massively successful numbers of enslaved Africans in attendance in one single church service, the only to spend huge sums (like $32,000 for the initial plans), and to have not only classes, but African American leaders, exhorters, and teachers.

83. White, *Southern Presbyterian Leaders*, 297. The old Anson Street Mission is now the Reformed Episcopal Church attended by master blacksmith Philip Simmons, now deceased.

84. Lois Simms, *A History of Zion, Olivet, and Zion-Olivet Churches 1850–1985 Charleston, South Carolina* (Mercury MicroComputer Products: Library of Congress, 1987), 2.

85. This issue of "having a place of honors" in the seating will be dealt with at length later in the chapter.

86. Lois Simms, *A History of Zion*, 1.

87. James O. Farmer, *The Metaphysical Confederacy: James Henry Thornwell and the Synthesis of Southern Values* (Macon, GA: Mercer University Press, 1986), 220–21.

88. White, *Southern Presbyterian Leaders*, 298.

89. Clarke, *Wrestlin' Jacob*, 149–50.

90. Kevin DeYoung, "Two Cheers for the Spirituality of the Church," January 31, 2019. The Gospel Coalition.

91. DeYoung, "Two Cheers."

92. Charles Irons, *The Origins of Proslavery Christianity* (Chapel Hill: University of North Carolina Press, 2008).

93. Willborn, "*Girardeau*," 99.

94. John Adger received an honorary Doctor of Divinity degree from the College of Charleston in 1853 for his work with the enslaved African population of Charleston. Clarke, *Wrestlin' Jacob*, 151.

95. W. F. Robertson, *History of Zion Presbyterian Church.* Vertical File, Churches-Presbyterian-Zion-Olivet, Avery Research Center for African American History and Culture. It should be noted here that between 1852 and December 1853 between Adger and Girardeau the Reverend Ferdinand Jacobs filled the pulpit at the Anson Street Mission. However it is clear to most historians of these churches that Jacobs was a replacement until the presbytery could secure Girardeau from his post in the Wilton Presbyterian Church. Girardeau was on everyone's mind to take up where Adger left off. Presbyterian historian Henry Alexander White noted that Jacobs was a "faithful shepherd and preacher."

96. W. F. Robertson, *"Dr. Girardeau Devoted to Negro Work," History of Zion Presbyterian Church.* Vertical File, Churches-Presbyterian-Zion-Olivet, Avery Research Center for African American History and Culture.

97. George A. Blackburn, ed. *The Life Work of John L. Girardeau, D.D., LL.D.: Late Professor in the Presbyterian Theological Seminary, Columbia, S.C.* (Columbia, SC: The State Company, 1916), 32.

98. Clarke, *Our Southern Zion*, 108–9.

99. Clarke, *Our Southern Zion*, 195. Gullah is a recognized language and not simply a dialect. It has its roots in the Krio language of Sierra Leone and has developed over centuries from a mixture of Indigenous African tongue, English, French, creole languages, and Spanish.

100. Clarke, *Wrestlin' Jacon*, 151.

101. Robertson, "*Dr. Girardeau*," in *History of Zion Presbyterian Church, by* W. F. Robertson. Vertical File, Churches-Presbyterian-Zion-Olivet, Avery Research Center for African American History and Culture.

102. White, *Southern Presbyterian Leaders*, 300–301.

103. Clarke, *Wrestlin' Jacob*, 145.

104. *Second Presbyterian Minutes of Session,* South Caroliniana Library, 2.

105. Willborn, "Girardeau," 16.

106. Douglas Kelly, *Preachers with Power: Four Stalwarts of the South* (Great Britain: St. Edmundsbury Press, 1992), 124.

107. John L. Girardeau, *John L. Girardeau Papers, 1825–1908*, "Letter of John L. Girardeau to Miss Emily M. Girardeau," May 15, 1846. Columbia: South Caroliniana Library.

108. Blackburn, *The Life Work of John L. Girardeau,* 27.

109. Karen Stokes, "John L. Girardeau and 'Big Zion': A Forgotten Chapter in South Carolina History," *Carologue: A Publication of the South Carolina Historical Society,* vol. 33, no. 1 (Summer 2017): 12.

110. Before pastoring at Anson Street Girardeau spent a significant amount of time at Wilton Presbyterian Church as well as in Adam's Run where he employed C.C. Jones's model of enslavement missions by visiting plantations and preaching in various churches on plantations.

111. White, *Southern Presbyterian Leaders*, 301.

112. Prefatory Notes, Thomas Smyth Papers: Second Presbyterian Church Papers: Records of Anson Street and Zion Church Kept by Dr. Girardeau, collection 24, box 5, folder 6. South Carolina Historical Society.

113. White, *Southern Presbyterian Leaders*, 301.

114. Stokes, "Girardeau and 'Big Zion,'" 13.

115. Stokes, "Girardeau and 'Big Zion,'" 13.

116. Willborn, "*Girardeau*," 102.

117. Clarke, *Our Southern Zion*, 195.

118. Jones, "Work among the Negroes,". 107.

119. Minutes of Session of Zion Presbyterian Church, June 5, 1858. Today a hotel is located where the old "Big Zion" Church was. There is a small plaque in front of the hotel commemorating Zion.

120. Clarke, *Our Southern Zion*, 195.

121. It is important to note that this observation or imagining is reflective of multiple conversations that Dr. Nick Wilborn and I have had standing in front of what is now a hotel on Calhoun Street where Zion Church used to exist. We would both remark on how shocking it would have been to White eyes to see a throng of enslaved African Americans exiting a massive church structure and onto Calhoun Street in the 1850s. Both of us believe that this symbol would have been startling to the White population of Charleston for a variety of reasons.

122. Randall Balmer and John R. Fitzmier, *The Presbyterians* (Westport, CT: Greenwood Press, 1993), 73.

123. Willborn, "*Girardeau*," 102.

124. Stokes, "Girardeau and 'Big Zion,'" 13.

125. John L. Girardeau, *Unpublished Notes of His Ministry,* Thomas Smyth Papers, 16; Willborn, "*Girardeau*," 121.

126. Boles, *Masters and Slaves*, 174.

Chapter 4: "We Are Marching to Zion"

1. Zion was literally an area in Jerusalem called the city of David, 2 Samuel 5:6-9 and 2 Chronicles 5:2.

2. Zion is also used figuratively as representing God's kingdom in Psalms 125:1, Hebrews 12:22 and Revelation 14:1.

3. Conley Smith, "Churches' Histories Documented," *Post and Courier*, Thursday, December 14, 1989. Also *Exercises Connected with the One Hundredth Anniversary of Second Presbyterian Church of Charleston, SC*, in Thomas Smyth Papers: Second

Presbyterian Church Papers Collection 24, box 4, folder 9, at the South Carolina Historical Society.

4. Stokes, "Girardeau and 'Big Zion,'" 13.

5. Stokes, "Girardeau and 'Big Zion,'" 14.

6. Adger, *My Life and Times*, 173; Blackburn, "Work Among the Negroes-Part III," *Life Work of Girardeau*, 101–3; Willborn, "Girardeau," 112.

7. Whites sat in the galleries of Girardeau's church, which was perhaps another reason for the Minute Men's anger.

8. Robertson, *Dr. Girardeau Devoted to Negro Work*.

9. *Second Presbyterian Minutes of Session*, South Caroliniana Library, 6.

10. Blackburn, "Work among the Negroes, Part III," 89–90.

11. Willborn, "Girardeau," 90–91.

12. Drago, *Charleston's Avery Center*, 25.

13. Willborn, "Girardeau," 129.

14. Willborn, "Girardeau," 130.

15. Boles, *Masters and Slaves*, 14.

16. Willborn, "Girardeau," 129–31.

17. Boles, *Masters and Slaves*, 13.

18. Willborn, "Girardeau," 129–31.

19. Boles, *Masters and Slaves*, 14

20. Boles, *Masters and Slaves*, 14.

21. Girardeau also included hymn recommendations to go with catechism questions.

22. Willborn, "Girardeau," 127.

23. Willborn, "Girardeau," 127.

24. Minutes of Zion Session Presbyterian Church, October 25, 1859; Willborn, "Girardeau," 136.

25. Zion-Olivet Papers, box 1, folder 1, Avery Research Center for African American History and Culture.

26. Boles, *Masters and Slaves*, 12.

27. Boles, *Masters and Slaves*, 9.

28. Clarke, *Our Southern Zion*, 153.

29. Clarke, *Our Southern Zion*, 153.

30. Clarke, *Our Southern Zion*, 196–97.

31. Clarke, *Our Southern Zion*, 153.

32. Clarke, *Our Southern Zion*, 193. Clarke went on to state that these southern churches' roll books showed that "when a slave joined a church, only the Christian name was listed, followed by 'servant of' or occasionally 'slave of,' 'London, servant of Tho. Bennett,' 'Judy, servant of Col. I. Bryan.'"

33. Clarke, *Our Southern Zion*, 193.

34. Clarke, *Our Southern Zion*, 197.

35. Zion Presbyterian, Minutes of Session, 1856.

36. Simms, *A History of Zion*, 2.

37. Clarke, *Our Southern Zion*, 152.

38. John Berkley Grimball Collection, letter dated November 27, 1859, South Caroliniana Library.

39. Joseph B. Mack, "Work among the Negroes, Part II," in George Blackburn, ed., *The Life Work and Sermons of John L. Girardeau* (Columbia, SC: State Company, 1916), 58.

40. Blackburn, *Life Work of Girardeau*, 61.

41. Blassingame, *Slave Community*, 93.

42. Boles, *Masters and Slaves*, 10.

43. Boles, *Masters and Slaves*, 7.

44. Quoted in John W. Blassingame, ed., *Slave Testimony: Two Centuries of Letters, Speeches, Interviews, and Autobiographies* (Baton Rouge: Louisiana State University Press, 1977), 642.

45. Blackburn, *Sermons*, 4–5.

46. Boles, *Masters and Slaves*, 10.

47. Clarke, *Our Southern Zion*, 235. Clarke went on to state, "With the end of the war, they met the challenge of drawing their congregations together once again, of forging new traditions and institutions as freed people, and of walking together along the difficult road between two worlds. That road, they believed, for all its ambiguity and difficulty, was the only road that led toward a still distant freedom and justice."

48. Boles, *Masters and Slaves*, 14.

49. Clarke, *Our Southern Zion*, 196.

50. While Clarke argued that much of this work at Zion enforced a "move toward the vision of a well-ordered, class-stratified society," I am not quite convinced that this education and development of a leadership within the African American community lent itself to the prevailing notions of order in Charleston of the 1850s. It seems that it turned those roles upside down in the sense that enslaved African Americans were not really dependent on Girardeau for a number of church duties and supplied their own leaders to teach, conduct funerals, and hold classes. Clarke's entire argument about Zion was that it reinforced Thornwell's notion of "regulated liberty" and was strictly paternalistic in that it "talked about the duties of and rights of masters as masters and the duties and rights of slaves as slaves, each in their own concrete place, each according to their God-given responsibilities." Indeed "it helped to legitimize the present order –with whites in control- even as it called for a new order. It provided a sense of identity, and it stood as a preserving counter-vision to the challenges of revolution, antislavery, and the disintegrative forces of the modern world. Thornwell's vision, in other words, was not only utopian, it was also profoundly ideological. Both the utopian and the ideological elements were held together in a single conceptual framework. That framework—a fusion of the world view and the ethos of the low country Reformed community—with its primary metaphor the middle way, led to the Anson Street church and to the experiment in paternalism that followed." This is a compelling

argument. However, how is it paternalistic to provide education and help create a leadership base for enslaved African Americans chosen from among and within their own community in a society that was trying to destroy any sense of a liberating leadership? How was it paternalistic to make one's own race (Whites) sit in the galleries while enslaved Africans were given the "place of honor" in the pews before the pulpit at Zion? Why were the Anson Street work and the work at Zion drawn along the same paternalistic lines when it was running counter, in a multitude of ways, to other paternalistic slave missions throughout the South? The work at Zion cannot be written off as only paternalistic when it is so distinct from slave missions and slave churches that did not acknowledge humanity, create an community-led leadership base, or acknowledge surnames in the roll books.

51. Boles, *Masters and Slaves*, 14.

52. John L. Girardeau, "Conscience and Civil Government: An Oration Delivered before the Society of Alumni of the College of Charleston on Commencement Day, March 27th, 1860," Pamphlets, College of Charleston Special Collections (Charleston, SC: Evans & Cogswell, 1860), 8–11.

53. John L. Girardeau, "Conscience and Civil Government," 8–11. It must also be noted that this type of missionary to enslaved persons existed in various places throughout the South. One example is of the Reverend James Smylie of Mississippi who "devoted his time exclusively to the religion of the negroes," and he "organized large classes for study and trained them to recite the whole of the Westminster Shorter Catechism. Smylie also prepared a catechism long before C. C. Jones's effort. This is in White, *Southern Presbyterian Leaders*, 304–5.

54. Boles, *Masters and Slaves*, 18.

55. Matthew 21:13 (English Standard Version Bible).

Chapter 5: "Still in Its Bud in Our Every Heart"

1. Boles, *Masters and Slaves*, 5, 17.

2. Boles, *Masters and Slaves*, 5, 17.

3. Boles, *Masters and Slaves*, 17.

4. Bowen Family Papers, Letter from John L. Girardeau to Clara Bowen from Camp on Sullivan's Island, Dated April 5, 1864. South Caroliniana Library, 2–3.

5. Bowen Family Papers, Letter from John L. Girardeau, 2–3. Girardeau spent time in Wallace's Brigade Infirmary where he wrote, "the two great armies of Lee and Grant are lying at ease, like two lions with their heads upon their paws eyeing one another. Sometimes a poor fellow is brought back shot through the head, but this is now of comparatively rare occurrence, as the men are a little more conservative than they used to be." Continuing with a rather humorous story of the difficult context of preaching in trenches, he wrote, "A few Sabbaths ago I had occasion to preach to the Holcombe Legion in the trenches. It had been tolerably quiet along the lines for some time previously, but after I had been preaching some time one of our batteries for some cause or

another fired a shot." In the midst of the firefight, Girardeau kept preaching to the men and wrote, "This drew a rapid fire of mortar shell from the enemy. They came whizzing and popping about us in proximity too near to be altogether pleasant. But after that I managed to keep straight. Imagine a preacher with pointed finger and earnest voice laying down a sentence and just in the midst of it, the man at whom he was intensely looking, steals a glance up into the sky, then dodges down and WHIRRR – POW! finishes the sentence." Girardeau continued to preach despite the disturbances and even asked the commanding officer if he should omit the hymn as the men were clumped together and the chances of them being hit were greater. The officer replied "'No, sir, you might as well go on!' So we did and sung while the mortar shells were roaring."

6. Thomas H. Law, "Pastorate after the War" in George Blackburn, ed. *Life and Work of John Lafayette Girardeau* (Columbia, SC: State Company, 1916), 133.

7. Willborn, "Girardeau," 177.

8. Willborn, "Girardeau," 179.

9. Stokes, "John Girardeau and 'Big Zion,'" 15.

10. Prefatory Notes, Thomas Smyth Papers.

11. Blackburn, *Girardeau*, 136. Erskine Clarke also wrote that "a bitter debate followed in which Gibbs sought under the Civil Rights Act to secure the building for the black members; the white trustees appealed to General Rufus Saxton of the FreedMen's Bureau for the return of the building; and John Adger appealed to the Northern General Assembly to oppose Gibb's action. The military authorities finally acted, returning the building to the white trustees with the stipulation that a school for blacks operated by the Northern Assembly be allowed to continue on the ground floor of the building. Girardeau, who had been preaching to the white congregation at Glebe Street, returned to the pulpit at Zion in January 1867, while continuing to be the pastor of the white Glebe Street congregation." Clarke, *Our Southern Zion*, 226.

12. Powers, *Black Charlestonians*, 210

13. Clarke, *Our Southern Zion*, 226. Clarke went on to state that African Americans came to Zion "from churches all over the city: From First Scots and Second Presbyterian, from Methodist Churches and Baptist Churches, and from First Colored Presbyterian (the congregation of Gibbs). They came from country churches too: Johns Island and Edisto, James Island and Wadmalaw. A few came from other parts of the state: from Sumter and Columbia and Spartanburg. Most, however, came not by transfer from another church but on examination, joining a congregation for the first time. They were all people on the move, working out the meaning of their new freedom. Within two years, four hundred blacks had joined Zion, and many more were worshipping there every Sunday."

14. Prefatory Notes, Thomas Smyth Papers.

15. Blackburn, *Girardeau*, 134.

16. Powers, *Black Charlestonians*, 209.

17. Powers, *Black Charlestonians*, 209.

18. Letter from Paul Trescot to John Girardeau, dated July 27, 1865, microfilm roll 160, South Caroliniana Blackburn Papers at the South Caroliniana Library.

19. Powers, *Black Charlestonians*, 210–11.

20. Willborn, *Girardeau*, 194.

21. Clarke, *Wrestlin' Jacob*, 178.

22. Willborn, "Girardeau," 190–91.

23. Willborn, "Girardeau," 192.

24. Willborn, "Girardeau," 193.

25. John Lafayette Girardeau. "Ecclesiastical Relations to Freedmen," *Southern Presbyterian Review* 18 (1866): 2.

26. Robert L. Dabney. *Discussions: Volume 2* (London, England: Banner of Truth Trust, 1891), 2:204.

27. Girardeau, "Ecclesiastical Equality of Freedmen," 4.

28. Girardeau, "Ecclesiastical Equality of Freedmen," 4.

29. Girardeau, "Ecclesiastical Equality of Freedmen," 4.

30. Girardeau, "Ecclesiastical Equality of Freedmen," 14.

31. In the twenty-first century in a multiethnic Presbyterian church in Jackson, Mississippi, there were still members who believed that an African American could not pastor White people. This mind-set has been in southern ecclesiastical bodies since Reconstruction. The individual who said this later repented and ended up sitting under the preaching and authority of an African American PCA teaching elder named Reverend Mike Campbell.

32. Girardeau, "Ecclesiastical Equality of Freedmen," 10.

33. Girardeau, "Ecclesiastical Equality of Freedmen," 5.

34. Girardeau, "Ecclesiastical Equality of Freedmen," 14.

35. Girardeau, "Ecclesiastical Equality of Freedmen," 5.

36. Lucas, *Dabney*, 145.

37. Lucas, *Dabney*, 24.

38. Lucas, *Dabney*, 101.

39. Lucas, *Dabney*, 31.

40. Lucas, *Dabney*, 102.

41. Robert L. Dabney. *A Defense of Virginia and the South* (Harrisonburg, VA: Sprinkle Publications, 1977), 145.

42. Eugene D. Genovese. *A Consuming Fire: The Fall of the Confederacy in the White Christian South* (Athens: University of Georgia Press, 1998), 95.

43. Lucas, *Dabney*, 135.

44. Smith. *In His Image*, 266.

45. Smith, *In His Image*, 239.

46. Smith, *In His Image*, 239.

47. Dabney, "Ecclesiastical Equality of Negroes," 200.

48. Dabney, "Ecclesiastical Equality of Negroes," 201.

49. Dabney, "Ecclesiastical Equality of Negroes," 202.
50. Lucas, *Dabney*, 146.
51. Dabney, "Ecclesiastical Equality of Negroes," 206.
52. Dabney, "Ecclesiastical Equality of Negroes," 206.
53. Lucas, *Dabney*, 149.
54. Dabney, "Ecclesiastical Equality of Negroes," 149.
55. Dabney, "Ecclesiastical Equality of Negroes," 203.
56. Lucas, *Dabney*, 149.
57. Dabney, "Ecclesiastical Equality of Negroes," 217.
58. Lucas, *Dabney*, 148.
59. Lucas, *Dabney*, 148.
60. Lucas, *Dabney*, 148–49.
61. Blackburn, *Life Work of Girardeau*, 143–44.
62. Blackburn, *Life Work of Girardeau*, 143–46.
63. Willborn, "Girardeau," 190.
64. Blackburn, *Girardeau*, 137.
65. Blackburn, *Girardeau*, 144.
66. Those who entered the ministry from Zion Church included the Reverends. James E. Fogartie, George A. Trenholm, W. G. Vardell, J. B. Warren, C. E. Chichester, and T.B. Trenholm. Thomas Law recalled, "All these Brethren, I venture to say, drew their inspiration and encouragement for the higher work from their consecrated and ever zealous pastor." Blackburn, *Life Work of Girardeau*, 147.
67. Willborn, "Girardeau," 203.
68. The seven individuals include Paul Trescot, John B. Mitchell, Sam Robinson, John Warren, Jacky Morrison, William Price, and William Spencer. In Prefatory Notes, Thomas Smyth Papers.
69. Willborn, "Girardeau," 203.
70. Willborn, "Girardeau," 203. W. F. Robertson also recorded "Charleston, July 6, 1869—At a meeting of the colored congregation of Zion Church, Charleston S.C., held this night and called for the purpose of considering the propriety of organizing them according to the plan recommended by the last General Assembly, the following resolution was adopted—Resolved—That this congregation accepts the plan of the Assembly and desire to be organizes accordingly thereto . . . Resolved that the session of Zion Church be authorized to carry out the plan above adopted."
71. A session would include teaching elders and ruling elders. A teaching elder has a formal seminary education and must be examined by the presbytery before receiving license to preach. A ruling elder is nominated by the congregation; examined in theology, the Bible; and church government by the session; and voted on by the congregation. If the vote passes the individual would then be ordained in a service with members of the session and even members of the presbytery present. It would

have been very significant to have White teaching and ruling elders in the Charleston Presbytery attend such a ceremony in 1869 and preside over the ordination of African American ruling elders who would then be equal voting members and colleagues in session and presbytery meetings.

72. Blackburn, *Life Work of Girardeau*, 150

73. Boles, *Masters and Slaves*, 18.

74. Prefatory Notes, Thomas Smyth Papers.

75. Willborn, "Girardeau," 205.

76. Powers, *Black Charlestonians*, 209–10.

77. Prefatory Notes, Thomas Smyth Papers.

78. Willborn, "Girardeau," 205.

79. Clarke, *Our Southern Zion*, 227.

80. William Banks Papers (1814–1875), Letter from John L. Girardeau to Reverend J. B. Mack, dated July 29, 1874, William Banks Papers (1814–1875), South Caroliniana Library, 2–4.

81. Blackburn, *Life Work of Girardeau*, 160.

82. Tennent Family Papers, Letter from John L. Girardeau to Dr. Charles Tennent dated June 6, 1878. South Caroliniana Library, 3–4.

83. Willborn, "Girardeau," 205

84. *Dr. Girardeau Devoted to Negro Work*. Part of Girardeau's legacy was that in April 1878 the *Records of the Charleston Presbytery* show that "the Zion colored church, Calhoun Street, Charleston, S.C., is still open and religious services are conducted twice every Sabbath by a Presbyterian minister, a minister, however, who is not in connection with our Presbytery.

85. *Dr. Girardeau Devoted to Negro Work*.

86. Clarke, *Wrestlin' Jacob*, 178

87. Powers, *Black Charlestonians*, 139.

88. *News and Courier*, "Exhibit Tracks Rise of Black Charleston Churches." Region section, February 21, 1988. Vertical File, Churches-Presbyterian-Zion-Olivet, Avery Research Center for African American History and Culture Vertical file, Churches-Presbyterian-Zion-Olivet.

89. *News and Courier*, "Exhibit Tracks."

90. *Post and Courier*, "Wallingford Presbyterian Church Being Torn Down." March 4, 1968. Holloway family scrapbook collection box 2, folder 1. Avery Research Center for African American History and Culture.

91. Clarke, *Our Southern Zion*, 244.

92. Clarke, *Our Southern Zion*, 244.

93. *Post and Courier*, "Wallingford Presbyterian Church." Reverend Woods also expressed in the article that "according to the records the first session of colored elders to serve the Presbyterian Church in South Carolina were ordained in this church.

94. *News and Courier,* "Exhibit Tracks."

95. Clarke, *Our Southern Zion*, 247. Clarke continued to argue for the continuity of antebellum education with the post bellum schools stating, "Beyond whatever formal education an elite free black such as Francis Cardozo was able to attain as a youth in Charleston, the Reformed community had head for generations the scholarly sermons of low country white preachers, had memorized with whites the questions and answers of catechisms, and had worshipped in churches that affirmed order, reasonableness, and simplicity and that deprecated emotionalism and disorder. They had had, in other words, adequate time over several generations and the needed context to have already internalized to a significant extent a Reformed tradition, in its world view, and its ethos."

96. *Post and Courier,* Conley Smith, "Churches' Histories Documented," Thursday, December 14, 1989, vertical file, Churches-Presbyterian-Zion-Olivet, Avery Research Center for African American History and Culture.

97. Thomas Holt, *Black Over White: Negro Political Leadership in South Carolina during Reconstruction* (Urbana: University of Illinois Press, 1979), 9.

98. Holt, *Black over White*, 11.

99. Holt, *Black over White*, 14

100. Clarke, *Our Southern Zion*, 241.

101. Sharon E. Garrett, Zion-Olivet Presbyterian Church (USA) Collection 1854–1992, January 20, 1993, vertical file, Churches-Presbyterian-Zion-Olivet, Avery Research Center for African American History and Culture.

102. F. P. Metz, 1971 Annual Review of the Zion-Olivet United Presbyterian Church in the USA by F.P. Metz, vertical file, Avery Research Center for African American History and Culture.

103. Willborn, "Girardeau," 205–6.

104. F. P. Metz, *1971 Annual Review.*

105. Souvenir Booklet, anniversary of Zion Presbyterian Church 1858–1948, vertical file, Churches-Presbyterian-Zion-Olivet, Avery Research Center for African American History and Culture.

106. *Post and Courier,* First Black Leader Chosen by Area Presbyterians," 1B February 3, 2002, 1B, vertical file, Churches-Presbyterian-Zion-Olivet, Avery Research Center for African American History and Culture.

107. *Post and Courier,* "First Black Leader."

108. F. P. Metz, 1971 Annual Review.

109. F. P. Metz, 1971 Annual Review.

110. Otis W. Pickett "Race and the Visions of John Lafayette Girardeau," *Southern Religion, Southern Cultures: Essays Honoring Charles Reagan Wilson* (Jackson: University Press of Mississippi).

Chapter 6: "The Evils Which Now Oppress Us"

1. Charles Regan Wilson, *Baptized by Blood: The Religion of the Lost Cause, 1865–1920*. (Athens: University of Georgia Press, 1980), 73.

2. David Blight, *Race and Reunion: The Civil War in American Memory* (Cambridge, MA: Belknap Press of Harvard University Press, 2001), 2.

3. John B. Boles, *Black Southerners, 1619–1869* (Lexington: University Press of Kentucky, 1983); Robert M. Calhoon, *Evangelicals and Conservatives in the Early South, 1740–1861* (Columbia: University of South Carolina Press, 1988); David B. Cheesebrough, *Clergy Dissent in the Old South, 1830–1865* (Carbondale, Southern Illinois University Press, 1996); Kenneth Moore Startup, *The Root of All Evil: The Protestant Clergy and the Economic Mind of the Old South* (Athens: University of Georgia Press, 1997); Edward R. Crowther, *Southern Evangelicals and the Coming of the Civil War* (Lewiston, NY: E. Mellen Press, 2000); Donald G. Mathews, *Religion in the Old South* (Chicago: University of Chicago Press, 1977); E. Brooks Holifield, *The Gentlemen Theologians: American Theology in Southern Culture 1795–1860* (Durham, NC: Duke University Press, 1978); James D. Essig, *The Bonds of Wickedness: American Evangelicals against Slavery, 1770–1808* (Philadelphia: Temple University Press, 1982); Paul Harvey, *Freedom's Coming: Religious Culture and the Shaping of the South from the Civil War through the Civil Rights Era* (Chapel Hill: University of North Carolina Press, 2005); W. Scott Poole, *Never Surrender: Confederate Memory and Conservatism in the South Carolina Upcountry* (Athens: University of Georgia Press, 2004); Charles Reagan Wilson's *Baptized in Blood: The Religion of the Lost Cause, 1865–1920* (Athens: University of Georgia Press, 1980); and *Religion in the South* (Jackson: University Press of Mississippi, 1985).

4. Wilson, *Baptized in Blood*, 66, 73–74.

5. Wilson, *Baptized in Blood*, 74.

6. Poole, *Never Surrender*, 56.

7. Pickett, "We are Marching to Zion," 91–101.

8. John L. Girardeau, College of Charleston Special Collections Pamphlets, "Confederate Memorial Day at Charleston, S.C.: Re-interment of the Carolina dead from Gettysburg" (Charleston, SC: W.G. Mazyck, printer, 1871).

9. Betram Wyatt Brown *Southern Honor: Ethics and Behavior in the Old South* (New York, NY: Oxford University Press, 1982).

10. Girardeau, "Re-internment," 6–7.

11. Girardeau, "Re-internment" 3.

12. Girardeau, "Re-internment," 6.

13. *The Westminster Confession of Faith* (Lawrenceville, GA: Committee for Christian Education & Publications), 96–97.

14. Girardeau, "Re-internment," 6.

15. Girardeau, "Re-internment," 8.

16. Girardeau, "Re-Internment," 7–8.

17. Girardeau, "Re-internment," 8.

18. Girardeau, "Re-Internment," 8.

19. Girardeau, "Re-Internment," 8–9.

20. Girardeau, "Re-Internment," 17.

21. Girardeau, "Re-Internment," 19.

22. Girardeau, "Re-Internment," 19.

23. Girardeau, "Re-Internment," 18.

24. Girardeau, "Re-Internment," 18.

25. Wilson, *Baptized in Blood*, 1.

26. Girardeau, "Re-Internment," 20.

27. Isaiah, Timothy 1:7, 1 John 4:18, Proverbs 29:25. ESV.

28. Mathews, "Jones Crusade," 318.

29. E.T. Thompson *Presbyterians in the South. 3 vols.* (Richmond, VA: John Knox Press, 1963).

BIBLIOGRAPHY

Primary Sources

Adger, John. Adger Family Papers, Presbyterian Historical Society, Montreat, North Carolina.

Adger, John B. "Human Rights and Slavery." *Southern Presbyterian Review* 2, no. 1 (March 1849): 569–86.

Blackburn, George A. Blackburn Collection, Reformed Theological Seminary, Jackson, MS.

Blackburn, George A. *The Life Work of John L. Girardeau*. Columbia, SC: State Company, 1916.

Blackburn, George A., ed. *Sermons by John L. Girardeau*. Columbia, SC: State Company, 1907.

Blackburn, George A., ed. *Sermons by John L. Girardeau*. Special Collections, College of Charleston Library, Charleston, SC.

The Charleston Evening Post, "Zion Redeemed by Congregation," 1933. Dabney, Robert L. *Discussions: Evangelical and Theological.* Vol. 2. London, England: Banner of Truth Trust, 1891.

Faris, D. S. "Reminiscences of The R.P. Church in South Carolina." In *Our Banner*, 341–49. Philadelphia: N. R. Johnston, 1875.

Girardeau, John L. *A Catechism for the Oral Instruction of Coloured Persons*. Charleston, SC: Evans and Cogswell, 1860.

Girardeau, John L. "Christ's Pastoral Presence with his Dying People." Sermon. Special Collections, College of Charleston. Charleston, SC.

Girardeau, John L. "Confederate Memorial Day at Charleston, S.C.: Reinterment of the Carolina Dead from Gettysburg." Ladies Memorial Association. Special, Collections, College of Charleston, Charleston, SC.

Girardeau, John L. "Conscience and Civil Government: An Oration Delivered before the Society of Alumni of the College of Charleston." Special Collections, College of Charleston, Charleston, SC.

Girardeau, John L. *Discussions of Theological Questions*. Richmond, VA: Presbyterian Committee of Publications, 1905.

Girardeau, John L. "Our Ecclesiastical Relations to Freedmen." *Southern Presbyterian Review* 18 (1866): 1–16.

Girardeau, John L. "Our Ecclesiastical Relations to Freedmen." *The Southern Presbyterian Review* 18 (1866): 1–16.

Girardeau, John L. "Palmer's Life of Thornwell." *Southern Presbyterian Review* 27, no 3. (July 1876): 512–38.

Girardeau, John L, Papers, South Caroliniana Library, Columbia, SC.

Girardeau, John L. *Sermons.* Edited by George A. Blackburn. Columbia, SC: The State Company, 1907.

Girardeau, John L. "The Suffering Seaboard of the South." *Southern Presbyterian Review* 27, no. 2 (April 1876): 199–227.

Girardeau, John L. *The Will in Its Theological Relations.* Columbia, SC: W. J. Duffie and New York: Baker and Taylor, 1891.

Haris, S. F. "The Theology of Dr. Girardeau." *The Methodist Quarterly Review* 37, no. 1 (April 1893): 29–45.

Hoge, Peyton. *Moses Drury Hoge: Life and Letters.* Richmond, VA: Presbyterian Committee of Publication, 1899.

Howe, George. *History of the Presbyterian Church in South Carolina.* Columbia, SC: Duffie & Chapman, 1870.

Howe, George. *History of the Presbyterian Church in South Carolina.* Vol. 2. Columbia, SC: W. J. Duffie, 1883.

Jones, Charles Colcock. *A Catechism of Scripture, Doctrine and Practice: For Families and Sabbath Schools, Designed also for the Oral Instruction of Colored Persons.* 3rd. ed. Savannah, GA: Thomas Purse, 1845.

Jones, Charles Colcock. *The Religious Instruction of Negroes in the United States.* Savannah, GA: Thomas Purse, 1842.

Jones, Charles Colcock. *Tenth Annual Report of the Association for the Religious Instruction of the Negroes in Liberty County, Georgia.* Savannah, GA: Office of P. G. Thomas, 1845.

Jones, Charles Colcock. *Thirteenth Annual Report of the Association for the Religious Instruction of the Negroes in Liberty County, Georgia.* Savannah, GA: Edward J. Purse, 1848.

Manual of the Second Presbyterian Church, Charleston, SC. Charleston: Steam Power Press, 1854.

Mcleod, Alexander, *Negro Slavery Unjustifiable: A Discourse.* New York: T&J Swords, 1802.

McClurkin, H. P., "Reminiscences of the Church in South Carolina." In *Our Banner*, 129–30. Philadelphia: N. R. Johnston, 1876.

Minutes of the General Assembly, PCUSAUS 1861–99. All of the following minutes are at the Presbyterian Historical Society now located at Columbia Theological Seminary in Atlanta, GA.

Minutes of the General Assembly, PCUSA. 1840–98.

Minutes of the General Assembly, PCUSA. 1896–1955.

Minutes of Presbytery of South Carolina. 1867.

Minutes of the Session, Zion Presbyterian Church, Charleston, SC. 1858–69.

Minutes of the Session, Zion Presbyterian Church, Glebe Street, Charleston, SC. 1869–75.

Minutes of the Session, Zion Presbyterian Church, 1936–45.

Minutes of the Synod of South Carolina. 1847–98.

Moseley, B. W. "Evangelization of the Colored People." *Southern Presbyterian Review* 2, no 2. (July 1858): 225–45.

Myers, Robert Manson, ed. *Children of Pride: A True Story of Georgia and the Civil War. Containing the Letters of Charles Colcock Jones.* New Haven, CT: Yale University Press, 1972.

Proceedings of the Meeting in Charleston, SC May 13–15, 1845, on the Religious Instruction of the Negroes, Together with the Report of the Committee, and Address to the Public. Charleston, SC: B. Jenkins, 1845.

Seabrook, Whitemarsh B. "An Essay on the Management of Slaves, and Especially, on Their Religious Instruction: Read before Agricultural Society of St. Johns Colleton." Charleston, SC: A. E. Miller, 1834.

Smythe, Thomas. Thomas Smythe Papers, Records of Anson and Zion Presbyterian Church. South Carolina Historical Society, Charleston, SC.

Thornwell, James Henry. "Slavery and the Religious Instruction of the Coloured Population." *Southern Presbyterian Review* 4, no. 1 (July 1850): 105–41.

Weyland, John, ed. *The Spirit Divided: Memoirs of Civil War Chaplains: The Confederacy.*

Wylie, Samuel Brown. *Memoir of Alexander Mcleod, D.D.* New York: Charles Scribner, 1855.

Zion-Olivet Presbyterian Church Papers. Avery Research Center for African American History and Culture, Charleston, SC.

Zion Presbyterian Church Communicants Roll Book, Presbyterian Historical Society, Philadelphia, PA.

Secondary Sources

Alvis, Joel L. *Religion and Race: Southern Presbyterians, 1946–1983.* Tuscaloosa: University of Alabama Press, 1994.

Armstrong, Maurice W., Lefferts A. Loetscher, and Charles A. Anderson, eds. *The Presbyterian Enterprise: Sources of American Presbyterian History.* Eugene, OR: Wipf & Stock, 1956

Atkinson, James R. *Splendid Land, Splendid People: The Chickasaw Indians to Removal.* Tuscaloosa: University of Alabama Press, 2004.

Axtell, James. *After Columbus: Essays in Ethnohistory of Colonial America.* New York: Oxford University Press, 1988.

Bailey, Kenneth K. "The Post-Civil War Separations in Southern Protestantism: Another Look," *Church History* XLVII, December 1977.

Bailey, Kenneth K. *Southern White Protestantism in the Twentieth Century.* New York: Harper and Row, 1964.

Balmer, Randall, and John R. Fitzmier. *The Presbyterians.* Westport, CT: Greenwood Press, 1993.

Barnes, Albert. *The Church and Slavery.* New York: Negro University Press, 1857.

Barnes, Gilbert Hobbes. *The Anti-Slavery Impulse: 1830–1844.* New York: Harcourt, Brace & World, 1933.

Berkhofer, Robert F. *Salvation and the Savage: An Analysis of Protestant Missions and American Indian Response, 1787–1862.* Lexington: University Press of Kentucky, 1965.

Blassingame, John W. *The Slave Community: Plantation Life in the Antebellum South.* New York: Oxford University Press, 1972.

Blum, Edward J., and W. Scott Poole. *Vale of Tears: New Essays in Religion and Reconstruction.* Macon, GA: Mercer University Press, 2005.

Boles, John B. *Black Southerners, 1619–1869.* Lexington: University Press of Kentucky, 1983.

Boles, John B. *The Great Revival: Beginnings of the Bible Belt.* Lexington: University Press of Kentucky, 1996.

Boles, John B. *Masters and Slaves in the House of the Lord: Race and Religion in the American South, 1740–1870.* Lexington: University Press of Kentucky, 1988.

Boles, John B. *The South Through Time: A History of an American Region.* Englewood Cliffs, NJ: Prentice-Hall, 1995.

Boles, John B., and Evelyn Thomas Nolen. *Interpreting Southern History: Historiographical Essays in Honor of Sanford W. Higginbotham.* Baton Rouge: Louisiana State University Press, 1987.

Boles, John B., and Charles R. Wilson eds. *Religion in the South: Essays.* Jackson: University Press of Mississippi, 1985.

Boorstin, Daniel J. *The Americans: The National Experience.* New York: Random House, 1965.

Brooks, James. *Confounding the Color Line: The Indian-Black Experience in North America.* Lincoln: University of Nebraska Press, 2002.

Butler, Jon. *Awash in a Sea of Faith: Christianizing the American People.* Cambridge, MA: Harvard University Press, 1990.

Calhoon, Robert. *Evangelicals and Conservatives in the Early South, 1740–1861.* Columbia: University of South Carolina Press, 1988.

Cheesebrough, David B. *Clergy Dissent in the Old South, 1830–1865.* Carbondale: Southern Illinois University Press, 1996.

Chisolm, J. Julian. *History of The First Presbyterian Church of Natchez, Mississippi.* Natchez, MS: Mcdonald's, 1972.

Christie, John W., and Dwight L. Dumond. *George Bourne and the Book and Slavery Irreconcilable.* Wilmington: Historical Society of Delaware, 1969.

Clarke, Erskine. *Dwelling Place: A Plantation Epic.* New Haven, CT: Yale University Press, 2005.

Clarke, Erskine. *Our Southern Zion: A History of Calvinism in the South Carolina Low Country.* Tuscaloosa: University of Alabama Press, 1996.

Clarke, Erskine. "Thomas Smythe, Moderate of the Old South." ThD diss., Union Theological Seminary, Virginia, 1970.Clarke, Erskine. *Wrestlin' Jacob: A Portrait of Religion in the Old South.* Atlanta: John Knox Press, 1979.

Cornelius, Janet Duitsman. *Slave Missions and the Black Church in the Antebellum South.* Columbia: University of South Carolina Press, 1999.

Crowe, Ronald Girardeau, and Elizabeth Lee Girardeau, *The Girardeau Family in the United States.* Corvallis: West Oregon Web Press, 1996.

Crowther, Edward R. *Southern Evangelicals and the Coming of the Civil War.* Lewiston, NY: E. Mellen Press, 2000.

Dabney, Robert L. *A Defense of Virginia and the South.* Harrisonburg, VA: Sprinkle, 1977.

Dabney, Virginius. *Liberalism in the South.* Chapel Hill: University of North Carolina Press, 1932.

Davis, David Brion. *In the Image of God: Religion, Moral Values and Our Heritage of Slavery.* New Haven, CT: Yale University Press, 2001.

Davis, David Brion. *The Problem of Slavery in the Age of Revolution: 1770–1823.* Ithaca, NY: Cornell University Press, 1975.

Davis, David Brion. *The Problem of Slavery in Western Culture.* Ithaca, NY: Cornell University Press, 1966.

De Graaf, Lawrence. "Race, Sex, and Region: Black Women in the American West, 1850–1920." *Pacific Historical Review* 1980.

Deloria, Philip. *Playing Indian* New Haven, CT: Yale University Press, 1998.

Denson, Andrew. *Demanding the Cherokee Nation: Indian Autonomy and American Culture 1830–1900.* Lincoln: University of Nebraska Press, 2004.

DuBois, W. E. B., ed. *Economic Co-Operation among Negro Americans*, Atlanta: Atlanta University Publications, no. 12, 1907.

Dumond, Dwight Lowell. *Antislavery: The Crusade for Freedom in America.* Ann Arbor: University of Michigan Press, 1961.

Edgar, Walter B. *South Carolina: A History.* Columbia: University of South Carolina Press, 1999.

Emerson, Michael O. and Christian Smith. *Divided By Faith: Evangelical Religion and the Problem of Race in America.* New York: Oxford University Press, 2000.

Engerman, Fogel. *Time on the Cross: The Economics of American Negro Slavery.* Boston: Little, Brown and Company, 1974.

Ethridge, Robbie F. *Creek Country: The Creek Indians and Their World, 1796–1816.* Chapel Hill: University of North Carolina Press, 2003.

Ethridge, Robbie F. *From Chicaze to Chickasaw: The European Invasion and the Transformation of the Mississippi World, 1540–1715.* Chapel Hill: University of North Carolina Press, 2010.

Ethridge, Robbie F., and Charles Hudson, eds. *The Transformation of the Southeastern Indians, 1540–1760.* Jackson: University Press of Mississippi, 2002.

Farmer, James O. *The Metaphysical Confederacy: James Henry Thornwell and the Synthesis of Southern Values.* Macon, GA: Mercer University Press, 1986.

Feldman, Glenn. *Politics and Religion in the White South.* Lexington: University Press of Kentucky, 2005.

Finkelman, Paul. *Defending Slavery: Proslavery Thought in the Old South: A Brief History with Documents.* Boston: Bedford/St. Martin's Press, 2003.

Foner, Eric. *Reconstruction: America's Unfinished Revolution.* New York: Harper and Row, 1988.

Fountain, Daniel L. "Long on Religion, Short on Christianity: Slave Religion 1830–1870." PhD diss., University of Mississippi, 1999.

Frank, Andrew K. *Creeks and Southerners: Biculturalism on the Early American Frontier. Indians of the Southeast.* Lincoln: University of Nebraska Press, 2005.

Frey, Sylvia R., and Betty Wood, *Come Shouting to Zion: African American Protestantism in the American South and British Caribbean to 1830.* Chapel Hill: University of North Carolina Press, 1988.

Genovese, Eugene D. *A Consuming Fire: The Fall of The Confederacy in the White Christian South.* Athens: University of Georgia Press, 1998.

Genovese, Eugene D. *Roll, Jordan, Roll: The World the Slaves Made.* New York: Pantheon, 1974.

Genovese, Eugene D. *The Slaveholders Dilemma: Freedom and Progress in Southern Conservative Thought, 1820–1860.* Columbia: University of South Carolina Press, 1992.Genovese, Eugene D. "Slavery Ordained of God: The Southern Slaveholders' View of Biblical History and Modern Politics." 24th Annual Fortenbaugh Memorial Lecture, Gettysburg College, Gettysburg, PA, 1985.

Genovese, Eugene D. *The Southern War: History and Politics in the Cultural War.* Columbia: University of Missouri Press, 1995.

Graves, Fred R. *The Presbyterian Work in Mississippi.* Sumner, MS: Sentinel Press, 1927.

Gray, Richard, and Owen Robinson. *A Companion to the Literature and Culture of the American South.* Malden, MA: Blackwell, 2004.

Greenberg, Kenneth S. *Honor and Slavery: Lies, Duels, Noses, Masks, Dressing as a Woman, Gifts, Strangers, Humanitarianism, Death, Slave Rebellions, the Proslavery Argument, Baseball, Hunting, Gambling in the Old South.* Princeton, NJ: Princeton University Press, 1996.

Hammond, Sue. "Socioeconomic Reconstruction in the Cherokee Nation, 1865–1870." *Chronicles of Oklahoma* 56 (1978): 158–70.

Harvey, Paul. *Freedom's Coming: Religious Culture and the Shaping of the South from the Civil War through the Civil Rights Era.* Chapel Hill: University of North Carolina Press, 2005.

Harvey, Paul. *Redeeming the South: Religious Cultures and Racial Identities among Southern Baptists, 1865–1925.* New York: Oxford University Press, 1997.

Harvey, Paul, and Edward J. Blum. *The Color of Christ: The Son of God and the Saga of Race in America.* Chapel Hill: University of North Carolina Press, 2012.

Hawkins, Hugh Ed. *The Abolitionists: Means, Ends, and Motivations.* Lexington, MA: D C Heath, 1972.

Haynes, Stephen R. *Noah's Curse: The Biblical Justification of American Slavery.* New York: Oxford University Press, 2002.

Heyrman, Christine. *Southern Cross: The Beginnings of the Bible Belt.* New York: Knopf, 1997.

Hiemstra, William L. "Presbyterian Missions among the Choctaw and Chickasaw Indians, 1845–1862," master's thesis, University of Mississippi, 1947.

Higginbotham, Evelyn Brooks. *Righteous Discontent: The Women's Movement in the Black Baptist Church.* Cambridge, MA: Harvard University Press, 1993.

Hildebrand, Reginald Francis. *The Times Were Strange and Stirring: Methodist Preachers and the Crisis of Emancipation.* Durham, NC: Duke University Press, 1995.

Hill, Samuel S., ed. *Encyclopedia of Religion in the South.* Macon, GA: Mercer University Press, 1984.

Hill, Samuel S. *One Name but Several Faces: Variety in Popular Christian Denominations in Southern History.* Athens: University of Georgia Press, 1996.

Hill, Samuel S. *On Jordan's Stormy Banks: Religion in the South: A Southern Exposure Profile.* Macon, GA: Mercer University Press, 1983.

Hill, Samuel S. *Religion in the Southern States: A Historical Study.* Macon, GA: Mercer University Press, 1983.

Hill, Samuel S. *Southern Churches in Crisis Revisited.* Tuscaloosa: University of Alabama Press, 1999.

Hollifield, E. Brooks. *The Gentlemen Theologians.* Durham, NC: Duke University Press, 1978.

Holt, Thomas. *Black over White: Negro Political Leadership in South Carolina during Reconstruction.* Urbana: University of Illinois Press, 1977.

Howard, Victor B. *The Conscience of Slavery: The Evangelistic Calvinist Domestic Missions, 1837–1861.* Kent, OH: Kent State University Press, 1990.

Howe, George. *History of the Presbyterian Church in South Carolina.* Columbia, SC: Duffie & Chapman, 1870.

Howe, George. *History of the Presbyterian Church in South Carolina.* Vol. 2. Columbia, SC: W. J. Duffie, 1883.

Hultkrantz, Ake. *The Study of American Indian Religions.* New York: Crossroad, 1983.

Isaac, Rhys. *The Transformation of Virginia, 1740–1790.* Chapel Hill: Omohundro Institute of Early American History and Culture, University of North Carolina Press, 1999.

Jenkins, Wilbert. *Seizing the New Day: African Americans in Post–Civil War Charleston*. Bloomington and Indianapolis: Indiana University Press, 1998.

Jennings, Francis. *The Invasion of America: Indians, Colonialism, and the Cant of Conquest*. Chapel Hill: University of North Carolina Press, 1975.

Johnson, Alonzo, and Paul Jersilid, eds. *"Ain't Gonna Lay My 'Ligion Down": African American Religion in the South*. Columbia: University of South Carolina Press, 1996.

Jones, F. D., and W. H. Mills, eds. *History of the Presbyterian Church in South Carolina since 1850*. Columbia, SC: R. L. Bryan, 1926.

Kelly, Douglass. *Preachers with Power: Four Stalwarts of the South*. Great Britain: St. Edmundsbury Press, 1992.

Kidwell, Clara Sue. "The Choctaws in Oklahoma: From Tribe to Nation, 1855–1870." *American Indian Law and Policy Series* no. 2. Norman: University of Oklahoma Press, 2007.

King, Duane H. *The Cherokee Indian Nation: A Troubled Nation*. Knoxville: University of Tennessee Press, 1979.

Lambert, Valerie. *Choctaw Resurgence: A Story of American Indian Resurgence*. Lincoln: University of Nebraska Press, 2007.

Lesick, Lawrence Thomas. *The Lane Rebels: Evangelicalism and Antislavery in Antebellum America*. Metuchen, NJ: Scarecrow Press, 1980.

Lewis, Bonnie Sue. *Creating Christian Indians: Native Clergy in the Presbyterian Church*. Norman: University of Oklahoma Press. 2003.

Libby, David J. *Slavery and Frontier Mississippi*. Jackson: University of Mississippi Press, 2004.

Littlefield, Daniel F. *Africans and Creeks: From the Colonial Period to the Civil War*. Westport, CT: Greenwood Press, 1979.

Littlefield, Daniel F. *The Chickasaw Freedmen: A People without a Country*. Westport, CT: Greenwood Press, 1980.

Litwack, Leon F. *Been in the Storm So Long: The Aftermath of Slavery*. New York: Knopf, 1979.

Litwack, Leon F. *North of Slavery: The Negro in the Free States, 1790–1860*. Chicago: University of Chicago Press, 1961.

Loveland, Anne C. *Southern Evangelicals and the Social Order, 1800–1860*. Baton Rouge: Louisiana State University Press, 1980.

Lucas, Sean M. *Robert Louis Dabney: A Southern Presbyterian Life*. Phillipsburg, NJ: P&R Publishing, 2005.

Macaulay, John Allen. *Unitarianism in the Antebellum South: The Other Invisible Institution*. Tuscaloosa: University of Alabama Press, 2001.

Maddox, Jack. "Presbyterians in the South, Centralization, and the Book of Church Order, 1861–1879." *Journal of Presbyterian History* 68, no. 1 (spring, 1990): 24–45.

Marsden, George. *Religion and American Culture*. San Diego: Harcourt Brace Jovanovich, 1990.

Marsden, George, Nathan O. Hatch, and Mark Noll, eds. *The Bible in America.* New York: Oxford University Press, 1982.

Mathews, Donald G. *Religion in the Old South.* Chicago: University of Chicago Press, 1977.

Mathews, Donald G. *Slavery and Methodism: A Chapter in American Morality, 1780–1845.* Princeton, NJ: Princeton University Press, 1965.

Mathews, Donald G., and Beth Barton Schweiger, eds. *Religion in the American South: Protestants and Others in History and Culture.* Chapel Hill: University of North Carolina Press, 2004.

May, Katja. *African Americans and Native Americans in the Creek and Cherokee Nations, 1830s to 1920s.* New York: Garland, 1996.

Mckivigan, John R., and Mitchell Snay. *Religion and the Antebellum Debate over Slavery.* Athens: University of Georgia Press, 1998.

McLeod, Alexander, *Negro Slavery Unjustifiable: A Discourse.* New York: T&J Swords, 1802.

McLoughlin, William G. *After the Trail of Tears: The Cherokees' Struggle for Sovereignty, 1839–1880.* Chapel Hill: University of North Carolina Press, 1993.

McLoughlin, William G. *Cherokees and Missionaries, 1789–1839.* New Haven, CT: Yale University Press, 1984.

Merritt, Jane T. *At the Crossroads: Indians and Empires on a Mid-Atlantic Frontier, 1700–1763.* Chapel Hill: University of North Carolina Press, 2003.

Miles, Tiya. *The House on Diamond Hill: A Cherokee Plantation Story.* Chapel Hill: University of North Carolina Press, 2010.

Minges, Patrick. *Slavery in the Cherokee Nation: The Keetowah Society and the Defining of a People, 1855–1867.* New York and London: Routledge, 2003.

Montgomery, William E. *Under Their Own Vine and Fig Tree: The African-American Church in the South, 1865–1900.* Baton Rouge: Louisiana State University Press, 1993.

Myers, Robert Manson, ed. *Children of Pride: A True Story of Georgia and the Civil War.* New Haven, CT: Yale University Press, 1972.

Naylor, Celia E. *African Cherokees in Indian Territory: From Chattel to Citizens.* John Hope Franklin Series in African American History and Culture. Chapel Hill: University of North Carolina Press, 2008.

Nelson, Timothy Jon. "Every Time I Feel the Spirit: Religious Experience and Religious Ritual in an African American Congregation." PhD diss., University of Chicago, 1997.

Noll, Mark. *America's God: From Johnathan Edwards to Abraham Lincoln.* New York: Oxford University Press, 2002.

Noll, Mark. *The Civil War as a Theological Crisis.* Chapel Hill: University of North Carolina Press, 2006.

Noll, Mark. *A History of Christianity in the United States and Canada.* Grand Rapids, MI: W. B. Eerdmans, 1992.

Noll, Mark. *The Old Religion in a New World: The History of North American Christianity.* Grand Rapids, MI: W. B. Eerdmans, 2002.

Oakes, James. *The Ruling Race.* New York: Vintage Books, 1983.

Ownby, Ted. *Subduing Satan: Religion, Recreation, & Manhood in the Rural South, 1865–1920.* Chapel Hill: University of North Carolina Press, 1990.

Perdue, Theda. *Slavery and the Evolution of Cherokee Society, 1540–1866.* Knoxville: University of Tennessee Press, 1979.

Pickett, Otis W. "'We Are Marching to Zion': Zion Church and the Distinctive Work of Presbyterian Slave Missionaries in Charleston, South Carolina, 1849–1874," MA thesis. College of Charleston, 2008.

Pitts, Charles F. *Chaplains in Gray: The Confederate Chaplain's Story.* Nashville, TN: Broadmen Press, 1957.

Powers, Bernard. *Black Charlestonians: A Social History, 1822–1885.* Fayetteville: University of Arkansas Press, 1994.

Raboteau, Albert. *A Fire in the Bones: Reflections on African American Religious History.* Boston: Beacon Press, 1995.

Raboteau, Albert. *Slave Religion: The "Invisible Institution" in the Antebellum South.* New York: Oxford University Press, 1978.

Rawick, Goerge P. *From Sundown to Sunup: The Making of the Black Community.* Westport, CT: Greenwood Publishing, 1972.

Reeves, Carolyn Keller, ed. *The Choctaw before Removal.* Jackson: University of Mississippi Press, 1985.

Robinson, William Childs. *Columbia Theological Seminary and the Southern Presbyterian Church.* Decatur, GA: Dennis Lindsay, 1931.

Ronda, James P. "The Sillery Experiment: A Jesuit-Indian Village in New France, 1637–1663." *American Indian Culture and Research Journal* 3, no.1 (1979): 1–18.

Ronda, James P. "We Are Well as We Are": An Indian Critique of Seventeenth-Century Christian Missions." *William and Mary Quarterly* 34, no. 1 (January 1977): 66.

Ross, Fred A. *Slavery Ordained of God.* New York: Haskell House, 1970.

Salisbury, Neal. *Manitou and Providence: Indians, Europeans, and the Making of New England, 1500–1643.* Oxford: Oxford University Press, 1982.

Salisbury, Neal. "Red Puritans: The 'Praying Indians' of Massachusetts Bay and John Elliot," *William and Mary Quarterly* 31 (1974).

Saunt, Claudio. *Black, White, and Indian: Race and the Unmaking of an American Family.* Oxford: Oxford University Press, 2005.

Scherer, Lester B. *Slavery and the Churches in Early America.* Grand Rapids, MI: William B. Eerdmans, 1975.

Schweiger, Beth Barton, and Donald G. Mathews, eds. *Religion in the American South: Protestants and Others in History and Culture.* Chapel Hill: University of North Carolina Press, 2004.

Sermett, Milton C., ed. *African American Religious History: A Documentary Witness.* Durham, NC: Duke University Press, 1999.

Shoemaker, Nancy. *A Strange Likeness: Becoming Red and White in Eighteenth-Century North America.* New York: Oxford University Press. 2004.

Shoemaker, Nancy. "How Indians Got to be Red" *American Historical Review* 102, no. 3 (June 1997): 625–44.

Simms, Lois A. *A History of Zion, Olivet, and Zion-Olivet Churches: 1850–1985.* Charleston, SC: Mercury Micro Computer Products, 1987.

Smith, H. Shelton. *In His Image, But . . . Racism in Southern Religion, 1780–1910.* Durham, NC: Duke University Press, 1972.

Smith, H. Shelton. "The Church and the Social Order as Interpreted by James Henry Thornwell." *Church History* 7 (June 1938).

Snay, Mitchell. *Gospel of Disunion: Religion and Separatism in the Antebellum South.* Cambridge: Cambridge University Press, 1993.

Sparks, Randy J. *On Jordan's Story Banks: Evangelicalism in Mississippi, 1773–1876.* Athens: University of Georgia Press, 1994.

Sparks, Randy J. *Religion in Mississippi.* Jackson: University Press of Mississippi, 2001.

Startup, Kenneth Moore. *The Root of All Evil: The Protestant Clergy and the Economic Mind of the Old South.* Athens: University of Georgia Press, 1997.

Stowell, Daniel W. *Rebuilding Zion: The Religious Reconstruction of the South, 1863–1877.* New York: Oxford University Press, 1998.

Street, T. Watson. *The Story of Southern Presbyterians.* Richmond, VA: John Knox Press, 1961.

Sturm, Circe. *Blood Politics: Race, Culture, and Identity in the Cherokee Nation of Oklahoma.* Berkeley: University of California Press, 2002.

Swanton, John R. *Chickasaw Society and Religion.* Lincoln: University of Nebraska Press, 2006.

Swartley, Willard M. *Slavery, Sabbath, War, and Women.* Scottdale, PA: Herald Press, 1983.

Thomas, Hugh. *The Slave Trade: The Story of the Atlantic Slave Trade, 1440–1870.* New York: Simon & Schuster, 1997.

Thompson, Ernest Trice. *Presbyterian Missions in the Southern United States.* Richmond, VA: Presbyterian Committee of Publication, 1934.

Thompson, Ernest Trice. *Presbyterians in the South.* 3 vols. Richmond, VA: John Knox Press, 1963.

Thompson, Robert Ellis. *A History of the Presbyterian Churches in the United States.* 3rd ed. Eugene, OR: Wipf & Stock, 1895.

Tindall, George Brown. *South Carolina Negroes, 1877–1900.* Columbia: University of South Carolina Press, 2003.

Tinker, George E. *Missionary Conquest: The Gospel and Native American Cultural Genocide.* Minneapolis: Fortress Press, 1993.

Tise, Larry E. *Proslavery: A History of the Defense of Slavery in America, 1701–1840.* Athens: University of Georgia Press, 1987.

Treat, James, ed. *Native and Christian: Indigenous Voices in Religious Identity in the United States and Canada.* New York: Routledge, 1996.

Tyler, Mark Kelly, "Bishop Daniel Alexander Payne of the African Methodist Episcopal Church: The Life of a 19th Century Educational Leader, 1811–1865." PhD diss., University of Dayton, 2006.

Wade, Richard C. *Slavery in the Cities: The South, 1820–1860.* New York: Oxford University Press, 1967.

Wallace, Daniel. *History of South Carolina.* New York: American Historical Society, 1934.

Waselkov, Gregory A. *A Conquering Spirit: Fort Mims and the Redstick War of 1813–1814.* Tuscaloosa: University of Alabama Press, 2006.

Wells, Samuel J., and Roseanna Tubby, eds. *After Removal: The Choctaw in Mississippi.* Jackson: University Press of Mississippi.

Welsch, Susan A. "Religion, Slavery, and Sectionalism as Shown in Southern Methodist Publications, 1844–1860." MA thesis, College of Charleston and The Citadel, 2002.

White, Henry Alexander. *Southern Presbyterian Leaders.* New York: Neale, 1911.

Willborn, C. N. "John L. Girardeau: Pastor to Slaves and Theologian of Causes." PhD diss., Westminster Theological Seminary, 2003.

Williamson, Joel. *After Slavery: The Negro in South Carolina during Reconstruction, 1861–1877.* Chapel Hill: University of North Carolina Press, 1965.

Williamson, Joel. *A Rage for Order: Black/White Relations in the American South since Emancipation.* Hanover, NH: University of New England Press, 1990.

Wills, George A. *Democratic Religion: Freedom, Authority, and Church Discipline in the Baptist South, 1785–1900.* New York: Oxford University Press, 1996.

Wilson, Charles Reagan. *Baptized in Blood: The Religion of the Lost Cause, 1865–1920.* Athens: University of Georgia Press, 1980.

Wilson, Charles Reagan. *Religion.* New York: Gordon and Breach, 1991.

Wilson, Charles Reagan. *Religion and the American Civil War.* New York: Oxford University Press, 1998.

Wilson, Charles Reagan, ed. *Religion in the South.* Jackson: University Press of Mississippi, 1985.

Wood, Peter. *Black Majority: Negroes in Colonial South Carolina from 1670 through the Stono Rebellion.* New York: Alfred A. Knopf, 1974.

Woodward, C. Vann. "The Northern Crusade against Slavery." In *The Abolitionists: Means, Ends, Motivations,* 177–96. Boston: D. C. Heath and Company.

Woodward, C. Vann. *The Strange Career of Jim Crow.* New York, Oxford University Press, 1955.

Wyatt-Brown, Bertram. *Lewis Tappan and the Evangelical War against Slavery.* Cleveland, OH: Case Western Reserve University Press, 1969.

Wyatt-Brown, Bertram. *Southern Honor: Ethics and Behavior in the Old South.* New York: Oxford University Press, 1982.

Yarbrough, Fay A. *Race and the Cherokee Nation: Sovereignty in the Nineteenth Century.* Philadelphia: University of Pennsylvania Press, 2008.

Zellar, Gary. *African Creeks: Estelvste and the Creek Nation. Race and Culture in the American West.* Norman: University of Oklahoma Press, 2007.

INDEX